3-30 8

THE CASE FOR THE WELFARE STATE

THE CASE
for the
WELFARE STATE

From Social Security to Social Equality

Norman Furniss

and Timothy Tilton

INDIANA UNIVERSITY PRESS

BLOOMINGTON AND LONDON

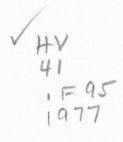

FIRST MIDLAND BOOK EDITION 1979

Copyright © 1977 by Indiana University Press

Manufactured in the United States of America

Library of Congress Cataloging in Publication Data
Furniss, Norman, 1944–
The case for the welfare state.
Bibliography:
1. Welfare state. 2. Public welfare. I. Tilton,
Timothy Alan, joint author. II. Title.
HV41.F95 1977 361.6 76-26414
cl. ISBN 0-253-31322-8
pa. ISBN 0-253-20230-2

2 3 4 5 81 80 79

CONTENTS

ACKNOWLEDGMENTS

For valuable critical, editorial, and secretarial assistance we express our gratitude to: Sam Beer, Jim Christoph, Sophie Dales, Vickie van Fechtman, George Furniss, Ed Greenberg, Hugh Heclo, Max Horlick, Charles Hyneman, Lennart Lundqvist, Trudi Miller, Barrington Moore, Jr., Alan Ritter, Sandy Roberts, Sue Rodman, Kathy Solt, Don Studlar, Martin Tracy, George Wright.

Research for this book has been facilitated by financial support from: American Philosophical Society, American-Scandinavian Foundation, Indiana University, National Endowment for Humanities, West European Studies Program at Indiana University.

INTRODUCTION

Social scientists now have an overwhelming interest in "policy studies." This term is singularly ill-defined, but it does connote at least a concern with the "output" of political institutions. Movements to develop social indicators and to engage in social experimentation exemplify the drive to evaluate and measure the impact of specific public policies. Thus far, however, these promising fields of study are too often locked into narrow behavioral, historical, normative, or descriptive styles of analysis which fail to confront the current issues of social policy. They lack the combination of a clear normative foundation and a general interpretative framework which together are necessary for the assessment of social policy. No one has stressed the need for this linkage better than Max Weber:

> The distinctive characteristic of a problem of social *policy* is indeed the fact that it cannot be resolved merely on the basis of purely technical considerations which already assume settled ends. Normative standards of value can and must be the objects of *dispute* in a discussion of a problem of social policy because the problem lies in the domain of general cultural values....[1]

Citizens trying to orient themselves within a fluctuating political world similarly require a solid base from which they can assess bewildering events and confusing policy alternatives. As John Plamenatz has written,

> The sophisticated man needs more than a set of customs and prejudices ... he needs a *practical philosophy*. He lives in a changing society, and he is socially mobile in that society.... He lives in a society where men strive deliberately to change their institutions. If he is not to feel lost in society, he needs to be able to take

his bearings in it; which involves more than understanding what a society is like and how it is changing. It also involves having a *coherent set of values* and knowing how to use them to estimate what is happening. . . .[2]

Modern citizens want and need to understand the major structural features and evolutionary tendencies of their societies. They want and need a general perspective with which they can evaluate the general contours of their societies, proposals for change, and their costs and benefits. It should be a primary goal of a democratic social science to help citizens take their bearings in society by providing them with descriptions of such general perspectives for ordering and evaluating political activity.

This book attempts to develop a perspective which will elucidate the structural characteristics and political possibilities of advanced western societies. We have tried to combine a clarity about normative standards with a rigor in presenting empirical findings in order to illuminate the major political choices available to advanced western societies. In this effort we find that classifications and evaluations of political regimes as "totalitarian" or "democratic," "capitalist," or "communist," "industrial" or "post-industrial" lack utility. The central phenomenon in advanced western nations is public intervention in economic markets and property relations; the central issue is the form and goal of this intervention. Price levels, capital investment, and the distribution of income and wealth have come to be regulated increasingly by conscious political decisions rather than by the play of market forces; the great political question is who will benefit from these decisions.

While most commentators loosely call all of these emergent societies welfare states, we prefer to distinguish three kinds of interventionist regimes, the corporate-oriented *positive state,* the *social security state* with its assurance of a minimum standard of civilized life, and the radically democratic and egalitarian *social welfare state.* Only the latter two properly qualify as welfare states. These ideal-typical constructs, we contend, offer three fundamental perspectives for policy choices from which scholars and citizens may choose.

While we consider each of these perspectives, our sympathies lie with the social welfare state. It alone offers the prospect of satisfying the need for a new political theory commensurate with the demands of a new era, and we sketch the groundwork for this political theory of the social welfare state.[3] We argue explicitly for the values on which it is based: human dignity, equality, liberty, democracy, security, solidarity, and economic efficiency. We show how its tools of budgetary planning, active labor market policy, and solidaristic wage policy can improve the functioning of a capitalist economy; how public services, progressive taxation, transfer payments, and—to a lesser extent—social insurance can redress the distributional inequity produced by unregulated markets; and how various modes of participation can enhance citizens' opportunities to supervise this apparatus and can give public guidance to community life. We then consider conservative and radical criticisms of welfare statist arrangements and conclude that neither of these critical thrusts seriously damages the case for welfare states and, in particular, the case for the social welfare state.

In order to demonstrate that our ideal-typical constructs are not airy fantasy, but the underlying bases of policy choice, we next compare the origins, structure, and performance of welfare policy in Britain, Sweden, and the United States. While the fit between these countries and our models is imperfect and approximate at best, Britain does illustrate the accomplishments and limitations of the social security state, Sweden the possibility of a social welfare state, and the United States the moral inadequacy of the positive state. This comparative survey shows that the standard American political categories of "radical," "liberal," and "conservative" obscure and limit the potential range of political possibilities. More important, it demonstrates that the advanced economic and social welfare policy of what we call the social welfare state, far from being detrimental to human welfare and political stability as many Americans imagine, actually promotes these two desirable ends.

The strength of the political theory of the social welfare state carries obvious implications for the United States. It mandates the nine-point program of social democratic reforms presented in Chapter Eight. This program conforms to Karl Mannheim's description of progressive reform; it tackles the system as a whole rather than simply tending to particular details. It addresses the genuine issues of contemporary western society: What concrete forms should social equality and social solidarity assume? What forms should public participation in political and economic decision-making assume? How can individual freedoms not only be maintained but expanded in an increasingly politicized society? The changes we recommend would not put an end to political controversy—ideologies would continue to flourish—but they would lead to a diminution of the cruel and normal politics first described by Thucydides in which "the strong do what they can and the weak suffer what they must."

THE CASE FOR THE WELFARE STATE

1

The Development and Structure of the Welfare State

The imprecise usage of the term "welfare state" may be perceived by considering the regimes to which it has been applied. In Germany, for example, the term has had the following applications: The Federal Republic has been labeled a welfare state on the basis of its elaborate system of social benefits. The term has been applied to Nazi Germany: "There can be no doubt that the base of Nazi politics was the politics of the welfare state."[1] And it has been found serviceable in describing the Second Reich; indeed many commentators trace the development of present welfare institutions elsewhere directly to the reforms undertaken by Bismarck.[2] Finally, the welfare state has been unearthed at least as far back as eighteenth century Prussia, the leaders of that nation employing police power to enforce rules that its subjects might not otherwise have followed.[3]

While it is possible to imagine a definition sufficiently inclusive to embrace systems as diverse as these, it would not be of much assistance to one attempting to "place oneself in the world" or to one engaged in policy debate. To give utility to the term we must construct a set of conditions that will identify the welfare state more precisely. We first distinguish between two conceptions of the "good life," both of which were advocated vigorously during the formation of nation-states in Western Europe in the sixteenth and seventeenth centuries—the good life for the individual, and the good life for the collectivity in which the individual is to find his place. Only states founded upon the first principle, we shall argue, should even be considered potential welfare states.

But if the foundation of the state is the good life for the individual, why should not individuals be allowed to get on with providing for their own security and well-being unfettered by governmental controls and social initiatives? The answer to this question is best given historically. We shall show that the bulwarks of autonomous markets and private property, upon which individual security and self-reliance were to rest, have, with the development of industrial society, been undermined. Not only have markets and property not functioned as originally conceived, but even the vision of the social order evoked by their *effective* operation has been found by many to be uninspiring.

These developments have led to an expansion of governmental activity in all polities aspiring toward the good life for the individual. Intervention aimed primarily at insuring economic stability and thus the self-interest of existing property holders we shall call the functioning of the *positive state.* The welfare state attempts in addition to establish surrogate forms of property for all those without an adequate basis for security and self-development. We conclude this chapter by distinguishing between two types of welfare states—the *social security state* which aims at a guaranteed national minimum; and the *social welfare state,* directed toward greater social and economic equality and toward a collective role in framing public policy.

The Good Life For Whom?

From the outset of the debate over the proper organizational principles upon which the emerging nation-states in Europe should be based, a key element of those advancing the position of the "good life for the individual" has been the development of the concept of private property. A major thinker who described its liberating qualities and who revealed its inherent difficulties was

2

Jean Bodin. In his major work, *The Republic,* Bodin began his discussion of property with what he perceived as a basic disagreement with a fundamental principle of ancient and medieval political thought—that man is naturally a social and political animal destined to life in society and achieving his essence only within it. Bodin contended the contrary, that families existed—and could continue to exist—apart from the state, which itself was nothing but the "lawful government of many families."[4] Since families were the basis of the state, it followed that "as foundations can of themselves stand without the form of a house . . . so also a family can be of itself without a city or Commonwealth . . . but a Commonwealth can no more be without a family than a city without houses, or a house without a foundation."[5]

For Bodin the family was the basis of the state; to put its essence into contention was to undermine the state itself. Commonwealths were "chiefly established to yield to every man that which is his own and to forbid theft, as it is commanded by the word of God who would have every man enjoy the property of his own goods. . . . *True popular liberty consists in nothing else, but in the enjoyment of our private goods securely without fear to be wronged, in honor, wife or family.*"[6] Bodin's message was to let the inhabitants forget about religious controversies and concern themselves with personal enrichment, while the government proceeded unimpaired in its duty to maintain order and secure property (by the punishment of theft). To employ an analogy of Hobbes', the construction of, and the subsequent respect for, hedges delimiting human behavior would be a good description of the sovereign's duty. Sovereignty, in fact, became defined by Bodin *in relation to* property. One could not exist without the other, or, as Bodin described:

> But however lands may be divided, it cannot possibly be that all things should be common among citizens, which for Plato seemed so notable a thing [that] . . . he deemed it would come to pass that these two words, Mine and Thine, should never more be heard amongst his citizens being in his opinion that cause of all discord and evils in a Commonwealth. But he understood not that by making all things common, a Commonwealth must needs perish: for nothing can be public, where nothing is private: neither can it be imagined there to be anything had in common, if there be nothing to be kept in particular.[7]

3

Given this statement, it is hard to conceive of sovereignty without property, a link with important implications for the holder of sovereignty. Not only are families basically complete in themselves and thus need only security, but also since the sovereign derives his existence from the Mine/Thine duality, he must respect the principle of private property. In short, order is maintained, the state is established, not to exalt the power of itself or of the idea it is supposed to represent, but to *maximize the opportunity for self-fulfillment by its inhabitants.* The distinctiveness of this formulation may be better conceived if it is contrasted with the later mercantilist doctrine.

The Good Life for the State

It is not necessary for our purposes to inquire into the subtleties of mercantilist thought or into the differences among its exponents. All factions were agreed on two basic points: first, national aims were distinct from, and superior to, individual interest; and second, these national aims were founded upon an export surplus.[8] National wealth was not, then, the sum total of goods and services produced internally; rather, wealth consisted of a nation's reserve position, plus or minus its current balance of payments account. Not all goods and services were weighted equally; only those contributing to the national end were valuable.

The achievement of an augmentation in national power represented by an increase in the previously defined national wealth was, moreover, predicated on the proper use of labor power. Far from wishing to establish an order that permitted the self-fulfillment of individuals, the mercantilists asserted that individual energies must be used for the self-fulfillment of the state. This aim helps explain a seeming paradox in mercantilist thought: If they adhered to a "labor theory of value," why was labor to be kept at subsistence level? Their answer was that in order to compete abroad, wages had to be kept as low as possible, and strong incentives must be given to work.[9]

From this line of reasoning followed the whole train of mercantilist prescriptions: the duty to labor, the need to create properly productive work, the stratagem of raising prices in good times so "excess" wages would be absorbed, the need to increase population at all costs, the proscription of frolic, the hatred of

4

"debauchery." This last sentiment is well represented by Daniel Defoe:

> There is a general Taint of Slothfulness upon our Poor. There's nothing more frequent, than for an Englishman to work till he has got his Pocket full of Money, and then go and be idle, *or perhaps drunk,* till 'tis all gone . . . he'll tell you honestly, he'll drink as long as it lasts, and then go to work for more.
> 'Tis the Men that *Won't work,* not the Men that can get no work, which makes the numbers of our Poor. . . .[10]

Whose Welfare?

The two positions of social organization—the good life for the individual, and the good life for the state—have more than an antiquarian interest. Both have been represented in the development of the European, and then the modern, state system. Only when the end of social organization is welfare for the people can we label it a "welfare state." It is not enough simply to interfere with market mechanisms or to infringe upon property rights, as the cases of the Soviet Union and Nazi Germany demonstrate. Rather, intervention must promote individual well-being. And because conceptions of individual welfare differ, political controversy flourishes. These considerations bring the question of values into the heart of the welfare state debate.

We also can develop further the inherent problem facing advocates of the "welfare for the individual." Their original aim was a deflection of activity away from what was considered sterile or disruptive political activity toward private (economic) gain. This project faced the immediate problem that individuals in fact were *not* autonomous, each secure in his own property. And the only force capable of "liberating" people to pursue private gain was the state, exalted for its own sake by their opponents. The tension again is seen clearly in Bodin, who posited sovereignty, the "most high, absolute and perpetual power over the citizens and subjects of a commonwealth," as the essential and unique element in the state.[11] In this situation the king/subject duality became the most vital in the state, transcending all degrees of the feudal scale. No one could demand special privileges of the sovereign, gazing down from the lonely heights of power. Indeed, it could hardly be otherwise, for sovereignty in order to be "absolute" and "most high" could not be mediated through a system not of its own creation, nor could it mean a priori something different for one person than for another. The condition of the good life for the individual, in short, depended for its fulfillment on the volition of the sovereign, a sovereign restrained from tyranny only by moral admonitions or by threats to "appeal to heaven."

Similar problems confronted admirers of various eighteenth century "enlightened despots." None of the chosen sovereigns (Frederick, Catherine, et al.) displayed what one could call a consistent moderation; nor were appeals to reason of much success in returning them to the proper path. Finally, the same tension in the development of the concept of private property, that the only force capable of securing it had also the power to destroy it, is found as well in Anglo-American constitutional interpretation. The classic case involved John Entick, an eighteenth century English pamphleteer, whose books and papers were seized by the crown in an effort to uncover subversive material. None was found; Entick was released and later sued on a charge of trespass. The judge, Lord Camden, found for Entick:

> The great end for which men entered into society was to secure their property. That right is preserved sacred and incommunicable in all instances, where it has not been taken away or abridged by some public law for the good of the whole. . . .[12]

In this decision we find the postulates and ambiguities of the "welfare for the individual" enshrined. People are conceived autonomously; the centrality of property is now presented as an axiom; only by "public law" can property be taken away or abridged (i.e., other individuals cannot). But should the "good of the whole" require it, the rights of property must yield. And since each individual was not in a position to decide this good, the central authority, "public law," is left to do so.

We do not mean to denigrate either the value or the historical achievements of this original welfare for the people position, which found its triumphant expressions in late eighteenth century constitutional and quasi-constitutional documents—the Declaration of the Rights of Man, the Declaration of American Independence, the American Constitution. Nor has the drive terminated. *Men* have been declared liberated; but a basic unit of traditional authority, the family, remained largely unemancipated. The individualization of women and children has not yet

6

fully occurred, and movement toward the goal has been halting. (Significantly, the methods used to attain "women's liberation" are the same as those used by men in the late eighteenth and early nineteenth centuries—central laws; decrees; in the United States, a proposed constitutional amendment.) At the same time, however, this autonomy has brought the danger of central tyranny, forestalled only "theoretically" by the proposed inviolability of private property. Moreover, as we shall now investigate, the link between private property and individual freedom has had further deleterious effects, particularly with the advent of the industrial revolution and the associated sanctification of the market. The development of the market and property system came to pose serious impediments for the acquisition by many of any individual autonomy at all.

The Problems of Unregulated
Markets and Property

Individual autonomy for all is an ideal that embodies many static qualities. It presumes a security of holdings. It is best conceived within an economic order not subject to wide fluctuations. And the admonition to avoid the distractions of politics and to embrace economics as the appropriate focus "of all worthwhile human endeavor"[13] makes sense only if the political realm refrains from social or economic intervention. All three are tenuous assumptions that were not in practice sustained. We shall look at the conflict between the operation of the market and property system, and the challenge to the classical liberal vision itself.

The Problem of Unregulated Markets

The advent of industrialization and the triumph of the market economy brought an approximation of the early liberal vision discussed above in which the political realm ceased to intervene in social relations and in which, in Polanyi's phrase, society became virtually an adjunct of the market.[14] The resulting pattern of economic development, it was soon noticed, took the form of a series of trade or business cycles, times of "boom" and "bust" which tended to become increasingly transnational in their impact. The effect of these cycles on the individual property holder, too often overlooked, was severe. It did not suffice, to use the famous adage, to build a better mousetrap to get the world to come to one's door. If trade was "bad," the best mousetrap in the world might not sell. Of what use then were the virtues of thrift, initiative, and self-discipline?

For years "liberals" and "socialists" considered business cycles within a capitalist economy inevitable. The most popular analogy seems to have been with the weather. Those caught in the rain had to make the best of it. With the mobilization during World War I, however, it began to be accepted, even in economic theory, that something (namely, government intervention) could be done to limit the damage brought on by a downturn of the business cycle. The policy proposals (budget deficits and public spending) and objections to the traditional remedy for depression (wage cuts) were advanced by the "Stockholm School" of Swedish economists and by John Maynard Keynes.

This change in the feeling of helplessness toward business cycles coincided with, and was of course stimulated by, the onset of the Great Depression, the gravest challenge yet to the capitalist economic order. What made the situation so severe was first of all the failure of the world's economies to rebound from the trough of the depression in the usual way. To be sure, after only a brief pause, new consumer industries continued and even accelerated their post-World War I advance. The radio, telephone, camera, and automobile not only continued to experience strong demand; their proper enjoyment necessitated investment in infrastructure on one side and spurred a legion of support facilities (shops, gas stations, repairmen) on the other.[15] The growth in consumer durables also enabled many countries to raise their industrial output over pre-Depression levels. In 1937, for example, industrial output was 49 percent above the 1929 level in Sweden, 34 percent higher in Denmark, 24 percent higher in Britain, and 16 percent higher in Germany. (Industrial output was 6 percent lower in Belgium, 8 percent lower in the United States, and 24 percent lower in France.)[16] With the exception of France, personal income also resumed an upward advance, albeit at a much slower rate.

On the other hand, these selectively favorable trends seemed outweighed by negative factors. To begin with, heavy industry appeared stagnated. World coal production never threatened 1929 levels; only in Germany was there a slight advance. Euro-

8

pean production of pig-iron and steel ingots had failed by 1939 to regain their level of a decade earlier.[17] The shipbuilding industry was decimated, as were industries such as cotton spinning that were forced to compete with new synthetic fibers. Associated manufacturing employment fared even worse. Whole industrial areas appeared destined for permanent attrition. In the northeastern United States, for example, 1939 manufacturing employment was at only 80 percent the 1923–1925 level in New York, 75 percent in Pennsylvania, 70 percent in Massachusetts.[18] Nor was alternative employment easy to find. Indeed, a high level of permanent unemployment seemed to be the particular curse of the Great Depression. In no democratic country did unemployment fall below 10 percent of the work force before 1939. Moreover, and this finding is perhaps even more disconcerting, the record of the 1920s had been only slightly better. In the eighteen years between 1921–1938 Sweden and Denmark had never achieved an unemployment level below 10 percent of the work force. Norway and Britain managed this feat only once, while Germany went through a series of wild gyrations—6.9 percent unemployment in 1925, 18 percent in 1926, 8 percent in 1928, 13 percent in 1929.[19] As a final negative economic sign, many economies experienced the pathological pattern of falling consumption. With falling consumption it was hard to see how demand could ever be stimulated sufficiently.[20] Taking the years 1923–1938 as a whole, this record strongly supported the Keynesian contention that left to its own devices capitalism was likely to generate equilibrium at less than full employment.

The repercussions of the inability of the system of unregulated markets to provide individual stability, or even general economic advance, were far reaching. Although the population of many countries (particularly in the United States and Britain) remained remarkably quiescent, there was a widespread feeling among social commentators and "progressive" politicians that a "middle way" had to be found between the waste and irrationality of unencumbered capitalism and the loss of liberty and individuality imposed by "totalitarianism." This "middle way" entailed the *reintervention of politics into the social and economic order.* Markets had to be regulated ("planning" became the emotive word of the 1930s), and property could not be considered inviolable if its exercise ran counter to plans for orderly economic development.

Just how established market intervention had become was revealed after World War II when most of the Western governments returned to the political control of conservative parties, many of which had campaigned on the platform of drastically reducing the government's economic role. None had any significant success. The reason has been well-described by Arthur Schweitzer:

> [This] inability to realize the conservative goals of a limited government and return to an automatic market system suggests two inferences. Negatively, the structure of markets has changed to such an extent that there is no longer any satisfactory and acceptable mechanism of self-regulation, bringing beneficial results to a majority of those affected by particular adjustments. Positively, the public economy in the United States is so well established that no political party can dare to assume the risk of destroying it.... *A government without economic functions is not regarded as desirable or feasible by any significant economic group in the country.*[21]

The effect on the system of private property was equally severe. The failure of unregulated markets to generate orderly economic advance brought government supervision not merely to forestall malicious use but to promote the economic good of the whole.

The Problems of Unregulated Property

Even the staunchest defender of the inviolability of property has difficulty in justifying, or even in entitling, its unrestricted use. The most obvious abuse of property rights is malicious activity that limits the ability of others to enjoy *their* property—the building of a high wall solely for the purpose of depriving a neighbor of air and light has been the classic case. It is a commentary on the belief in the tangible unity of the concept of property that such activity was long declared beyond the compass of the law, but gradually during the nineteenth century it became proscribed—in France in 1850, in the United States in 1889, in Germany in 1896.[22] More significant were injunctions against the use of property in situations in which others could not be expected to protect themselves. Regulation of hours of labor for children was initiated as early as 1802 in Britain; protection for women followed later. The discovery of "public health" and communicable diseases entailed further restrictions. It was one thing if unsanitary conditions tolerated by an individual brought on his own ill health, but if his disease then spread to an innocent neighbor, it seemed time for public authority to step in with minimum standards and demands. More broadly, it has often been thought proper to regulate or prohibit one's liberty to promote or participate in activities deemed at variance with official public morality—drugs, alcoholic beverages, gambling, and prostitution.

While these reforms could—and did—modify the "natural" outcome of property relations, they remained within the spirit of the classical liberal profession of individual autonomy based on the ownership of private property. With the further development of the unregulated market economy, however, the automatic (nonpolitical) nature of these rights became increasingly challenged as it was discovered that industrial society spawned a large number of individuals without property and without realistic hope of acquiring any, and that the fluctuations of business cycles robbed people, "through no fault of their own," of the security and independence that the ownership of property was supposed to bring.

The social and economic changes occasioned by the growth of heavy industry made the moral exhortations of unconstrained individualism simply not relevant to the lives of the bulk of what came to be called the "working class." Meanwhile, the "men of property" soon came to be viewed understandably as conservative and hypocritical. The system of private property itself, which had only recently been seen as such a liberating force that its establishment received the appropriate German term *Befreiungsgesetzgebung* ("liberation-legislation"), was now deemed a great bulwark of the class system. As a final irony, the collective output of the individual "wills" of property owners, the industrial towns, seemed the triumph not so much of "individual energy" as of inhuman forces. Manchester, for example, was compared by outside observers to an "awful machine," "the entrance to hell," "an industrious spider," "a noisome labyrinth"—surely this town, the first city of the industrial age, could not be the product of human design![23]

When investigators turned their attention to a systematic study of the inhabitants of these urban centers, the inadequacy of property as a basis for individual action was brought into even sharper focus. In the first place, there was unearthed a whole substratum of direct casualties of the industrial system—the unemployed, the marginally employed, the disabled and infirm, and vagrants. These groups together were found by Booth to comprise more than 20 percent of the entire population of London in the 1880s.[24] Perhaps even more disturbing was the finding that "steady" industrial workers also went through a "cycle of poverty," with the vast majority totally unable to accumulate any significant assets of any kind and thus being forced to live in total destitution when not fully employed (that is, when sick, thrown out of work, or too old to labor).[25] Nor have the industrial advances of the last seventy years eliminated these problems. The demands of industrial society continue to produce marginal and expendable groups, and even those who devote themselves to a lifetime of toil for the industrial order are often as unable as were the inhabitants of York in 1900 to acquire any property of monetary importance. As we shall see in Chapter Seven, of those retiring in the United States in 1969, over one-third had a net worth (including home equity) of less than $5,000; almost 60 percent had less than $15,000. In short, we note again that property rights have to be attenuated to allow for orderly economic growth and that markets must be circumscribed if the system of private property is to provide a basis of security and independence for the bulk of the population.

A final problem of unregulated property is found in the tendency toward the concentration of productive property in corporations and the associated weakening of the bond between ownership and control.[26] These corporations are able and very willing to impose prices and conditions. And their domination of the market increases; in the United States the two hundred largest corporations controlled over 60 percent of the assets of manufacturing firms in 1970; the number had been one thousand as late as 1941.[27] These developments have put the sanctity of private property in jeopardy. It is one thing to say that someone has the right to run his affairs as he pleases. But should a manager for General Motors be accorded the same leeway over assets that are not his? Is there not a place for public authority to direct the management toward politically determined goals?

More narrowly, the concentration of capital has made others besides the working class potential nonaccumulators of assets— small businessmen, shopkeepers, and farmers become insecure as well. Once again we are faced with the dilemma of Bodin and the other early liberal writers. Then, the goal of setting men free from political coercion in order to pursue private, economic gain required the massive intervention of state authority and thus potentially *increased* the sphere of politics. Now, the goal of a widespread system of private property designed to limit political action may rest on state support and guarantees. We shall explore this issue further in Chapter Three.

Loss of Collective Purposes

Unregulated markets and unfettered property rights, functioning within the liberal conception of private satisfaction, frustrate the pursuit of collective goals. Pollution that does not immediately threaten public health may, for example, be objectionable and well worth proscribing. But it is hard to see how such a task could be carried out under a system of free markets and property guarantees.[28] It is not even easy to subject the polluter to a tax since he may not gain any monetary value from the pollution.

The end result is a bias toward what Galbraith and earlier writers have termed "private affluence and public squalor," squalor measured not in terms of public spending levels but in the quality of public life that modern society seems to produce. We mentioned earlier the opinion of a number of contemporary observers that from the very beginning the individual property owners who created Manchester factory by factory, house by house, had somehow lost control of the whole. This feeling grew with the spread of urban blight, with the "uglification" of formerly aesthetically pleasing spots. Surely, it was argued, something must be done about this situation, and however this "something" might vary from writer to writer, there was general agreement that the system of private property posed a formidable barrier. The concern for the public good is strengthened by the tendency toward economic segregation. Given a choice, individuals of high income and assets will tend to congregate together to the exclusion of the less well off.[29] And on what basis consistent

13

with the principle of property rights should individuals *not* be given this choice? But if they are, what then becomes of collective feeling or collective purpose?

These questions raise the general issue of the adequacy of the liberal vision in the modern world, specifically the separation of politics from society and the focus of legitimate individual interest on the latter. In the first place, as we have shown, politics *has* reentered social and economic life, and in an instrumental sense has become a practical affair. More broadly, politics and the pursuit of collective goods can assume new significance for the citizen. He may come to see the flaw in the early liberal estimate of politics and resolve to become politically active as a means of developing his or her character.

To see the potential involved from another direction, we recall the fears expressed as early as the middle of the nineteenth century that economically directed individualism has presaged the advent of naked philistinism, of materialism run mad, that it has broken down important social relationships like the family, and that it has made a mockery of altruistic and social values. This is not to advance the solution of an irrational subordination of the individual to the collectivity, but rather it is to recognize the reciprocal ties and responsibilities between the individual and society. The problem from the viewpoint of the individual is evoked by Hillel's questions:[30]

> If I am not for myself, who will be for me?
> If I am only for myself—then what am I for?

And again, in sorting out the complexities involved in such a relationship, the vision of a society consisting of individuals each secure in his property and relating to each other only through the impersonal medium of the market provides at best limited guidance.

Types of State Responses

No modern, democratic state has failed to address the difficulties resulting from the operations of unrestrained markets and property. All governments have attenuated property rights, both productive and nonproductive, and all have intervened in various ways in the operations of the "market." In this sense we have indeed experienced the historical failure of what Wolin calls the "liberal cluster of assumptions and propositions" to insulate society from politics. Or, to put the matter another way, we have experienced the end of laissez-faire capitalism. If any sustained departure from this model is deemed an instance of "socialism" or "the welfare state," then either or both are clearly established everywhere. But, to repeat, this formulation is unsatisfactory because it precludes the ability to make elemental and essential distinctions. Specifically, the major issue is not that all states have a policy of intervention, but that different states employ different policies for different purposes. Abstracting from the historical record, we can aggregate these different forms of intervention in three "models": the *positive state,* the *social security state,* and the *social welfare state.* For each we shall describe the type of intervention employed, the groups benefiting from the intervention, and the vision inspiring the thrust of public policy.[31]

The Positive State

The primary aim of the positive state[32] is to protect the holders of property from the difficulties of unregulated markets and from potential redistributive demands. The policy orientation is toward *government-business collaboration for economic growth,* what Gramm calls the "symbiotic relationship between the business, legal, and political communities."[33] In this relationship, business has ceded much of its ability to make unhindered market decisions in return for financial assistance at home and political support abroad. Also applied is a *minimalist full-employment policy*— that is, there is a concern to keep employment high enough to assure high levels of consumption and business activity. There is consternation when unemployment hits sectors of the labor market controlled by organized labor, whose support is conducive to the smooth operation of the government-business cooperation. There is equal concern that the demand for labor not be so strong as to bid up its price and extend the influence of unions.

In the field of "welfare," there is a disinclination to do anything inconsistent with economic "efficiency."[34] This interest puts major emphasis on *social insurance programs.* These programs are founded on actuarial principles (with occasional help from general revenues) and are designed to even out income over a person's "life cycle" and to spread the risk of unemployment and illness from the individual to the general population. For those benefiting from the services of the positive state, these programs have the attraction that potential redistribution from the rich to the poor is deflected to noneconomic categories (the young to the old, the healthy to the sick). Social insurance has the further advantages of tying the destiny of wage earners to the destiny of the state and of encouraging proper work habits. It cannot be said that the "proletariat has no country" if the nation is overseeing and often contributing to a plan that would provide unemployment and retirement benefits. And since one has to make certain minimum and periodic payments to qualify for assistance, systems of social insurance in effect institute a form of compulsory savings and provide a strong incentive to conform to a regular life of work. The goal corresponds generally to what Titmuss labels the "residual welfare model": welfare policy "is to function as a means of social control."[35]

In sum, this model entails considerable government intervention in the economy and restrictions on business activity. From the perspective of those who consider any form of government intervention the touchstone of improper public policy, the positive state becomes indistinguishable except in degree from the types of welfare state. We shall consider this position when we discuss the "conservative critics" of the welfare state. From our perspective, however, the positive state is not a welfare state because it does not perform the elemental function of a welfare state which is to guarantee surrogate forms of property for all citizens and not to restrict the benefits of autonomy and independence to those whom the economic order favors. Rather, the beneficiaries tend to be those who, under conditions of laissez-faire, one would expect would prosper most readily. The vision of the positive state is one of rugged individualism within the context of balanced economic growth and protection of corporate interest.

The Social Security State

In discussing the social security state we must first make a distinction between economic and social policy. To provide for macroeconomic growth the social security state advances the tool of government-business cooperation described above. *"Maximalist" full employment* is pursued, through public employment as a last resort. In social policy the social security state embraces the welfare state ideal of guaranteeing surrogate forms of property for all. And the important objective of a *guaranteed national minimum* is introduced.

A guaranteed national minimum is intended to overcome the limitations inherent in a welfare policy based on social insurance provisions. Programs of social insurance are designed for workers in steady employment who are, however, subject to cyclical unemployment and who are not able to accumulate sufficient assets to provide for a decent retirement. These programs cannot, except at the loss of insurance principles, be stretched to cover the casualties of the industrial order—the chronically sick and disabled, single parent families with small children, workers with no or unneeded skills. Effective assistance to this group entails a broader conception of the national interest than that which would lead to advocacy of social insurance. The public commitment to a guaranteed national minimum for every citizen, the provision of benefits for all "adequate in amount, that is to say enough for subsistence without other resources, and adequate in time, that is to say as long as the need lasts,"[36] marks a momentous step in the direction of collective responsibility for individual maintenance. It makes plain the failure of a system of private property to provide universal security and the duty of the state to fill the void. The historical circumstances under which this principle arose are detailed for Britain in Chapter Five.

The elaboration of the national minimum makes it perfectly possible to abolish poverty conceived as the absence of basic subsistence. If the minimum line, "subsistence," is placed at a level commensurate with the minimum expectations of society, and if the level is then raised to conform to advances in the standard of living, and if no one for any reason is permitted to fall below this floor, then decent security "from the cradle to the grave" can be said to have been achieved. This security, as we shall see concretely in our studies of Britain and Sweden, is not in the least impossible for public policy to accomplish either by supplementing social insurance with government payments and services for those not qualifying or (even better since it does not so easily isolate the casualties of the industrial order for invidious comment) by labeling all benefits up to minimum levels "insurance" and then permitting specific plans to supplement them. Statements like "the poor will always be with us" are nonsense. Incomes may always be arranged in the form of a pyramid, but there is no reason why the base of the pyramid need go below a recognized minimum.

There is a final point concerning a guaranteed national minimum that, because of its importance for the welfare debate in the United States, should be stated explicitly. A guaranteed minimum, in the words of the Beveridge Report, is to be given "*as of right*" to every citizen. A recognized level of benefits is not something to be granted or withheld at public whim. Benefits from social insurance funds and general revenues cannot assume the surrogate form of property if their recipients must assume a proper political or moral posture, or if they cannot count on receiving requisite assistance in the future.

These economic and social policies are intended to be of direct benefit to every citizen. This vision is not a priori hypocritical. Rather, as we shall maintain in Chapter Three, it represents a modern and noble version of the Liberal Ideal. Although the specter of a thoroughgoing social and economic egalitarianism haunts many conservative critics of the social security state, the governing principle is clearly not equality but equality of opportunity. In the words of the Beveridge Report, "the state in organizing security should not stifle incentive, opportunity, responsibility; in establishing a national minimum, it should leave room and encouragement for voluntary action by each individual to provide more for himself and his family."[37]

The Social Welfare State

The contrast between the vision underlying the social security and the social welfare state is evident when we juxtapose Beveridge's words to the argument of Ernst Wigforss, one of the leading Swedish Social Democratic theoreticians. For Wigforss, the wage earner

> cannot readily agree to that view of the welfare state that is now frequently put forth, that it should secure a minimum livelihood for all, but allow whatever goes beyond this to be won through each individual's or each group's asserting itself in an unlimited competition for standards, wealth, and power. That spirit clearly conflicts with the ideas that both the trade union movement and social democracy seek to follow in their public

18

labors . . . that it still shall be the labor movement's ideas of equality, cooperation and solidarity, that shall set their stamp upon society's continuing transformation.[38]

To actualize this vision requires a different policy mix from that animating the refurbished liberalism of the social security state. In economic policy government-business collaboration becomes an expedient that at least in theory can, and should, be transcended. And the goal of full employment is to be realized more by *government-union cooperation* in the labor market than by public works.[39]

Equally important are two new policies, *environmental planning* and *solidaristic wages*. We use the term "environmental planning" in its most comprehensive sense as the regulation of property to preserve amenities, the prohibition of activities resulting in unacceptable levels of pollution, urban planning, and the development of "new towns"—in sum, an effort to inject social and collective values into a society founded, as it must be, on the good life for the individual. The tension between these concerns is obvious, but so was the tension between the liberty of the individual property owner and the aggregate outcome of this liberty which often seemed a product of demonic design. And while these efforts have been far from uniformly successful, when made in other than random fashion, they have blurred the dichotomy between "private affluence and public squalor" without labor direction or expropriation.

The phrase "solidaristic wage policy" was developed by the Swedish Trade Union Confederation, the Landesorganisationen (LO).[40] The purpose of this policy is to counteract the tendency toward the concentration of assets and income and to bring as many of the low paid as possible within the organization. The mechanism to achieve these ends has been a series of national employer-union wage agreements in which there has been a concerted effort (1) to narrow differentials among groups in the labor market and (2) to extract for labor a larger relative piece of the national income. This policy entails the active participation of the labor organization in wage and employment decisions and thus helps extend economic control beyond the administrative-business elite. The purpose of this tool is more social solidarity, more equality. What the solidaristic wage policy strives for is the establishment of a relative level below which wages may not go (equivalent in conception to the policy of the national minimum), and then the progressive *collapse* of the income pyramid from the bottom toward the top.

In social as well as in economic policy, the social welfare state aims to promote equality and solidarity. It seeks not merely to produce a guaranteed minimum for its citizens, but to achieve a general equality of living conditions. The primary social policy instrument for attaining equality is the substitution of public services for social insurance programs and public assistance in the provision of health care, child-rearing facilities, legal services, and the like. Public services give benefits to all, making no distinction as to whether the recipients can or cannot pay for these services, or whether they have contributed to the appropriate insurance programs. Through this procedure public services remove important sectors of social life from the influence of the market.

This vision and the policies associated with it portend for the first time a *broadening of the locus of power.*[41] The social welfare state does not intend merely to extend benefits to the underprivileged and to raise benefits relatively over time. There is in addition an effort to bring previously underrepresented groups into the formation of economic and political policy. The ultimate aim is to shift decision-making power from employer to employee,[42] and (the two are not necessarily compatible) to increase citizen participation within all decision-making organizations.

The Future Political Agenda

None of the three types of interventionist states is historically inevitable; there is even some counterevidence to the proposition that welfare provisions expand as a nation's per capita income rises.[43] The absence of historical determinism heightens the significance of current political debate. We can dispense with such arid topics as the formal ownership of the means of production, the staple of discussion between "communism" and "capitalism." Instead, we are able to raise issues such as the following: What sorts of government intervention in market and property relationships are desirable? Does the transition toward a national minimum or a classless society jeopardize individual autonomy and incentives? Can the reforms necessary to establish a social welfare state be implemented in advanced capitalist societies? Or if one desires "real social equality," does the capitalist generation of economic wealth within what is basically a capitalist economic order make the dream impossible?

In the succeeding chapters we shall pursue these questions from two directions. We shall attempt to isolate and discuss the value positions implicit in the current political debate by contrasting the critics with the defenders of the welfare state. We shall then be in a position to differentiate between the two types of welfare state and to describe how specific welfare policies operate in Britain, Sweden, and the United States. We shall conclude with suggestions for forming an American welfare state.

2

Justifying the Social Welfare State

Two tasks confront anyone bent on justifying a particular form of social organization. The first is to state clearly and to defend vigorously the basic values that a society should seek to embody; the second is to specify the major social institutions and policies required to achieve those ends. Such justifications need not guarantee utopias in order to be successful; they need only demonstrate the relative superiority of one set of values, institutions, and policies over alternative sets. To express the point more specifically, one can make the case for the social welfare state without contending that it constitutes a panacea for all social ills. The social welfare state might well retain sufficient blemishes to show that it is the product of imperfect human beings, but if its imperfections are relatively fewer than alternative systems—even if it is "the worst of all possible systems, save all others that have been tried"—then the case for it would be compelling.

These considerations determine the strategy of this chapter. After briefly noting the undeveloped and ambiguous character of welfare state theory and noting possible techniques for justifying a social welfare state, it will be necessary first to examine the value preferences that undergird the social welfare state. Second, the major institutions and policies required to achieve these values will be considered. The analysis then turns to the problem of implementing the social welfare statist program. The justification developed here pertains to only one type of welfare state, the social welfare state; the reader may wish to work out the closely related case for the social security state.

The Neglect of Theory

To date no coherent and persuasive case for the welfare state exists. Its appeal is pre-theoretical; it, more than its rivals, conforms to elemental standards of justice and decency. The absence of a dominant theorist or of a single commanding system of thought endorsing the welfare state has been documented again and again. "The social philosophy behind the welfare state is vague and inchoate," writes Sidney Hook.[1] Maurice Bruce, in his history of the welfare state in Britain, observes that his country's welfare institutions have not been constructed according to a clear theoretical design; rather "there is very little evidence, at any stage in the evolution of the Welfare State, of the direct influence of a political philosophy setting out to remake society."[2] The Swedish writer Gunnar Adler-Karlsson suggests that his countrymen suffer from a similar poverty of theoretical guidance. Noting the lack of "any accepted *theory* of the middleway economy in Sweden," he claims only that the Swedish Social Democrats have acted "*as if*" they adhered to such a theory.[3] Piet Thoenes expresses similar dissatisfaction with the condition of welfare state theory: "A remarkable feature of the welfare state," he observes, "is that nobody has the courage to propagate it properly and completely. To the socialist it is nothing but semi-socialism, to the liberals only semi-liberalism."[4] On even the most basic questions the proponents of the welfare state can muster no more than negative and incomplete answers. What are its ends? How does it conceive of welfare:

> As a matter of fact, there are very few concrete pronouncements about this; the Welfare State was brought into being after a world crisis and a world war, in a period of scarcity in which it was patently obvious to everybody what it was they did *not* want, and that was: danger, hunger, thirst or cold, unemployment, dictatorships or squandering of either food or talents.[5]

The conclusion is plain: The welfare state has yet to develop a single coherent and compelling theory to guide its political practice.

Instead of one satisfactory justification for the welfare state, a variety of partial and mutually inconsistent arguments circulate in the political debate of advanced industrial societies. These arguments rest on a variety of metaphysical and moral premises. They emphasize different aspects of welfare statist organization. Their eclectic and protean character, however unattractive for the political theorist in search of coherent theory or the policy maker in need of well-grounded advice, does carry certain political advantages. For in modern representative systems popular agreement on basic principles, religious, political, or economic, cannot be assumed; no single metaphysical or moral system is so dominant that it can provide a consensual foundation for political theorizing. In these societies a political argument, to be persuasive, must appeal to a variegated audience of citizens entertaining distinct and often contradictory fundamental assumptions. Under these conditions the major criterion for effective political argument is not strict logical consistency, but the capacity to elicit general agreement and support. The appropriate symbol for brilliant argument ceases to be the sharp, precisely structured arrow to aim at opponents and becomes instead a series of nets, large, loose, a bit tattered, but designed to capture as many different sorts of political fish as possible. Current arguments for the welfare state have this broad, eclectic quality. None offers a systematic defense of welfare statist institutions comparable to the great intellectual enterprises of Plato, Aquinas, Hobbes, or Rousseau, but together they do attract a broad spectrum of voters.

The current arguments for the welfare state have developed primarily as criticisms of the liberal and socialist traditions. In an early article Gunnar Myrdal argued that justifications for social welfare policy flowed from two distinct sources—a socialistically inclined liberalism and a liberalized socialism. The pure strains of traditional liberalism and socialism, Myrdal argued, rejected social welfare policy as a solution for social ills. "If one examines the two major ideological currents that have come down to us from the Enlightenment—liberalism and socialism—one will find that neither of them expresses to any great extent aspirations to social welfare policy—in fact scarcely even so much as the more patriarchal and religiously tinged variants of the old estate ideology (*'ståndsideologien'*)...."[6] Only through a "softening up" of these traditional doctrines could a distinctive social welfare ideology emerge.

Classical liberalism had maintained that efforts to improve the lot of the underprivileged, however well-intentioned, would prove fruitless. Efforts to eliminate or even to moderate class distinctions were doomed to fail because they contravened the natural economic laws to which society must conform. For this claim Malthus's pessimistic demography stood as the primary authority. According to his argument social reforms that improved the living standards of the impoverished classes would stimulate population increases that would in turn drive living conditions downward once again; thus in the long run social welfare policy was self-defeating. This doctrine of the futility of reform afforded traditional liberalism a comfortable escape from the logical implications of its egalitarian assumptions; it could denounce advanced social welfare policy as unavailing as well as immoral.

Not until economists like John Stuart Mill and Adolf Wagner questioned the fundamental principles of classical liberal economics was the way cleared for a coherent liberal case for social welfare policy. Mill accepted the validity of classical economics for the sphere of production and, on the whole, for the sphere of exchange, but denied its claim that the prevailing distribution of property resulted from the ineluctable working of economic laws. The property system was a work of men, and men had the right and eventually the duty to alter it. For Wagner, too, society's mechanisms for distributing resources were not sacrosanct, but open to manipulation for the purpose of eliminating gross disparities in living conditions. Furthermore, these improvements could endure, for advances in birth control technology provided the means to limit increases in population and the resultant oversupply in the labor market; with the availability of contraceptive devices the Malthusian argument lost its force. Traditional liberal teachings could now assume a "social" and "interventionist" thrust; modern liberalism would consider private capitalism efficient for the production of goods, but in need of modification in its patterns of distribution. The affinity between this view and the social security state's emphasis on reforms in the distributive rather than in the productive apparatus of society (in contrast to classical Marxism's prescription) is obvious.

Traditional socialism, both in its utopian and Marxist forms, was, in Myrdal's view, also uninclined to social welfare policy. Utopian socialism insisted upon a revolution in social values, not simply social reforms. Piecemeal improvements in living conditions, carried on within the existing social order, could not suffice; even worse, they would perpetuate an inherently evil system. Similarly, classical Marxism, with its emphasis upon the historical inevitability of a revolutionary crisis within capitalist society, a catastrophe which would usher in the socialist era, left little scope for a conscious, ameliorative social policy. Such a policy could flourish only when the doctrine of the *necessity* of a revolutionary transformation had lost its force. The revisionist socialists, with Bernstein at their head, "softened up" the traditional doctrine in just this way; they denied the inevitability of the proletariat's growing impoverishment and of capitalism's collapse. They discerned within capitalist structures and parliamentary democracy a resiliency and adaptability that would permit the gradual realization of socialism through a steady procession of reforms in social welfare policy.

Writers in the "softened-up" traditions tended to assume liberal or socialist values rather than to argue for them. This invocation of values that were held to be universally valid had three drawbacks: It prevented the formation of a complete and coherent case for the welfare state. It obscured the specific meaning attached to such broad terms as liberty and equality. And finally, it permitted the coexistence of two general variants of welfare statist arguments—liberally tinged arguments for the social security state and socialistically tinged arguments for the social welfare state. A thorough consideration of these inconsistencies and ambiguities, however intriguing in its own right, falls outside the scope of this volume. It suffices for the present to note the current disjointedness of the arguments for the welfare state, a condition explicable by the varied ideological origins of such arguments, but a situation that must be remedied if the welfare state is to be placed on a secure theoretical footing.

The Problem of Justification

A satisfactory justification for the welfare state could start from a variety of philosophical premises. A social contract theorist

26

attracted by Rawls' *Theory of Justice* could easily alter minor portions of Rawls' argument and generate a case for either the social security state or the social welfare state. He might argue, for example, that the maximin psychology of Rawls' rational men really dictates not a society based on the difference principle (all social values are to be distributed equally unless an unequal distribution is to everyone's advantage), but one based on an assured (high) minimum standard of material provision. Alternatively, he might contend that persons who rated self-respect as the most important of primary goods might establish a more egalitarian society, perhaps even one based on the principle of redress, rather than allow the potentially great inequalities sanctioned by the difference principle.[7]

Similarly utilitarianism, particularly negative utilitarianism, offers grounds for constructing justifications for the welfare state. Indeed much of social welfare policy—early factory legislation and child labor laws, public assistance, public health measures, public housing legislation, unemployment and disability insurance, and full employment policy—has been implicitly or explicitly based on the premise that it will eradicate or ameliorate intolerably painful conditions. Negative utilitarian arguments for a social security state would concentrate on eliminating the most obvious causes of physical distress—grinding poverty, inadequate nutrition, insufficient medical care, and the like. To justify a social welfare state the negative utilitarian would stress in addition the psychic and material pain resulting from inequality and alienation and the need to remedy these conditions through egalitarian reforms.

The third great current of modern Western philosophy, historical idealism, might also provide a basis for advocacy of the welfare state. Without vast distortion Hegel himself may be read as having advocated a somewhat eccentric welfare state, organized on corporate lines, bent on rationality, and dedicated to resolving the conflicts and remedying the deficiencies of a capitalist economy. One might also argue (with somewhat less warrant) that the course of modern history demonstrates that the world's most advanced industrial societies are becoming welfare states rather than capitalist or socialist states.

The development of these systematic justifications for the welfare state, grounded on the three most important moral and philosophical systems of modern Western political theory, remains a stimulating but largely unfulfilled assignment. Completed, it would offer inducements for the proponents of these traditions to give allegiance to the welfare state, but for those who do not share the particular intellectual perspective enbodied in a specific tradition, a justification in its (say, negative utilitarian) terms would be unconvincing. Thus any defense of the welfare state which aims at general acceptance must be couched not in any particular "conceptual framework," but in the values that are poured into this framework. Social contractarians must always specify the nature of an appealing contract, utilitarians the nature of the good, and historical idealists the nature of historical progress, and in doing so they infuse their systems with the values that they advocate. These values must be accepted, if one is to accept the ensuing political recommendations.

The Values of the Social Welfare State

Values are not capable of being scientifically demonstrated. They are choices that people must make according to their own conceptions of "right" and "wrong," "good" and "evil." These conceptions may be the product of social environment, rational deliberation, emphathetic imagination, or other factors. Whatever their sources, however, values are not simply irrational preferences or matters of taste; values can be defended with arguments and moral appeals. These arguments and appeals serve two purposes: to persuade persons that the value preferences underlying a particular type of state are superior to alternative sets and thus to establish tests whereby the performance of governments can be evaluated.

The values that form the basis and constitute the appeal of the social welfare state are equality, freedom, democracy, solidarity, security, and economic efficiency. Intrinsic to each of these is the fundamental assumption of individual human worth and dignity. This list of values is not meant to be complete—the social welfare state bears no animus against love, truth, and beauty—but only to indicate the primary political objectives that distinguish the welfare state from other regimes. Nor is the list intended as a rank ordering of values. The relative priorities and trade-offs among these objectives are not a matter for a priori determination, though the social welfare state does differ from alternative social orders in the interpretations and the emphasis that it gives to particular values like equality and solidarity.

What distinguishes the social welfare state from traditional liberal forms of social organization is above all the prominence it gives to the value of *equality*. Equality in itself is a formal value; to give it content, one must answer the question, equality of what? equality in what respects? Equality embraces numerous specific considerations like the right to education, equality before the law, equality of personal respect, equality of political and economic influence, but the core of the principle, as social welfare statists conceive it, is the conviction that all persons have the same right to live a full and satisfying life. "Equality's special position lies in the fact that its content consists just in that claim for everyone's equal right."[8] Equality in this sense is an end in itself, an essential attribute of a just society.

This concept of equality goes beyond the liberal idea of equal opportunity. It mandates more than simply an equal start or the right to compete on equal terms. Not only is the liberal ideal virtually impossible to implement without sharp redistributions of power and wealth, but it can easily lead to a meritocratic society stratified on the basis of differential personal accomplishment, however accomplishment is defined.[9] The social welfare state's conception of equality requires a society free from class barriers, not merely at the beginning of an individual's life but throughout it.

This view of equality does not imply or endorse the elimination of personal differences; on the contrary it envisages a society in which individual development is no longer hampered by the obstacles imposed by a class society. Its goal is not the society Kurt Vonnegut satirizes in his short story, "Harrison Bergeron," a society which condemns Vonnegut's ballet-dancing hero to a life in shackles in order to satisfy the envy of his less agile fellows. Rather, the social welfare state hopes to create an environment in which any person is free to fulfill aspirations to a legitimate career, regardless of sex, wealth, or family background, and to receive compensation for his or her activities that is comparable with that of his or her fellow citizens.

Nor does the egalitarian ideal require a society in which all economic activities receive equal remuneration; such a situation would be virtually impossible because of differences in family structures and it would fail to account for persons with special needs. What equality does require in the economic sphere is the elimination of differentials in reward so large that they create social classes. In the United States this principle would mandate a substantial narrowing of the distribution of personal wealth and income. Through sharply progressive inheritance and wealth taxes the possibility of possessing a large fortune would have to be eliminated. Incomes might be limited to a range between twice the national mean and one-half of the national mean. This range (roughly $7,500 to $30,000 for a family of four) would permit a wide variety of life styles, but would make the existence of social classes distinctly harder to maintain. Differences of occupation would remain, but they would not determine a person's life chances. These changes would bring the United States closer to one of the finest models of the classless society, the family, a form of social organization in which the differences in personal capacity or status are not allowed to override the common bonds of kinship and affection.

This conception of equality as an end in itself has strong roots in Western thinking. Christianity views all humankind as members of a divine family in which harlots receive consideration equal to that of religious potentates. A recurrent theme of secular political thought holds that because human beings have similar basic needs (for air, food, shelter, love, and the like), that they consequently merit similar regard; Rousseau, in rejecting the notion that the rich had special needs, pointed out that a grandee like a goatherd has only two legs and one belly. A variant of this argument contends that men's similar abilities justify equal treatment. Hobbes puts the case on prudential grounds by pointing out that no human is so superior to another that he can be totally free from the fear of death by that person's hand. Finally, modern democratic and legal principles mandate equal treatment of citizens in the crucial areas of voting and legal treatment.

Greater equality is not merely an end in itself, however; it is also desirable as a means to other important goals. For R. H. Tawney equality opens the way for right relationships among human beings; it creates the basis for fellowship. Genuine cooperation and friendship, freed from social constraint, can only take place between equals.

30

Great disparities in standards and influence complicate and poison relationships and communication between individuals and groups. . . . Equalizing conditions of life then becomes a means of changing human relationships, of creating a better social climate.[10]

Fraternal association requires equality; it is incompatible with class cleavages.

Equality can also be commended as a means to economic efficiency. Contrary to the assertions of the prominent American economist, Arthur Okun, the relationship between equality and efficiency is not that of a "big trade-off."[11] This contention has long been a staple of conservative criticisms of the welfare state, but its factual basis is negligible. Okun himself concedes that progressive taxation has little effect upon incentives to work and to invest. He presents virtually no evidence to support the claim that equality undermines economic efficiency and even introduces several cases where equality enhances efficiency; the record on equalized employment opportunity in particular "illustrates the general possibility that what is good for equality may be good for efficiency."[12] Swedish Social Democrats, following the lead of Gunnar Myrdal, have long argued that it is grossly inefficient to allow only the better situated members of society to develop and employ their talents. Groups that lag behind, unable to use their abilities to contribute to the common good, hinder the attainment of economic efficiency as well as social justice. Inequality wastes "human capital."

Equality also serves as an instrument for expanding freedom. Equality promotes freedom by reducing the opportunities for the powerful to coerce the weak and by expanding opportunities for the poorer strata of society. The social welfare state aspires to free citizens from the pressure of external circumstances, class handicaps, and economic insecurity through more equal distribution of economic and political resources. As the Alva Myrdal report to the Swedish Social Democratic Party argues:

. . . it is inequality, class distinctions, which pigeonhole people and limit their opportunities to shape their lives freely. A more equal distribution of resources, influence and opportunities for choice increases variety in society and in the life of the individual. There is strong reason to believe that promoting equality of opportunity gives more scope to human individuality, for each person to shape his life according to his own ability and not along lines dictated by class.[13]

The demand for equality thus leads to a demand for equal freedom as well.

This concept of *freedom* as autonomous choice, as the equal right of each individual to determine his or her manner of life, is a second crucial value in the social welfare state. Freedom is not an abstract and indivisible quality, as both everyday language and much scholarly discussion imply, but embraces a multitude of individual freedoms: freedom of speech, freedom of religious belief (or disbelief), freedom of physical movement, of career choice, styles of interior decoration, recreational pastimes, and so on. Not all of these freedoms are equally important; a complete list of any free person's liberties would range from the indispensable (freedom of movement) to the trivial (the choice of Brut or Old Spice after-shave lotion).

Nor are all liberties compatible with one another. The budding rock group's freedom to practice directly challenges the neighborhood's right to occasional tranquillity. Often, as in this case, questions of freedom resolve into questions of freedom for whom. In resolving this issue, it may be necessary to restrict a freedom available only to a particular group in order to achieve a broader or more important freedom.

Liberties can always be expressed as freedom from particular restraints, as MacCallum's useful formula emphasizes:

> Whenever the freedom of some agent is in question, it is always freedom from some constraint or restriction on, interference with, or barrier to doing, not doing, becoming, or not becoming something. Such freedom is thus always *of* something (an agent or agents), *from* something, *to* do, not do, become, or not become something. . . .[14]

The character of restraints and their necessity vary with time and circumstance. The twentieth century American may be free to drive an automobile, but a relatively unimpeded journey depends upon motorists' general adherence to traffic laws; the medieval peasant had neither this freedom nor the necessity of such restraints. Whatever the historical situation, however, a satisfactory

32

balance of individual liberties can be attained only by the presence of some restrictions.

A well-ordered political freedom cannot be the freedom to do just as one chooses. Because "freedom for the pike means death for the minnows,"[15] the pike must be restrained, if the minnows are to be free. As Hobhouse properly insists:

> The first condition of universal freedom ... is a measure of universal restraint. Without such restraint some men may be free but others will be unfree. ... Law, of course, restrains the individual; it is therefore opposed to his liberty at a given moment and in a given direction. But, equally, law restrains others from doing with him as they will. It liberates him from the fear of arbitrary aggression or coercion, and this is the only way, indeed, the only sense, in which liberty for an entire community is attainable.[16]

Because the practice of unlimited individual discretion leads to mutual conflict, societies must either impose some restraints or suffer severe internal disorder.

In *Evolutionary Socialism* Edward Bernstein tried to define what restraints the Social Democrat regards as legitimate:

> The aim of all socialist measures, even of those which appear outwardly as coercive measures, is the development and the securing of a free personality. Their more exact examination always shows that the coercion included will raise the sum total of liberty in society, and will give more freedom over a more extended area than it takes away.[17]

This calculation of personal freedoms encounters many of the same problems as Bentham's felicific calculus, but the social welfare state supplies guidelines that run contrary to the practice of liberal society, though not to the spirit of liberal thought: Every agent is to count equally in the calculus; no one's liberties take precedence. Any restraints imposed must contribute to personal development and personal autonomy. Finally, public restraints are intrinsically no better and no worse than the restraints imposed by private individuals.

In practical terms this conception of freedom means that the social welfare state supports the traditional civil liberties supposedly upheld in bourgeois society, but does not grant the liberal argument that public intervention in the economic activities of private individuals must result in a diminution of freedom. The freedom of the marketplace, and particularly the individual's freedom to accumulate wealth, property, and power, must yield to more general claims for freedom from concentrated private power. The proponent of the social welfare state cherishes the core of the liberal conception of economic freedom—free choice of vocation, the opportunity to exercise personal initiative and responsibility, and to organize one's own work activities—but believes that in the absence of public measures only a small segment of the population can enjoy these freedoms. If the laborer is to benefit from a modern version of the liberal values of productive freedom, economic independence, and active participation in his work, if he is to be liberated from dependence upon the vagaries of an unregulated market economy and freed from the arbitrary economic power of his employer, then the state must intervene on his behalf—"even if the individual may thereby be deprived somewhat of his precious rights, both to become a millionaire and to starve to death."[18]

The social welfare state's conception of freedom also entails rights to participate in the making of critical political and economic decisions, and here the discussion of freedom merges into consideration of a third essential value, *democracy*. The social welfare state does not define democracy as an electoral struggle between competing elites or regard its demands as satisfied merely by agreement between public policy and public opinion. These conceptions of democracy have two serious flaws. They do not permit a sufficient measure of citizen participation in the formation of policy, and they confine democracy to the narrowly "political" sphere rather than allowing it to flow over into economic institutions.

The social welfare statist starts from the same premises as John Stuart Mill:

1. Only if all citizens can participate in the process of making decisions can there be any assurance that everyone's interest will be considered.
2. Participation trains one to develop the capacity to defend his or her interest.
3. Participation expands the personality by raising it above con-

34

cerns of mere self-interest to a sense of responsibility for the welfare of the whole.

It follows that politics is not the business of an elite, but a concern for all interested citizens. Democracy requires that in addition to the traditional democratic rights of discussion and voting citizens as individuals have the opportunity to participate in local government, in the administration of social welfare policy, in professional and labor organizations, and in the organization of their labor.

Liberal democracy triumphed in the struggle against monarchical political rule; social democracy aims to extend these same democratic values into economic and social life. Economic and organizational power free from control or responsibility conflicts with the democratic idea; the exercise of such power must be subjected to public regulation and dispersed among the citizenry. Men and women must have the right to influence their own working conditions. In addition, investment decisions, the key determinant of the economic future, cannot remain the prerogative of a narrow managerial elite.

This effort to generate a communal responsibility for the common life leads naturally to the aspiration toward *solidarity* (*cooperation, fraternity, community*), a fourth social-welfare state value. A new and social democratic society would strive to realize the condition implicit in the Latin root of socialism: *socius,* comrade. It would aim to replace the acquisitive sentiments and exchange relations of capitalism with sympathy and fraternity, the competitive atmosphere with cooperative impulses. It would endeavor to create conditions that would allow an outlet for non-economic impulses currently shackled by the present system of production: for example, the sense of comradeship, cooperative enterprise, and social feeling unmarred by competition for prestige.[19] The model and inspiration for this new spirit remains the solidarity of trade union members; its tangible expression the extension of social insurance and public services guaranteeing every citizen a secure standard of civilized life.

This emphasis upon solidarity and community sharply distinguishes social welfare statism from liberal individualism. Liberalism arose as a protest against the stifling bonds of the feudal order; it strove to expand the individual's field of activity

35

and to reward him or her according to personal contributions. Individual merit emerged as the legitimate standard of just distribution. In the process of liberation, however, individual rights and rewards became increasingly divorced from social service, creating what Tawney has called "the acquisitive society," a society characterized by personal striving, competition, and neglect of the socially disadvantaged. Social Darwinism presented the most uncompromising version of this individualist creed.

This acquisitive individualism is flawed. No individual can readily lay claim to benefits on the basis of his individual character. He or she does not "deserve" the natural gifts of intelligence, beauty, or skill; these derive from genetic factors over which the individual has no control. Nor can the individual claim full credit for the development of a valued personality, for as Hobhouse says, "the life of the individual . . . would be something utterly different if he could be separated from society."[20] Outside of society the individual's chances to develop speech, mature special talents, establish lucrative enterprises, and learn the social graces would be greatly impaired; the chance to unfold his or her personality to the full would be eliminated. It follows that no individual achieves maturity without the assistance of others and accordingly humility is in order in estimating one's own "personal" contribution to society and claims against it. Liberal individualism, while it properly warns of the dangers of cloying conformism, errs by artificially isolating the person from his social circumstances.

Security, a fifth essential value, expresses not only the fraternal bonds among members of the social welfare state, but it reflects a distinctive view of human beings.[21] To the social democrat, man is a frail but creative being. Distinctly lower than the angels, his fragile constitution falls prey to all manner of physical and social ills. His body is prone to decay, deformation, and illness, not according to regular and invariable formulas, but in eccentric, arbitrary, and accidental ways. In addition to the natural obstacles he confronts, his social existence subjects him to innumerable and unforeseeable hazards. A momentary lapse in concentration at the steering wheel or a miniscule failure in medical technology can abruptly and irrevocably extinguish the spark of his being. And although the rich possess certain modest advantages in this struggle with the vagaries of nature and social organization, they too face the threat of capricious death or incapacitation.

An unregulated capitalist economy only increases the perils of human existence. The early industrial worker, deprived of ownership of his means of production and possessing little in the way of savings, subject to the fluctuations of the labor market, and exposed to the threat of debilitating injury at his workplace, led an existence that was precarious in the extreme. The conditions of capitalist production have improved, but capitalist economies still undermine human welfare by producing below the level of production that is technically feasible, by failing to cushion workers against the effects of declining industries, and by creating an "underclass" of those unable to find employment within the productive system.

But frail man is also creative. Through the development of social insurance and public services he can abolish privation, provide redress to the handicapped for the injustice of nature, and secure the position of the aged, disabled, and bereaved. At its best social welfare policy can even prevent distress. Nearly half a century ago Gunnar Myrdal argued that social welfare policy ought to move beyond treating the symptoms of social ills to a preventive program that would forestall the occurrence of social disorders.[22] By anticipatory measures society might curtail the problems that result from unemployment, urban slums, illiteracy, and the like. Social welfare states like Sweden and even positive states like the United States now have institutions and policies that partially achieve the aim of preventive social policy—security against the distress occasioned by the normal tragedies of human life and by the incompetent organization of social life.

The provision of social and economic security is closely linked to the functioning of the economy. Without a high level of material production, the surplus necessary for the operation of social insurance programs and public services will not be available. Accordingly the social welfare state places a high premium upon *economic efficiency,* not as an end in itself, but as a means to increase human welfare. Its hope (as yet undemonstrated) is that satisfying labor, cooperative social relations, and productive efficiency are not mutually incompatible. Unlike the British Fabians described by Moynihan,[23] the proponent of the social welfare state goes beyond questions of distribution and redistribution. He also strives to ensure that the economy functions as efficiently as possible. Economic efficiency, he believes, is not the natural result of the free play of market forces, but comes from conscious public efforts to maintain a high and steady level of aggregate demand, to alleviate production "bottlenecks," to restrict oligopolistic inefficiencies, and to correct the market's incapacity to deal effectively with externalities such as pollution. Again the social welfare statist places his faith in human creativity, this time in humankind's ability to organize the economy so as to achieve optimal efficiency and productivity.

Even if one grants the desirability of these six values—equality, freedom, democracy, solidarity, security, and economic efficiency—questions may still arise about their mutual compatibility. Just as all of an individual's desires may not be realizable because of possible tensions among them, so a society may not be able to satisfy completely all of its aims. In erecting the apparatus to provide economic security, the social welfare state may create bureaucracies that challenge its democratic aims. On the whole, however, the compatibility of the six values is great and conflicts among them minor. The social-welfare statist conception of welfare is more coherent than its critics will allow. Liberty and equality, as social welfare statists conceive of them, complement rather than compete with one another. Security establishes a basis for free action rather than undermining individual autonomy. Equality promotes economic efficiency. On such conceptual and empirical grounds one is entitled to claim that there is no radical disjuncture among social-welfare statist aims, though conflicts at the margin may persist.[24]

Social-welfare statist values owe much to the socialist tradition and hence differ only marginally from socialist values. The social welfare statist may be rather more skeptical about prospects for a harmonious cooperative social order and somewhat more willing to allow modest differences in wealth, income, prestige, and power, but his real argument with the socialist concerns the proper means to attain these values. With the liberal, however, he differs fundamentally, except on the goals of economic efficiency and civil liberties. Whereas the liberal stresses the private life of individuals, and regards them as driven by insecurity and self-interest, the social welfare statist regards humans as social beings, destined to live together in security and harmony and to find satisfaction in their common life as well as in their private possessions. The liberal's theory of justice bestows rewards according to "merit" or "achievement" as liberal society defines them; the social welfare statist theory emphasizes equality. The liberal fears concentrated political power and tries to restrict the scope of the political; the social welfare statist, while respecting the notion of a balance of social powers, tries to democratize authority rather than privatize it. In short, the social-welfare statist's conception of human welfare differs from the liberal view in espousing a more organic concept of society, a more egalitarian concept of justice, and a more democratic solution to the problem of political power.

The Means of the Social Welfare State

The social welfare state differs from traditional liberalism and socialism not only in its conception of human welfare, but also in the means it employs to enhance the people's welfare. The case for the social welfare state thus derives not only from the values it professes, but from the relative superiority of its social techniques over those of liberal capitalism and state socialism. Its idiosyncratic combination of budgetary planning, active labor market policy, solidaristic wage policy, social welfare legislation, progressive taxation, community planning, and democratic participation permits it to avoid the major failings both of an unregulated capitalist economy and of excessive reliance upon the nationalization of industry. An adequate presentation of the merits of the social welfare state therefore demands a brief analysis of the flaws of liberal economics and of the limits of the case for nationalization.

Liberal economics has generated a body of thought which purports to show that a price system operating through free markets allocates resources efficiently and distributes goods justly. The actual performance of free market economies cannot dissuade the true defenders of this faith, for they argue— correctly—that modern western economies, rife with oligopoly and political intervention, fail to satisfy the conditions of the classical competitive model. In fairness, then, one must confront their model on its own theoretical ground.

Liberal economic theory rests on a number of critical assumptions: that buyers and sellers have perfect information, that there are no transportation costs involved in the dispersion of goods, that there are no barriers to the entry of firms into new markets, and other similarly unrealistic conditions. That these assumptions do not hold and cannot hold in any actual economy is a troubling feature of the liberal case, for if these assumptions do not hold, the remainder of the argument for justice and efficiency does not follow. Nonetheless, the implausibility of these assumptions is only the beginning of difficulties for the liberal case. It also fails in at least four other respects.

First, liberal economics has difficulties in making adequate provision for collective goods like national defense, public highways, and public parks. Provision for these goods must be made outside the market through public organization of the latent demand for these services. Private consumers, in a country of even modest size, are simply incapable of organizing this kind of demand within the confines of the market; they must turn to public instruments.

Second, the private market is incapable of reflecting adequately the social costs or external diseconomies of various productive and consumptive activities, as a ravaged natural environment testifies. In the long run society bears the cost of sludge in Lake Erie, minimal land reclamation in eastern Kentucky, and throwaway beer cans in national parks, but the market itself imposes no immediate cost upon the producers of these offenses.

Third, the market system does not guarantee full employment of productive resources, a point classically demonstrated in Keynes' *General Theory*. Keynes pointed out that capitalist economies were not self-correcting, as Say's Law had maintained, and that without public supervision and intervention they were likely to come to equilibrium below acceptable levels of output, employment, and efficiency. Insufficient purchasing power among the great mass of consumers, the disappearance of the wage flexibility required by classical economies, but above all the vagaries of the entrepreneurial disposition to invest destroyed the prospect of perpetual prosperity and full employment.

These three limitations undercut liberal economics' claim to efficiency; a fourth consideration shatters its pretensions to just distribution of income and wealth. Lester Thurow observes that:

> In market economies, individual preferences determine market demands for goods and services and as a consequence determine the market distribution of income—but individual preferences are weighted by economic resources *before* they are communicated to the market. An individual with no income or wealth may have needs and desires, but he has no economic demands. To make his personal preferences felt, he must have economic resources.... If income and wealth are not distributed in accordance with equity, individual preferences are not properly weighted. *The market quite efficiently adjusts to an inequitable distribution of purchasing power.* [Our italics.][25]

Consequently to claim that the market distributes incomes and rewards justly begs the question. The market merely reflects the previous distribution of wealth and resources. It offers no sanctification for that distribution itself. On this point the defenders of liberal capitalism remain mute, for the skewed distribution of wealth and resources makes a mockery of their claims about justice.

Both on grounds of efficiency and justice liberal economics fails. A market economy needs a visible public hand to steer it—to make provision for collective goods, to force accounting of social costs, to maintain full employment, and to render the distribution of wealth and income more nearly equal. The social welfare state does not abolish markets, but confines them to the functions they perform best—the general allocation of resources and registration of consumer preferences. It establishes limits and controls upon the private sector and plans and coordinates the public sector. It does not endorse either laissez-faire competition or a thoroughly planned economy, but combines competition, planning, and the price system in the synthesis known as the mixed economy.[26]

Just as the social welfare state rejects the liberal strategy of free and unregulated markets, so it rejects the traditional socialist nostrum of nationalization. For years the equation of socialism with public ownership of the means of production was automatic, and for many socialists it still is so. Nationalization served as a magical formula for eliminating all the malign features of capitalist society. It was to accomplish eight important changes:

1. Eliminate class differences based on property ownership.
2. Abolish glaring extremes of poverty and wealth.
3. End class conflict by removing the cause of strife.
4. Eliminate exploitation of labor.
5. Subject the economy to democratic control.
6. Ensure the economic security of working families.
7. Produce rapid increases in the standard of living.
8. Solve the psychological problems and alienation associated with industrial labor.

British experience shows that nationalization per se does not necessarily bring about these results. The experience of the Soviet bloc confirms this point and demonstrates in addition that state socialism can be more tyrannous than private capitalism. In short, nationalization has proved to be no panacea for the social ills of capitalism.

Nationalization is not a sufficient means of accomplishing socialist reforms, and it may not even be a necessary one. The record of contemporary welfare states, and that of Sweden in particular, suggests that the unattractive features of capitalist society may be dismantled piecemeal with as good or better results and with much less tumult than through nationalization. Gunnar Adler-Karlsson describes the Swedish process this way:

> What Swedish socialism has done, and is still doing, is thus to take away, or to regulate, a number of those functions which the capitalists themselves regulated earlier, and still regulate in many other capitalist countries, especially in the United States.
>
> Thus, we have not had a total socialization of ownership, but instead a selective socialization of some of the most important functions inside the totality of functions which we call ownership. We have limited the rights of the owners of the means of production to use their goods in an unsocial way. . . .
>
> Furthermore, an important feature of this way of looking at reality is that it enables us to realize that division of power which is so eagerly desired. When ownership is considered as an indivisible concept, only one owner can be imagined. But when ownership is considered as consisting of a number of functions, these can be divided between different subjects or "partial" owners. When this is done the balance of power in the economic

field can be retained, and the temptation to abuse too great a power concentration can be checked.[27]

This notion of property as a "bundle of rights" allows the parceling out of various rights to different owners and consequently obviates the need for wholesale nationalization. The resulting dissemination of rights permits hybrid forms of social organization that can combine many of the advantages of both private and public ownership. The social welfare state retains the option of nationalizing industry, but relies primarily on other means.

The other means divide naturally into the following categories:

1. Economic policies to improve the efficiency and wage distribution of a market economy: Keynesian budgetary planning, active labor market policy, and solidaristic wage policy.
2. Social policies to compensate for the insecurity and inequity of a market economy: public services, social insurance, transfer payments, and progressive taxation.
3. Measures to enhance public control of community life: interest group representation, influence over investment decisions, industrial democracy, and community planning.

Upon these techniques rest the social welfare state's claims to organizational superiority.

A preeminent objective of social-welfare statist economic policy is full employment. Jobs, rather than unemployment insurance, are the first defense against unemployment. Consequently, the social welfare state endorses the Keynesian prescription for public regulation of aggregate demand. In particular the public hand must attempt to secure a high and steady level of investment, stimulating investment in periods of slack and damping it down during rapid expansion. This public manipulation does not extend to ownership of the nation's capital *stock;* it regulates only the *flow* of investment. The social welfare state shares to a substantial degree Keynes' faith that "capitalism, *wisely* managed, can probably be made more efficient for attaining economic ends than any alternative system yet in sight...."[28]

A sustained high level of demand will generate a high rate of economic growth, but economic growth is a mixed blessing. It both produces burgeoning new industries and condemns old and inefficient industries to destruction. In the process workers must cope with the gales of creative destruction; they must find new employment, a task which often requires retraining and relocation. Here active labor market policy enters the picture. In addition to securing a high overall level of employment, labor market policy attempts to ease the pangs of assuming new employment by providing job information, retraining, mobility allowances, aid for the handicapped, day care facilities, and the like. In its most advanced form active labor market policy extends these services to workers who are already employed so as to increase their choice of livelihood and their potential productive efficiency.

Once a high level of employment has been achieved, the next task is to ensure an equitable distribution of wages. Solidaristic wage policy occupies the forefront in this campaign. The principle behind solidaristic wage policy is simple; the national distribution of wages is to be guided toward greater equality by raising the level of the lowest paid workers. The emphasis falls upon establishing a more just distribution of rewards before, rather than after, taxes and transfers. This method of raising the incomes of low wage employees has the advantage of avoiding any possible stigma attached to the receipt of public charity.

These measures to improve the operation of the labor market run up against an inevitable limitation, however; they do not benefit persons who cannot enter the labor market—children, the aged, the ill, and the severely handicapped. For these persons and similarly situated groups society must adopt social policies to ensure adequate provision. The social welfare state presumes that certain needs are so basic to all its citizens that they must be provided as public services; education, health care, legal aid, and recreational facilities are the outstanding examples. These services, financed from general revenues, are provided free or at nominal rates and as rights of citizens.

Social insurance provides a second mechanism for securing citizens the basic necessities of life. Schemes to protect citizens against loss of income through old age, illness, disablement, and unemployment are a central feature of welfare state organization. Transfer payments outside the insurance network are a third means of ensuring citizens decent housing (housing allowances), adequate income (guaranteed income or public assistance), and resources to meet the needs of children (family allowances). These programs may simply redistribute resources between

44

generations (e.g., from working families to retired persons), a "horizontal" redistribution that does not markedly change the overall distribution of income and thus conforms to the pattern of the social security state. The social welfare state aims at a "vertical" redistribution of resources through progressive taxation of incomes and wealth. High progressive taxes and the elimination of loopholes are deemed essential to curb concentrations of private power and to promote equality.

Because of the increased scope of public policy, it is essential that citizens have full opportunity to participate in policy formation if democracy is to be realized. The social welfare state therefore strives to enhance the role of interest group representation, solicits public commentary upon policy proposals, and expands opportunities for participation in local government and the administration of social welfare. Among existing states, Sweden has perhaps gone furthest in this direction. David Jenkins argues, for example, that the private interest organizations constitute a kind of second government.

> In the normal democratic process the people elect their representatives in the parliament, who then presumably express the will of the people through their management of the government. In Sweden the people also elect their representatives in the organizations, who then push for the interests of their members.... The second government may, indeed, be more powerful than the first one, but it would be difficult to say that it is any less responsive to the will of the people as a whole, especially since the existence of equally powerful organizations expressing opposite points of view means that they act as a check on one another's opportunities to abuse their power.[29]

This system of corporatist representation, together with the presence of investigative commissions and remiss procedures, offers mechanisms to supplement the formal apparatus of representative democracy. Together with opportunities to participate in local politics and administration, such institutions offer the best hope of revivifying parliamentary democracy.

The social welfare state also seeks to democratize economic life. It seeks to ensure greater public influence over investment decisions by a variety of means: increased public investment, state investment banks, investment of public pension funds according

45

to publicly determined criteria, experiments with novel forms of public ownership, placement of public representatives on corporate boards of directors, and restrictions on private advertising. At the level of the individual firm the social welfare state promotes experiments in industrial democracy that will secure workers' participation in the determination of their working conditions.

Finally, the social welfare state attempts to remove community development from the hands of real estate speculators and business interests. The residential environment is a matter for collective planning rather than haphazard private development. The consumers of housing, the citizens themselves, must have opportunities to participate in planning and must be able to employ instruments such as building controls, zoning codes, and long-term land purchase rights to enforce their policies. Public planning must also provide for more collective amenities such as child-care centers, health-care facilities, bicycle paths, and recreational areas so that a healthy and attractive living environment is ensured.

The institutions and policies just discussed do not exhaust the repertoire of social-welfare statist instruments; the present purpose, to reiterate, is to stress the features that raise the social welfare state above its competitors. This brief survey exposes the underlying assumption that neither piecemeal gradualism nor sweeping utopian measures can suffice, but rather that individual problems must be approached pragmatically within the framework of a more general conception of human welfare and social planning.

If this sketch of the values and the means of the social welfare state has been at all successful, the reader should be persuaded that much contemporary political discussion is hopelessly outmoded. The central problem of present-day politics is not the choice between "totalitarianism," "fascism," and "democracy," as one venerable textbook suggests. Nor is the formal ownership of the means of production—the crux of the debate between "capitalism" and "communism"—the central political issue. The real challenge is how to create institutions which insure public welfare and popular participation within advanced industrial societies.

The preceding discussion provides the general outlines of the social welfare statist response to this challenge. The reader, relying upon the discussion of the social security state in Chapter One, can readily work out the distinctive features of the social security-statist position. This alternative formulation places rather less stress upon the values of equality, solidarity, democracy, and economic efficiency, rather more upon security and equality of opportunity. In consequence it gives less emphasis (or none at all) to such measures as solidaristic wage policy, public control of investment, and industrial democracy. It prefers social insurance arrangements to the provision of public services. In general, it offers a future more in accord with liberal than with socialistic ideals.

Implementation

In addition to his primary obligations of stating and defending values, institutions, and policies, the proponent of a political program should examine the obstacles to attainment of his desired objectives and anticipate how to circumvent these difficulties. Indeed the task of justifying the social welfare state would remain incomplete without some reflection upon the means of bringing it into existence. The diversity of political conditions in advanced Western societies defies any attempt at a detailed strategic plan—the means of implementation will necessarily vary from country to country—but some general remarks on strategy and tactics are in order.

First, the social-welfare statist strategy is not a revolutionary one, but relies primarily on nonviolent and parliamentary means. This commitment reflects disenchantment with the results of Leninist violence and Stalinist terror. It rests on the assumption that conflict among social classes is less than total, that some grounds for political compromise exist, and that consequently terror and revolution are not needed to alter capitalist society. It also stems from the conviction that legitimate and enduring social changes require broad democratic support. Successful reformist efforts in Scandinavia and elsewhere reinforce this commitment to gradualism.

This preference for relatively peaceful reform does not mean that the social welfare statist underestimates the power and intransigence of established interests or the costs of gradual social change. He is well aware that entrenched capitalists seldom yield

47

on matters of substance without compulsion; it follows that he is quite prepared for some social tumult when it is required to extract concessions. He has no desire to precipitate revolution, but the possibility of avoiding it eventually depends upon the willingness of the "establishment" to make the necessary compromises in timely fashion. The social welfare statist also realizes that his gradualist course prolongs the agony of the socially disadvantaged; he defends the delays reluctantly, not by any claims that they are ideal, but only on the grounds that his strategy is the surest and least painful available. Because neither he nor the revolutionary can make any definitive calculation of the relative costs and benefits of gradualism versus revolution, the commitment to his strategy is in part an act of faith, but it originates primarily in his conviction that violent conflict is an unlikely seedbed for a fraternal society.

The social welfare statist discerns some basis in present attitudes for attracting converts to his program. People in advanced industrial societies resist paying taxes for social welfare programs, but they enjoy receiving the benefits and in general they approve of the rationale for these measures. Even in the United States, where the welfare state has made the least ideological headway, citizens accept the need for essential welfare state policies. Harold Wilensky, while noting a hard residuum of sentiment against aid for the unneedy and undeserving, points out that reliable polls "clearly show wide acceptance of proposals for national health insurance, federal government responsibility to do away with poverty, and increased spending on urban renewal. . . ." He adds that

> . . . the adult population discriminates among welfare-state policies: if the beneficiaries seem to work for it (earnings-based pensions, prepaid medical insurance), it is good, and big majorities of the respondents in national cross-section samples generally support an actual or a proposed program. If the benefit is unearned or perceived as unearned (AFDC, unemployment compensation), it is bad, and majorities typically reject the program.[30]

The social welfare statist believes it possible for skillful politicians to exploit these sentiments to build support for his platform because it coincides in considerable measure with people's desires for equality, freedom, democracy, solidarity, security, and economic efficiency; the near-triumph of the Nixon Family Assistance Plan and the growing consensus for a national health program in the United States confirm him in these views.

Third, the strategy of the social welfare statist coincides with the rational self-interest of citizens in ways that other political recommendations cannot. The preservation of the natural environment and the improvement of the social environment are in the interest of every citizen, but they require an active government operating on an advanced conception of human welfare. The provision of adequate energy affects every citizen, but the events of recent years show that this responsibility cannot be left to a cartel of multinational resource companies, but must be pursued by a government committed to the values of solidarity and economic efficiency. The availability of job opportunities in an increasingly high-skilled and automated economy does not result automatically from the operation of a mystical invisible hand, but only through conscious public policy. Security against the multiplying risks of advanced industrialism becomes an increasingly desperate and futile undertaking for the isolated individual. Finally, a sense of participation and mutual responsibility can come only from the increased role that the social welfare state offers the citizen. If citizens can eventually be brought to act in their rational self-interest, they will declare a preference for the social welfare state.

Here this abbreviated case for the social welfare state must rest. Only its distinctive conception of human welfare based on the values of equality, freedom, democracy, solidarity, security, and economic efficiency, its superior techniques of social organization, and its commitment to essentially nonviolent parliamentary reform offer a reasonable prospect for coping with the current and emerging crises of advanced industrial society.

3

The Conservative
Critique of the
Welfare State

Any attempt to categorize views opposed to those presented in the previous chapter immediately confronts numerous problems of terminology. Without undue effort, it is possible to list twenty distinct "isms" from which to critique the welfare state position: anarchist, conservative, corporate, egalitarian, liberal, libertarian, leninist, marxist, maoist, neo-conservative, neo-liberal, neo-marxist, new left, radical, reactionary, socialist, statist, syndicalist, theocratic, traditionalist. And even this bewildering array excludes the formulations of individual writers that could be used to judge the broad legitimacy of public policy—for example, the "difference principle" of John Rawls which states that social and economic inequalities are just only if they benefit the least advantaged group or the "entitlement principle" of Robert Nozick which states that individuals are authorized to dispose of what they have acquired or have been given provided their holdings do not constitute a de facto monopoly of something vital to the sustenance of others.[1] As a final complicating element, many concepts (e.g., "liberalism") change in content not only over time, but from country to country and from spokesman to spokesman.

To avoid the complications of an elaborate taxonomy, we return to the simple and unobtrusive classification of "conservative" and "radical." The radical critique, set forth in the next chapter, can be summarized as one which, while seeing the welfare state as an advance over the conduct of liberal capitalism, nevertheless argues that the reorientation has not been sufficient, and that further changes are needed, particularly in the process of economic production. The conservative critique consists of two separable components—"practical," and "philosophical." The latter is itself usefully divided between "organic conservatism" evoking "traditional" virtues and "modern" conservatism best described as a presumption in favor of (minimum position) or an unswerving commitment to (maximum position) the virtue of laissez-faire.

Of these major conservative thrusts, the "practical" is probably the most often heard in the United States. It is also the least interesting. It generally assumes the form, "would that this could be so": It would be nice, of course, to have full employment guarantees, but such a policy would make the population workshy. Sure, universal health care is a fine ideal, but it would bankrupt the country, and so on. These sentiments have been voiced ever since the notion of social reform was first broached in the United States; they continue to be the staple of most editorial pages. They can also be briefly disposed of. There is no evidence that the social reforms implemented in the United States over the last forty years have destroyed incentives or lessened the accumulation of wealth. Likewise, most European countries, with far more extensive welfare provisions than exist in America, have maintained since World War Two lower rates of unemployment and higher rates of productivity. Recently, Switzerland and Sweden passed the United States in income per capita. In short, if the only thing "practical" conservatives worry about is that the welfare state "won't work," we can all sleep peacefully.

We shall elaborate on these points when we describe the system of welfare provision in Britain and in Sweden. In this chapter we undertake a review of the more important, "philosophic" component of the conservative critique. First, we consider traditional arguments in favor of a conservative position. We find these arguments at best irrelevant for a critique of the welfare state. Second, we construct (because it is not done well in the literature) the case for "modern conservatism." While we find that the arguments in its favor cannot totally be sustained, the minimum position in particular can offer a coherent critique of the social welfare state. It can also generate concrete proposals for moving society more in line with its ideal.

Organic Conservatism

"Organic conservatism" describes the notion that the "natural" ordering of a society is the correct one—what has been is right. A strong argument can be made that it is not really necessary to work out this homily under a separate heading. To do so accords it a dignity it does not deserve.[2] We nonetheless persevere because the premises of organic conservatism are widely propounded and, more importantly, because they often intrude into "modern conservative" critiques. To isolate organic conservatism if only to discard it might be a service.

The pantheon of organic conservatism may be reduced to the following: Tradition, Order, Deference, God. Society is (ought to be) organized on the principles of a natural and recognizable hierarchy. Those at the bottom do (ought to) follow the lead of their betters. God, meanwhile, confirms and sustains the whole plan, and He is never more pleased than when He sees everyone in his proper station. This vision is unlikely to win many popular plaudits. When given even a modicum of substance, the canons appear either silly or a threat to the liberties most people hold dear. As Edith Efron concludes, seen abstractly, the Conservative creed seems reducible to one sentence, "God made society this way, Grandpa liked it this way, so it should remain this way"— hardly a case over which serious thinkers need tarry long. On the other hand, if one considers what might actually occur should this position achieve any political standing, the effect could be less amusing:

> What kind of a philosophy was this, I wondered, that cannot grasp the primacy of the individual mind, its right to self-assertion, to thought, to value judgments, to self-interest—its right to flout tradition, if that tradition is fatuous or irrational, its right to repudiate authority, if that authority is imbecile or immoral, its right to destroy order if that order is unjust or malignant? What kind of a mind was it that perceives society— *any* society—as some sort of irreducible Holy Unit to be respected, obeyed, and revered—while viewing the individual as

some eternal private in Life's Army who must say Yes, sir, Yes, sir, until he dies?[3]

The basic reason why any serious effort to institute the organic conservative premises of Tradition, Order, Deference, and God is inherently coercive is that the social order in all advanced industrial countries is *completely antithetical to its aims.* Men would have to be forced to be enslaved. And efforts to keep them subjected would entail the permanent placement of a restraining state and social apparatus—witness the speedy disintegration of the pretenses of "corporatism" in Portugal following the death of Salazar and the neutralization of the secret police.

It is this changed social situation that accounts for the fundamental difference *in effect* between modern conservative writers discussing the virtues of authority, order, and discipline, and similar views propounded in the past, for example, by Edmund Burke. When Burke spoke of "the great primeval contract of eternal society, linking the lower and the higher natures, connecting the visible and the invisible world. . . ."[4] he may, according to one's normative outlook, have been expounding mischievous doctrine, but he was at least abstracting from a social situation in which a large portion of the population did indeed lead lives that bore some resemblance to an organic order.[5] That is why Burke could recommend that we "should approach to the faults of the state as to the wounds of a father, with pious awe and trembling solicitude."[6] Modern organic conservatives cannot really make this statement (although they often do, particularly if the "fault" involves some tax loophole favorable to the rich) because the state is not founded upon principles compatible with their perception of the proper order.

Conservatism and Laissez-faire

The commitment to laissez-faire (the presumption of individual preferences constituting the only valid data, of individuals acting rationally in their own interests, and of the desirability of free market solutions to social problems) constitutes the primary element of the conservative challenge to the welfare state. This position, as we shall construct it, rests most securely on the assumption that we shall never know enough of man's preferences and future actions to make meaningful global social decisions, and the positing of certain rights as inviolable. As we shall see, neither of the two emerges from critical scrutiny unscathed, but enough of each remains to provide a powerful challenge to the social welfare state in particular. Before undertaking this construction and its critical review, we might note the obvious: The tenets of laissez-faire have been historically associated with classical liberalism, a link retained in economic theory.[7] In countries like the United States which have no well-developed conservative heritage, the new nomenclature, in line with popular definition, should cause few problems and should not be construed invidiously.[8]

The Inevitability of Ignorance

In this argument the focus is on the empirical: Whatever moral judgments one wishes to offer, men must be left free because only in this way can societies grow and prosper. Freedom is generally divided into two arenas—economic and social. In both, the interventions of public authority are likely to wreak havoc unless carefully circumscribed. In economic affairs this proposition has drawn its inspiration from the works of Adam Smith and his successors. Baldly, their essential dictum was that "individuals can always undersell the government" because the government has no notion of real costs and (because it is a monopoly) no incentive to discover them.[9] A host of instances have been offered in support, usually presented in the paradoxical form that intervention in the market system produced results exactly the opposite of what was intended. Adam Smith, for example, recounted that the British government, anxious to encourage the production of herring both to lower its price and to help out "depressed areas" in Scotland, put a bounty on the catch. This stratagem failed, however, to lower the price of the fish because it rewarded total production and not marginal cost reduction. If anything, the price rose. Nor should it be imagined that individual fishermen profited from the government handouts. "The usual effect of such bounties is to encourage rash undertakers to adventure in a business they do not understand, and what they lose by their own negligence and ignorance, more than compensates all that they gain by the utmost liberality of government."[10]

As can be seen by this example, Smith does not question the

intentions of government. They can be good or bad, and we can probably assume the former. But however well meaning, government intervention flounders on the rock of ignorance. One cannot be omniscient enough to discern all the relevant variables. It is this argument that led to the widespread belief that socialism could never be a viable economic system:

> Socialism . . . as a scheme for supplying the material wants of the community as seen at a glance to be totally incapable of adjusting the relation between supply and demand. I have suggested the practical test. If any Socialist were asked, "Suppose Socialism established now, how many suits of clothes, and of what quantities will have to be in stock for the township of Little Pedlington on the 1st of next June?" either he could not answer the question at all, or he would be compelled to fall back upon the device of a uniform. . . . Until Socialists can answer these questions, . . . Socialism has simply no *locus standi* as a practical scheme for the supply of material wants.[11]

And if this conclusion was appropriate for Socialism it held a fortiori for the "Communism" established in Russia in 1917. The immediate postwar period revealed a "misery [such as] has never been the lot of a people within so short a time in modern history." This misery, the *Economist* remarked, "is largely caused by the Soviet Government" and its rejection of economic laws.[12]

Considerations of the inevitability of ignorance were stated to be equally strong in social relationships as well. Just as the government or the collective society could not determine the proper price of corn, so it could not regulate the proper place of social classes, the proper form of morality, the proper reward for toil. As Maitland argued, "The most powerful argument [for liberty] is *based on the ignorance, the necessary ignorance, of our rulers*. . . . The statesman has to consider the good he may do by interfering on the right side, the evil he may do by interfering on the wrong side, and also the probability of his knowing which the right side is. The most convincing pleas for *laissez-faire,* and the most convincing pleas for religious toleration, are those which insist *a priori* on the great 'probable error' of any opinions on matters of religion and matters of political economy, and those which relate *a posteriori* the history of the well-intentioned failures of wise and good men."[13] This reasoning has been developed recently by

Hayek, from whom we take the subtitle of our section: "[T]he case for individual freedom rests chiefly *on the recognition of the inevitable ignorance of all of us* concerning a great many of the factors on which the achievement of our ends and welfare depends."[14]

It should not be assumed from this discussion of the negative necessity of freedom and liberty (without them economic and social life would stultify and regress) that no tampering with the natural order was justified. On the contrary, most advocates of laissez-faire from Adam Smith onward have declared that to the extent that governmental or collective actions could be shown to produce more efficient results than the market, they should be undertaken. The state is thus afforded a role larger than that of "night watchman" and can legitimately undertake such functions as the provision of public goods.[15] Similarly, to state that government meddling makes the situation worse is not to say that man's only obligation is to buy cheap and sell dear. Pure hedonism is not sufficient social cement; in the long run a lack of individual sympathy harms the interest of all.[16] Still less should it be supposed that adherence to the belief in the inevitability of ignorance automatically accompanies an outlook of facile optimism toward contemporary life. This constantly expressed charge of nineteenth century critics has been answered on a number of occasions.[17] What is at stake, it was maintained, was not the present order at all but the potential for future progress. As bad as the present may be, it is a classic case of throwing the baby out with the bath water to urge on this account a halt to natural social development. This point, well stated by Herbert Spencer, also served as the main argument against wholesale "welfare state" reforms of the 1930s—by disrupting social change they would merely universalize misery:

> The present social state is transitional, as past social states have been transitional. There will, I hope and believe, come a future social state differing as much from the present as the present differs from the past with its mailed barons and defenseless serfs. . . . My opposition to socialism results from the belief that it would stop the progress to such a higher state and bring back a lower state.[18]

How Inevitable is Ignorance in the Modern World?

The fundamental problem of the critique thus far described should be apparent—it rests on empirical demonstrations that, no matter how telling during the nineteenth century, have now become severely attenuated. The case is more obvious in economics, both theory and practice. The paradoxical comments on collective bungling have been reversed and it is now the private person who cannot plan rationally for the future! This reasoning was developed fully by Keynes. In his *General Theory of Employment, Interest and Money* Keynes offers the following problem: If a businessman cuts wages, will he increase his profits? One would suppose the answer to be "yes" since labor is an important part of production cost and a reduction would bring a lower price for the good. If we remember, however, that the businessman operates in a competitive system, his wage cut will be matched by those of others, bringing not just a return to the previous situation, but, because the level of aggregate demand is lower, a possible redistribution of real incomes *from* the entrepreneur *to* the rentier whose income is fixed. In other words, far from helping the businessman, a decision to cut wages could well result in a net loss.[19] This situation, Keynes argues, is precisely what occurred during the Great Depression—a vicious spiral, exacerbated, not relieved, by the sum of individual initiatives.

The position of public expenditures is also reversed. It will be recalled that public authorities had been charged with turning economic activities, even the most promising, to a loss. If, however, the primary goal is the maintenance of aggregate demand, it hardly matters *what* government spends its money on so long as it spends enough. Thus the paradox that endeavors absurd for private enterprise to contemplate can become essential elements of the economic structure. Keynes underlines this point in a famous passage from the *General Theory:*

> If the Treasury were to fill old bottles with banknotes, bury them at suitable depths in disused coal mines which are then filled up to the surface with town rubbish, and leave it to private enterprise on well-tried principles of *laissez-faire* to dig the notes up again (the right to do so being obtained, of course, by tendering for leases of the note-bearing territory), there need be no more unemployment and, with the help of the repercussions, the real income of the community, and its capital wealth also, would probably become a good deal greater than it actually is. It would indeed, be more sensible to build houses and the like; but if there are political and practical difficulties in the way of this, the above would be better than nothing.[20]

Finally, the end result of the superiority of public and private cooperation over a reliance on private rationality alone has been demonstrated concretely in the upsurge of prosperity since World War II, by the disinclination of any major political party in any Western nation to revert to pre-Depression economic practices, and by the advent of the "post-market" economy. To use Shonfield's phrase, "wisely managed capitalism" has become the order of the day, with the emphasis as much on "managed" as on "capitalism."

As regards social planning, the situation is more ambiguous. On the one hand, it has been shown that physical planning (the direct bureaucratic allocation of resources and labor) is inefficient and particularly susceptible to public wrath. The latest instance of this failure of physical planning concerns the "energy crisis." Distribution by quotas or by rationing—except as an emergency measure—is likely to be counter-productive.[21] In addition, it has been found that the more direct forms of "social engineering" (the term employed by many welfare state theorists before the discovery of appropriate euphemisms) have had little or no impact on social life.

Population policy is another good example. Social theorists and political leaders during the 1930s were worried about the long-range consequences of a dramatic fall in the birth rate. It was feared that the outcome would be a stagnant, stultified social life dominated by a gerontocracy. This fear helped mobilize political support (especially in countries like France with large, historically hostile neighbors) for a system of family allowances.[22] After the war, the birth rate did indeed rise, and the link with the newly instituted children's allowances was widely made. It has since been discovered, however, that this correlation was fortuitous. Family allowances are a great aid in alleviating some forms of poverty, but they seem to have no statistically significant impact on family size.[23] And so great has been the change in popular mores that reformers now insist on the *lack of association* between the birth rate and children's allowances in order not to be charged with furthering population growth.

While the above examples attest to the difficulties inherent in direct social control, they should not be thought to imply the hopelessness of more indirect forms of social management. Spatial planning (launched in Britain in 1946 with the Town and

Country Planning Act and carried to its furthest extent, perhaps, in the Netherlands)[24] has made some strides toward reducing the gap between private affluence and public squalor by directing the location of new industry, preserving parks and "green spaces," instituting pollution controls—in short, in sponsoring a decent collective environment. The benefits of these more modest efforts may be seen best in the field of urban housing. Historically, urban development had been thought too vital a matter to be left to private whim. The urban areas of seventeenth and eighteenth century Europe, so much admired today (Nancy, Edinburgh, Bath), do not attest to the merits of "free enterprise," but to the sensibility of city planners who laid street patterns, determined housing styles, and invited leading architects to submit comprehensive master plans.[25] It was only in the mid-nineteenth century that the provision of housing was arrogated by private builders. The result was apparent in the mean row houses in Britain and the barrack accommodations in Germany constructed in the late nineteenth century, and, more recently, in the suburban sprawl in the United States. Meanwhile, architects and what few "planners" remained turned their attention to homes for the rich or to grandiose public and corporate headquarters.

The evils of leaving the amount and type of housing to the vagaries of the "market" had become well documented by the end of the nineteenth century, and a few steps toward town planning were launched before World War II, especially in Britain.[26] Serious public action, however, did not commence until after the war, and at its best it has involved the restoration and preservation of old, *already planned,* urban areas as often as the construction of "New Towns."[27] Both of these activities are made easier by a welfare state which incorporates the idea of shared public and private property and legitimizes intervention for the promotion of a decent collective life. Even in the United States, however, the value of coordinating and shaping urban growth is becoming apparent. The idea of "urban planning" is constantly evoked and sometimes implemented.[28] Again, the proposition of the "inevitable ignorance of all of us" has been severely circumscribed.

Finally, we turn to the overlap between economic and societal development. Our previously made distinction has been artificial to a certain degree since planned changes in economic life have important social impacts. To give only one example: If, as in France and the German Federal Republic, it is decided to spur economic growth by facilitating the movement of labor off the land and into more profitable pursuits, the social consequences will be vast. Rural population will fall, some occupations will be artificially stimulated, reeducational facilities must be offered, and transportation must be reoriented. Seen from the perspective of public planners, planning assumes a pervasive guise. It is not only in economic affairs, therefore, that the inevitability of ignorance makes laissez-faire *empirically questionable* as a better means of progress. In social development, as well, there is the legitimate hope that a context, an environmental framework, can be established that will be supportive both of a higher level of collective life and of a better fulfillment of private volitions.

Reality Denied

It has been necessary to spend some time developing the "inevitability of ignorance" position because, being essentially an empirical argument, it must be confronted and tested on empirical grounds. In this test we found the claim partially controverted—that is, the experience of the last fifty years has shown that purposeful social and economic planning *can* (but not always will) produce outputs in line with its stated goals and in directions most people would consider "good." This conclusion is important particularly for American readers, because of the persistent exposition of the view that nothing has really changed since Adam Smith. In the United States the bunglings of "pointy-headed bureaucrats" continue to be blown up into examples of the eternal validity of the law that each is the best judge of his own interest. Grand homilies, resting on no discernible basis whatever, continue to be delivered:

> Individual effort [is] the very prerequisite for progress. . . . In the welfare state the individual is not only induced to be lazy, but he is also considered to be unable to take care of himself. The healthy are treated as if they were sick, the mature as if they were children. The physically fit are made psychologically ill, and the naturally independent are made artificially dependent. Individuals become spoiled and lose self-confidence.[29]

In fact, there seems nothing like the picture of someone receiving money or goods at taxpayer expense to excite grand exercises in social causality:

> In all likelihood it was probably no coincidence that the wave
> of redistributive legislation in the 1960's was followed by un-
> precedented outbursts of civil disturbances that rocked the
> country from end to end and left deep scars that may not heal
> for many years.[30]

Finally, and here we take up, not for the last time, topics raised
in the first two chapters, the whole history of efforts to address
social problems seriously and purposefully which is either ignored or ridiculed. On the question of the inevitability of poverty,
for example, a writer reputedly skilled in logical argument
recently began a section entitled "the dilemma of poverty" with
the comment that "in the United States, adults whose income is
less than half of the median are judged to be poor, regardless of
the absolute size of their income." This judgment (which the
author deplores, but which does make an approach toward the
abolition of poverty perfectly feasible) is followed in the next
paragraph by the conclusion that the "war against poverty" cannot be won because "anything but a totally equal distribution of
income necessarily puts some people at the top and others at the
bottom. Just as the top group will be called rich, the bottom group
will be called poor."[31] Similar pronouncements (usually not pre-
ceded by statements which refute them) are issued regularly on
the nonutility of collective social action, with one distinguished
scholar finding that "the serious problems of the cities will continue to exist in something like their present form for another
twenty years at least. . . . Even if we could afford to throw the
existing cities away and start from scratch, matters would not be
essentially different, for the people who moved into the new
cities would take the same problems with them. . . . [And] the
tendency of [government] programs will be to prolong the problems and perhaps even to make them worse." Relief must come,
as before, from economic growth, demographic change, and
from what Edward Banfield calls "middle-and-upper-classifica-
tion"—in sum, on the "hidden hand" of untrammeled market
forces.[32]

These conclusions may speak soothingly to those who are rea-
sonably contented and who do not wish their conscience to
interrupt their repose. But they perform no service to the conservative critique, because they obscure the following reasonable

conclusion that could be drawn logically from the evidence presented: Let us admit that organized collective action can and often does yield outcomes congruent with its original purpose. Let us admit in addition that many of these outcomes have occasioned socially beneficial developments. Nevertheless, the factor of ignorance remains a powerful force. It is wise, therefore, to assume a laissez-faire position until it can be demonstrated that collective action can produce desirable and efficient results.

Natural Rights

People have long attempted to show that men have certain rights, and not certain others, and that these rights ought not to be abridged by public authority. Now it must be admitted that these attempts—that of John Locke is the most relevant for our purposes—have been challenged on historical and logical grounds, on their scope (why not one more right or one less?), and on their presumption of inalienability (cannot rights be balanced, their content seen as a collection not as a unity, etc.?). Nor are the difficulties resolved by simply declaring that certain, basically Lockean, rights are ordained and then, as Robert Nozick seems to do, asserting that they ought not to be violated, without entering into the slippery business of describing how they arose or even what exactly they are.[33]

Nonetheless, in a spirit of prudence and reasonableness, the following case can be proposed: The Western world has been well served by the enshrinement of classical liberal rights in constitutions and legal codes. The freedom of individual conduct, combined with the responsibility for the effects this conduct might cause, has increased productive human enterprise, lessened the number of religious wars, undermined the notion of a feudal hierarchy, and encouraged social mobility. This legacy, which is basically the legacy of laissez-faire, leads one to advocate extreme caution in tampering with individual rights in the name of some public purpose. To be sure, some rights may need to be restricted. And others—especially some form of "freedom from want"—might be added to take into account the changes in property distribution brought about by the industrial revolution (and discussed in Chapter One).[34] Such additions might well secure broader support for more "classical liberal" concerns.

When combined with the truncated but still viable notion of

collective ignorance of private volitions, laissez-faire has some obvious assets. Its supporters can maintain that those wishing to restrict individual liberty, as defined by Locke and other "classical" writers, are obliged to demonstrate that collective gains will significantly outweigh losses, both empirical and normative.[35] The attractiveness of this argument is evident not only in the general movement for decentralization and community control but also in specific proposals for social reform that, it is hoped, might move the welfare state toward the most feasible maximization of liberty.

Accommodation to the Welfare State and Beyond

The first advantage of jettisoning the weight of claims to moral and empirical superiority is that it enables our refurbished conservative critique to consider the welfare state in practical terms and, in particular, to recognize its positive achievements. A certain amount of management is useful to sustain aggregate demand and to ensure full employment; it is also to the good that the more unfortunate members of society receive public assistance, provided, of course, that the costs do not become more than the economic system can bear and that the recipients do not become "work shy." It also becomes possible to inject a valuable historical perspective: The welfare state made a special contribution during the crisis period of capitalism when it was necessary for social peace, if nothing else, to ease the burden of the shift from exclusive reliance on heavy industrial production to a mixed more "service oriented" economy.[36]

This said, the conservatives can now stress the dangers of the welfare state losing sight of its original purpose—which, they can maintain, should be to make individual liberty a reality for all. This reality is often pictured in terms of choice. If, for example, a child suffers from malnutrition when young, he may have physical and mental disabilities that would effectively preclude a large array of choices in the future. Some choice must be restricted now so that more might be opened up later. On the other hand, if restrictions outweigh opportunities, the "reform" should not be undertaken. Given an ongoing welfare state,[37] this approach yields two types of political strategies which we can label minimum and maximum. At a minimum the aim is to keep the state at what we have termed the "social security state" level: assurance of a safety net below which no one could fall but above which one must climb on his own efforts. It could be one purpose of the modern conservative critique to retain this conception—to make sure that the operating principle of the welfare state remained not equality, but equality of opportunity beyond the basic level. A related minimum aim could be to assure that the provisions of the social security state were attuned, as far as possible, to considerations of the "market":

> The phrase "free-for-all" has sometimes been pressed into ser-
> vice to discredit the proposition that the changing forces of
> supply and demand should be reconciled by movements in
> price. Yet... in the absence of price suppliers must ration
> consumers by reference to wholly arbitrary criteria.... It would
> be a miracle if the highly imperfect political system were to lead
> to a division of "free" resources among alternative uses in a way
> that corresponded to the changing opportunities, needs and
> preferences of the varied consumers of differing public serv-
> ices.[38]

The major determination here is whether the programs neces-
sary to achieve the social security state are public goods, that is, goods whose benefits are indiscriminate and which are consumed equally by all. Those that are not (and specific cases, e.g., health services, are difficult to decide on an all-or-nothing basis) might better be constructed as much along market lines as possible.[39]

This attempt to restructure the provision of welfare services slides into the maximum goal of a complete reorientation of the system itself. If one can define the safety net or the "National Minimum" in almost all instances in money terms, why is it not possible to abolish the notion of "services" altogether and substi-
tute cash payments to those below the minimum level? Help would be concentrated, not generalized, and the impetus toward the development of the collectivist impulses of the welfare state would be stultified by the dismantling of controls and much of the bureaucracy. The means to accomplish these ends is available in the form of a negative income tax, direct payment of additional monies to individuals or groups whose income as determined by the tax system falls below a specified amount. As justified by Milton Friedman:

[We] might all of us be willing to contribute to the relief of poverty, *provided* everyone else did. We might not be willing to contribute the same amount without such assurance.... Suppose one accepts, as I do, this line of reasoning as justifying governmental action to alleviate poverty; to set, as it were, a floor under the standard of life of every person in the community. There remains the question... how ... so far as possible the program should, while operating through the market, not distort the market or impede its functioning.... The arrangement that recommends itself is the negative income tax.... It is directed specifically at the problem of poverty. It gives help in the form most useful to the individual, namely, cash. It is general and could be substituted for the host of special measures now in effect. It makes explicit the cost borne by society.[40]

The idea of a negative income tax has more than an abstract interest. It has been offered as a major way of relieving poverty in the United States in the form of "income maintenance" or of a "guaranteed minimum income." It was put forward by the Conservative Government in Britain in the form of a "Tax Credit Plan." These proposals—by substituting cash for public services, the individual for the collectivity, a minimum equality of opportunity for the drive for egalitarianism, the market place for the political arena—pose a major practical challenge to the development of the welfare state. The conservative critique has now escaped some of the difficulties of the concept of the inevitability of ignorance and is able to promote an alternative that maximizes freedom from restraint, defined in cost-benefit terms.

The Resurrection of Private Property

It should be recalled from our discussion in Chapter One that private property had been posited as the major defense of the liberal state against potential state aggrandizement at least since Jean Bodin, and that the sanctity of property was enshrined in a host of nineteenth century legal codes and constitutional provisions. The assault of the welfare state on the sanctity of property and the inability of most working class individuals to acquire property as a natural outcome of their productive labor has led some to revive the idea of T. H. Green: Failing spontaneous acquisition, property should be "secured by society."

The reasoning is the same as that employed in favor of the negative income tax: The power of the state must be used not only to ward off further "collectivism," but also to promote the positive value of social solidarity and social peace that cannot be relied upon as a matter of course. The ramifications of this argument, however, go well beyond the goals of "accommodation." It can be expected that the wide dissemination of property and the opportunities opened up for self-development might implant a liberal society in which the bulk of the population had a profound stake.[41] The difference can be seen most strikingly in the array of benefits: "Accommodation" offers money to be spent in a market situation over which the individual has no more control than before. A refurbished version of private property, on the other hand, would institute schemes of profit sharing, co-determination of industries, subsidies to private home buying. That is, to give to each individual as much nonproductive property as possible, supplemented by an extensive dispersal of industrial responsibility.

Together, the accommodation and property strands of a conservative critique founded on a bias in favor of laissez-faire attest to its continuing relevance and force. While recognizing the obligation to construct the social structure on certain minimum guarantees, and while acknowledging that the unimpeded unfolding of social and economic development will not necessarily provide them, there is an effort to free the individual, insofar as practicable, from governmental or social pressures, and *to return to a state of fundamental individual responsibility.*

4

Radical Criticisms of the Welfare State

While conservatives decry the activities of the welfare state and castigate them as subversive of personal liberty and social order, radicals belittle the extent of the changes wrought. They point to the persistent inequalities of wealth and income within welfare states, the emphasis on material consumption, hierarchical direction in government and industry, the unsatisfying character of work and working environments, the absence of a sense of community, and the prevalence of waste and of ecological destruction. The reforms instituted have not "fundamentally" altered the contours of capitalist society, the radical critic argues; at best these measures ameliorate the repellent features of capitalist society—at worst they render the "system" more tolerable and stable, thereby retarding the arrival of the essential destruction and transformation of bourgeois society. The burden of the radical critique is that the welfare state remains a class society characterized by inequality, authoritarian decision-making, alienation, and irrationality; the welfare state is capitalism disguised by window dressing.

The Radical Patrimony

The radical critique of welfare statist arguments has a long and distinguished ancestry. Even before the advent of Bernstein's revisionist socialism, Marx was polemicizing against deviations from proper socialist theory and practice. In his *Critique of the Gotha Program,* an analysis of the platform of the united socialist party in Germany, Marx condemns the program's emphasis upon the "fair distribution of the proceeds of labor" and its neglect of the relations of production. He argues that an equitable distribution of goods can only be achieved by a radical restructuring of productive relations, since the mode of production determines the distribution of goods.

> The capitalist mode of production, . . . rests on the fact that the material conditions of production are in the hands of non-workers in the form of property in capital and land, while the masses are only owners of the personal condition of production, of labor power. *If the elements of production are so distributed, then the present-day distribution of the means of consumption results automatically.* If the material conditions of production are the cooperative property of the workers themselves, then there likewise results a distribution of the means of consumption different from the present one. Vulgar socialism (and from it in turn a section of the democracy) has taken over from the bourgeois economists the consideration and treatment of distribution as independent of the mode of production and hence the presentation of socialism as turning principally on distribution. After the real relation has long been made clear, why retrogress again? (*Our italics.*)[1]

With this argument Marx denies that the "socialization of consumption" advocated by such supporters of the welfare state as Alva Myrdal can be effective.[2] Later in the *Critique* he reinforces the argument that successful socialism cannot result from governmental modification of patterns of distribution. To create a genuinely communist society the state must undergo a revolutionary transformation; in a capitalist society it necessarily remains "a committee for managing the common affairs of the whole bourgeoisie" and as such hardly comprises a suitable instrument for redistributing property, income, and power.[3]

The most powerful and comprehensive early polemic against the doctrines of gradualist, reformist social welfare policy is Rosa Luxemburg's *Reform or Revolution,* a vigorous indictment of Bernstein's case for an evolutionary socialism.[4] In her defense of scientific socialism Luxemburg concentrates her fire on the central assumption of Social Democracy—that gradual reforms without revolution can reshape capitalist society. Her basic argument is that reforms within a capitalist environment are bound to be tainted, ineffective, and inadequate. They can only succeed in propping up and reinforcing the essential structures of capitalist society, an intolerable result since the proper goal of the socialist movement is not the reform of capitalism, but the realization of socialism—not the diminution of exploitation, but the total suppression of the system of wage labor.

No reformist instrument can operate effectively within capitalist society, Luxemburg argues. The trade unions cannot suppress the capitalist law of wages; they cannot alter the size of the supply of labor or the demand for labor, the principal determinants of the price of labor. They cannot influence the process of production itself. At best they can defend their previous gains and ensure that they receive the full market price for their labor. If they succeed in raising wages further, Luxemburg implies, the capitalists will simply pass the additional costs along in higher prices. For Luxemburg these propositions are not transitory contingent facts, but necessary consequences of capitalist organization.

Cooperatives, the other economic instrument of the workers' movement, are similarly condemned to frustration when they operate within a capitalist framework. Subjected to the exigencies of competition on the market, the cooperative enterprise must either regulate itself with all the rigor and absolutism of a private capitalist firm or go under. Luxemburg pinpoints the dilemma of the cooperative enterprises: Either they "are obliged to take toward themselves the role of the capitalist entrepreneur—a contradiction that accounts for the usual failure of production cooperatives . . . or, if the workers' interests continue to prevail, [they] end by dissolving."[5]

Trade unions and cooperatives constitute the economic instrumentalities of reformism; parliamentary democracy, its principal political means. But for Luxemburg the notion of working through bourgeois democratic institutions is a snare and a delusion:

> . . . the present State is not "society" representing the "rising working class." It is itself the representative of capitalist society.

69

> It is a class State. Therefore its reform measures are not an application of "social control," that is, the control of society working freely in its own labor process. They are forms of control applied by the class organization of Capital to the production of Capital. The so-called social reforms are enacted in the interests of Capital.[6]

Parliaments can only reflect the interests present in society, and in capitalist society bourgeois interests dominate. The bourgeoisie infuses ostensibly democratic forms with the content of its own class interests. Should its capacity to control the outcome of democratic procedures be threatened, the bourgeoisie will promptly shed its adherence to democracy. "That is why the idea of the conquest of a parliamentary reformist majority is a calculation which, entirely in the spirit of bourgeois liberalism, preoccupies itself only with one side—the formal side—of democracy, but does not take into account the other side, its real content."[7]

Luxemburg concludes that the revisionists' tools—the unions, the cooperatives, and the parliamentary party—cannot effect the suppression of capitalism. They can only institute reforms that ameliorate and strengthen the institutions of capitalist society. Consequently the reformist program merely prolongs the existence of capitalism; what is required is the recognition that reformist efforts are only means in the struggle for the destruction of capitalism, the seizure of power by the workers, and the social revolution.

Lenin in *What Is to Be Done?* argues a similar case. The revisionists in Europe and the "economists" in Russia postpone the essential democratic and socialist transformation of society by neglecting to organize for a climactic political struggle. Lenin characterizes the fundamental doctrines of his revisionist opponents in the following manner:

> Social-Democracy must transform itself from a party of social revolution into a democratic party of social reforms. This political demand has been surrounded by Bernstein with a whole battery of quite well co-ordinated "new" arguments and considerations. The possibility of providing a scientific basis for Socialism and of proving its necessity and inevitability from the point of view of the materialist conception of history was denied, as were the facts of increasing misery, proletarianization,

and the sharpening of capitalist contradictions. The very conception of "the ultimate aim" was declared bankrupt, and the idea of the dictatorship of the proletariat was rejected absolutely. The difference in principle between Liberalism and Socialism was denied. The theory of the class struggle was repudiated on the grounds that it was inapplicable to a strictly democratic society, governed according to the will of the majority, etc.[8]

These central principles of reformism Lenin repeatedly condemns as "opportunistic" and attacks his opponents for aspiring to be a democratic party of reforms rather than a revolutionary socialist party.

The thrust of Lenin's attack is clear: Capitalist society prevents a harmony of social interests and a peaceful social order. Reforms within this liberal capitalist framework can never be adequate. Economic gains cannot replace the need for the political reconstruction of society along socialist lines. These arguments, like those of Marx and Luxemburg, emphasize that the state in capitalist society cannot be a neutral instrument of social improvement, but must remain—until its overthrow—a tool for bourgeois domination. Government intervention can establish only a positive state, or at best a social security state, but not a social welfare state. Reforms can improve the conditions of the working population, but not to such an extent that the political, economic, and social supremacy of the ruling class is endangered. Inequalities of wealth and power sufficient to maintain social classes will remain despite reformist efforts. This line of argument, the central theme of Luxemburg and Lenin, continues to constitute the basis of much radical criticism of the welfare state.

It is possible to distinguish at least three separate strands of this common theme of radical protest. The first, *the empiricist critique,* largely accepts the value premises of the social welfare state, but calls attention to its failures in achieving its objectives. These criticisms, which customarily originate with radical Social Democrats, concentrate on the empirical imperfections of existing welfare states. The second strand, *the structuralist critique,* also generally accepts social-welfare statist values, but contends that welfare statist means can never be sufficient to realize these ends. The basic contention is that the defects of the welfare state are unavoidable because of its reliance upon private capital, meritocratic motivation, and representative democracy. These structural flaws mean that welfare states must fail to create a democratic and egalitarian community, and consequently more decisive measures, possibly violent revolution, are required to socialize production and democratize administration. The third variant of radical protest is a mélange of criticisms that may be loosely termed *the new leftist critique*. Though generally rooted in the writings of the young Marx, this position emphasizes the psychological and cultural costs of the welfare state rather than its structural flaws. It rests on a conception of human welfare sufficiently distinct from that of even the most advanced social welfare state that it concludes that even if welfare states were to realize their most progressive aims, the results would still be unsatisfactory. This most fundamental of radical criticisms will be considered after attending to the modest empiricist critique and the more traditional structuralist critique.

The Empiricist Critique

In the late 1950s and early 1960s radical observers of an empiricist bent began noticing a disturbing trend—the much ballyhooed redistribution of income and wealth that had occurred during and shortly after World War II was coming to a stop; in fact, the trend indicated a broadening of class differentials. This conclusion ran strongly counter to the conventional wisdom which held that governmental policies were redistributing resources in favor of wage earners and poorer income groups. Full employment, the expansion of public services, and highly progressive tax structures were thought to have created consistently greater social equality—to such an extent that in the eyes of conservative critics, the incentives essential to capitalist production were being jeopardized. Just as the celebrations and denunciations of these egalitarian tendencies were rising to a crescendo, however, evidence mounted to show that the rhetoric was remote from social developments.

The most intelligent assessment of the situation came from Richard Titmuss. In his 1962 study of *Income Distribution and Social Change* Titmuss argued against the assumption that a natural movement of social forces was carrying British society toward a greater equality of incomes and standards of living. No "natural law" operated to ensure a more egalitarian future; on the contrary, Titmuss concluded, "there is more than a hint from a number of studies that income inequality has been increasing since 1949 whilst the ownership of wealth . . . has probably become still more unequal and, in terms of family ownership, possibly strikingly more unequal, in recent years."[9]

Titmuss based this finding upon a critical analysis of the statistics used in analyzing income distribution. He maintained that statistical measures had failed to keep pace with the ability of the wealthy to avoid taxation. By concentrating on individual rather than family incomes official data obscured the interfamilial transfers that allowed the very wealthy to spread their incomes among a number of persons. By defining income in the traditional sense of disposable cash, the statisticians ignored the arrangements made by many of the rich to receive income in kind (expense accounts, stock options, paid vacations, and the like) and to defer it over time (through pension benefits and trusts for their children). As Titmuss correctly noted,

> Long-run developments in family relationships and fiscal law; the shifting alignment of forces controlling access to a power system as distinct from individual property rights; the transformation of individual benefits in cash into family benefits in kind; the changing individual age cycle of earning and non-earning; the spreading and splitting of "income" over life and over the lives of several generations; the metamorphosis of income into capital; the growth of rewards in the form of tax-free payments and the use of credit facilities; all these make "cash in hand" less necessary for the business of daily life for certain classes and living on overdrafts, trusts and other forms of command-over-resources more fiscally rewarding if, at times, perhaps a little irksome.[10]

These developments allowed the rich to understate their incomes, and thus partially to escape the incidence of highly progressive tax rates. In consequence, a greater portion of the burden of financing the social services fell upon the poorer sections of the community and the redistributive effects of social welfare policy declined accordingly.

In an article published in 1958 Brian Abel-Smith had already argued that the middle class was relatively more successful than the working class in exploiting the services provided by the welfare state. Who had profited from the creation of the welfare state?

> I am going to suggest that the major beneficiaries of these changes have been the middle classes, that the middling income groups get more from the state than the lower income groups, that taxation often hits the poor harder than the well-to-do, and in general that the middle classes receive good standards of welfare while working people receive a Spartan minimum.[11]

Though he conceded that his evidence on the financing and utilization of public services was incomplete and unsystematic, Abel-Smith was able to show that middle-class parents received proportionately more benefit from the educational system and that they used the health service more often and received more expensive care. Furthermore, he argued that the quality of services for the most disadvantaged, and especially for the mentally ill, was grossly inadequate.

The discovery that the welfare state did not guarantee a continuing erosion of class barriers stimulated a vast critical literature documenting the persistence of social inequality. Inequalities of income and wealth were demonstrated, and the associated inequality of educational and economic opportunity convincingly portrayed. Poverty was rediscovered. The limited possibilities of entry into the political and economic elite received renewed confirmation and the enbourgeoisement thesis came under heavy criticism.

Neither these social developments nor the critical scholarship that followed was confined to Britain. In the United States Gabriel Kolko in his study of *Wealth and Power in America* reached conclusions similar to those of Titmuss. In the embryonic American welfare state Kolko found beneath the myth of equality great continuing inequalities of income, wealth, consumption, security, and incidence of unemployment. Taxation, he argued, had not mitigated the fundamentally unequal distribution of rewards. Kolko claimed for his study that it "refute[d] the basic assumption of universal abundance in America, which figures so centrally in current social thought."[12] In a similar vein Piven and Cloward argued that the welfare system functioned not to relieve distress, but to maintain social order.[13] Michael Harrington stimulated the investigation, if not the relief, of the human desolation and waste in *The Other America;* by his estimate forty to fifty million Americans remained outside the affluent society.[14]

In Sweden the discovery of persistent poverty and a declining rate of equalization of resources came as an especially bitter pill, given the government's touting of its successes in extending social welfare, yet the facts shortly became plain to all but the most partisan observers. Evidence accumulated that from about 1948 into the early 1960s no substantial changes in income distribution had occurred.[15] The progressivity of the tax structure was called in question. The unions and their allies discovered the existence of "the low-income problem," a somewhat sanitized Swedish term for what other countries called the poverty problem. A massive research effort with government support proceeded to document the existence of a stratum of poorly paid, irregularly employed, little educated persons whose political and cultural opportunities lagged behind those of the rest of the population and whose life chances and economic opportunities remained significantly below those of their fellow citizens.[16]

Meanwhile, separate studies disclosed that precisely this stratum, the least advantaged, benefited least from the welfare state. Walter Korpi and Gunnar and Maj-Britt Inghe demonstrated that numerous Swedes were falling through the safety nets provided by the welfare state.[17] Despite all the successes of social welfare policy, the need for revisions and elaborations to cope with continued hardship and to adapt to changing social circumstances remained. One of the most effective critics, Par Holmberg, wrote:

> Certainly the reforms in social insurance—for example the important increase in the national pension in 1948—brought with them declines in the need for social assistance in the years immediately following such reforms. But other circumstances in social developments have always occasioned opposing increases in the need for assistance for people not included by the particular reforms.[18]

As in Britain, social welfare policy in Sweden did not provide a lasting, once-and-for-all solution for the social problems of capitalist society, nor was even the most successful of welfare states able to eliminate an underclass of the socially disadvantaged. Capitalism's inherent tendency toward social inequality eroded the effects of welfare policy measures if these policies were not constantly adjusted to changing circumstances.

In comparison with the effort to document the persistent social inequalities of the welfare state, the attention given to inequality of political influence has been scant. Whether this neglect stems from the intellectuals' conviction that a substantial degree of paternalist manipulation is both legitimate and necessary for the welfare state's smooth operation is a question that cannot be resolved here. Social scientists scrutinize with inordinate zeal the degree and content of electoral participation, and to a lesser extent they examine the employee's involvement in the control of the firm or bureaucracy, but virtually never do they relate their findings to the welfare state as a specific form of social organization. Only a few observers indebted to the syndicalist tradition or inspired by the vision of a participatory democracy have discerned political failings in the welfare state without at the same time calling for a revolutionary solution. One is Ernst Wigforss, the elder statesman of Swedish Social Democracy, who has argued for more than fifty years that "industrial democracy" must accompany the other paraphernalia of the welfare state: Without chances for active participation in the direction of his work life, the employee's emancipation is incomplete. The amount of subsequent careful empirical work concerning participation in the governance of the enterprise and of the local community as a feature of the welfare state is, however, remarkably modest.

These studies and others like them document both the persistence of social inequality in welfare states and the emergence of new kinds of inequality. Remarkably few of them have any developed theoretical base; in general their approach is strictly empirical. What is the distribution of income? wealth? tax burdens? educational attainment? unemployment? Such are the questions asked. The origins of the distribution of resources and burdens in social structures and processes have received little attention, save from exceptional investigators like Titmuss. Likewise many of these studies avoid recommendations for policies that would alleviate the conditions they describe; nevertheless, if one assumes the desirability of a classless or at least more egalitarian society, the phenomena they disclose are genuine flaws of the welfare state. To the social welfare statist

76

they are not, however, systemic flaws inherent in this form of social organization. They do not result of necessity from the welfare state's reliance on private capital. They do not require a new type of social order, but further reforms within the existing society—a greater redistribution of resources and more specifically targeted programs of social assistance. To more radical observers these continuing imperfections in the welfare state may denote congenital flaws, but to the social welfare statist they merely indicate the need for completing his agenda—to move beyond the positive state to the social security state and the social welfare state.

The Structuralist Critique

The major radical critics, relying on the Marxist tradition, argue that the persistence of social and political inequality is not merely a contingent or accidental feature of welfare states, but a *necessary* consequence of their organizational structure. Thus the prominent American socialist, Michael Harrington, argues:

> There are three basic reasons why the reform of the welfare state will not solve our most urgent problems: the class structure of capitalist society vitiates, or subverts, almost every such effort toward social justice; private corporate power cannot tolerate the comprehensive and democratic planning we desperately need; and even if these first two obstacles to providing every citizen with a decent house, income and job were overcome, the system still has an inherent tendency to make affluence self-destructive.[19]

Here the ills of the welfare state are traced to inherent structural features; they must persist, the argument runs, because the welfare state does not make a sufficiently thorough break with liberal capitalist society. Indeed many radical critics argue that the welfare state is not a distinct social type, but merely a subspecies of capitalist society. They single out various aspects of capitalist society that remain entrenched within the welfare state to subvert the possibilities of egalitarianism and democracy. Only the three most powerful of these arguments will be scrutinized here.

The first argument is that the welfare state still contains the tendency to generate a potentially "unmanageable surplus," that is, a surplus of current output over current consumption that cannot be employed either for investment or increased consumption. In traditional Marxist analysis, the capitalists create this surplus by exploiting the workers to obtain the "surplus value" the workers create. This acquisitive activity eventually leads to a capitalist "catastrophe" that ushers in the socialist society. More recent critics, perhaps chastened by the delayed arrival of this catastrophe, offer a subtler version of this argument. The welfare state, with its dependence upon private enterprise, continues to produce an expanding surplus by exploiting the workers, but this surplus is not unmanageable. The dominant political forces within the welfare state have learned how to absorb the surplus through wasteful private consumption and public spending on war materials. The surplus can be managed, but not for humane purposes; because of the entrenched interests of private capital, war and waste—not social needs—exhaust the surplus.[20]

The most careful presentation of the unmanageable surplus argument occurs in the first four chapters of Paul Baran's *The Political Economy of Growth*.[21] Baran's argument is twofold: First, societies based on a capitalist economy fail and *must fail* to produce as large a surplus as they might and, second, the surplus that is produced is not and *can not* be devoted to rational social objectives because of the opposition of vested interests. Capitalist forms of production, Baran correctly observes, reduce the surplus below its potential by permitting "excess consumption" among middle and upper income groups; by employing unproductive workers such as stock brokers, tax evasion specialists, and advertising personnel; and by underemploying human and capital resources. That each of these phenomena involves waste is undeniable; what is debatable is the contention that this kind of waste is an unavoidable feature of the welfare state, particularly the social welfare state. It can certainly be argued that redistributive taxation would reduce wasteful consumption; that restrictions upon advertising and changes in financing of investments would cause a decline in the population of socially unproductive workers; and that expansive fiscal and labor market policy would ensure full employment of labor and capital. The question is: Are these developments possible without a revolutionary transformation of capitalist society?

Traditional Marxist criticism denies that they are. The dominant interests of the capitalist sector, the Marxists maintain, will have both the power and the will to resist the curtailment of their essential privileges. The changes in question are not physically impossible, for a socialist society is deemed fully capable of effecting them, but they are politically impossible because capitalists still hold the levers of power. Just which levers constitute the critical source of capitalist power varies from theorist to theorist. For Marcuse it is the ability to set the "background conditions" of public debate and thus to bias the formation of public opinion and public policy.[22] The French critic of Social Democracy, André Gorz, ascribes the power of private capital to its ability to withhold essential investment: "Here we come to the root of the capitalist system: if capital can not get what it considers a sufficient reward, it goes on strike."[23] For other writers, such as Ralph Miliband, a host of factors combine to frustrate gradualist reform efforts: the bourgeois composition of the civil service, the bourgeois "hegemony" over the mass media and educational institutions, and the economic sanctions that the international capitalist community can impose on deviant governments.[24] The thrust of these arguments is clear: Private capital subverts democratic government by distorting the formation and impact of public opinion and by eroding its sovereignty over economic affairs.

These private sources of power certainly operate to protect the position of private capital; the radical critics can easily adduce cases like the American oil companies' refusal to invest in further refining capacity without assurances of a "proper regulatory climate," the mineral companies' investment strike after Saskatchewan sharply raised their taxes in 1974, and the destabilizing outflow of capital under various Labour governments in Britain. But these instances do not prove the radical case; the radical critic has to demonstrate not merely that these levers of private capital sometimes work, but (1) that they *always* work sufficiently to preserve capitalism and (2) that only revolution can eliminate them. Neither the evidence nor rational deduction permits the stronger conclusion.

Reformist governments have carried out policies that have not only benefited the disadvantaged, but that have sapped the rights and privileges of private capital as well. The Social Democratic governments of the Scandinavian countries, the French Popular Front government, and the Labour ministry of 1945 all effected significant redistributions of income and power. In each case Social Democratic governments assumed office when depression or war had greatly eroded the legitimacy of the traditional capitalist order. Under these circumstances reformist politicians were able to restrict the capitalists' legal prerogatives (such as setting the length of the work day), to nationalize industry, to establish public health services and public insurance programs, and even to assume direction of some of the nation's investment. None of these reforms is trifling. Each permits a more humane employment of the national surplus. To claim that these measures only stabilize the system of private economic management is nonsense, for not only do they bring immediate material improvement to the under classes, they also remove the capitalists' means of defense. They strip away the rights of private property in the same way that legislatures traditionally stripped away the rights of monarchs. As a Swedish new leftist theoretician concedes, "The essentially socialist element in social welfare policy . . . is that it removes large sectors of social life from the power of the market mechanism."[25] In short, the historical record indicates that the obstacles that private capital poses to a beneficent use of community resources can be overcome through reformist measures.

Where, then, does the radical argument go wrong in its claim that only revolution can institute fundamental changes in capitalist society? It errs in its factual estimate of the power of private capital; capital's power does not always overwhelm the legal enactments of a democratic majority. It is simply not always true, as André Gorz claims, that "suffrage confers the right to govern, but not the power to do so."[26] Equally important, however, is a faulty psychological assumption that underlies the logic of the radical argument: the a priori assumption that the capitalist's fundamental desire is to make profits. Only this assumption that profits are dearer to the capitalist than life itself allows the radical to insist that the capitalist will defend his privileges to the death. Certainly such dedication is possible and has occurred, but it is by no means the only possible outcome. The private capitalist, the master of economic calculation, often possesses sufficient rationality and awareness of his self-interest to prefer to grant concessions rather than to court martyrdom (or even danger) in the defense of profits. The dubious psychology of the Marxist radical makes him incapable of offering cogent analyses of such developments as the passage of the Reform Act of 1832, the democratization of Sweden in 1918–1921, and most important for the present purpose, the proliferation of modern welfare states.[27] The same inability to comprehend the psychological basis of reformism destroys his argument that a gradualist transformation of capitalist society is impossible.

In lieu of reformism the Marxist radical advocates revolution. This strategy, as candid Marxists confess, leads to curious difficulties: If capitalism is so firmly entrenched, how can revolution succeed? And, if sufficient force to carry out a revolution can be amassed, then why can the essential policies not be implemented without violence?

The same difficulties plague a more recent theoretical essay steeped in the tradition of Marxist economics, James O'Connor's *The Fiscal Crisis of the State*. O'Connor argues that the state in capitalist (welfare) societies must try to fulfill two mutually contradictory functions, the "accumulation" and "legitimation" functions; that is, the state must seek both to promote profitable accumulation and to maintain the loyalty of the classes which suffer from such accumulation. In pursuing these activities governments must spend at a rate that outstrips their ability to finance their expenditures. They need to support private business through social investment and through social services and insurance programs that lower the costs of doing business. They must cover the costs of pollution. They must underwrite the welfare expenditures and the violence needed to pacify domestic and foreign populations. "Society's demands on local and state budgets seemingly are unlimited, but people's willingness and capacity to pay for these demands appear to be narrowly limited."[28] Neither wealthy capitalists nor the working class is willing to pay more taxes and the result is a chronic fiscal crisis and incipient tax revolt.

The economic and political foundations of O'Connor's argument differ sharply from Baran's. Rather than capitalism's generating a vast and potentially unmanageable surplus that governments must devise wasteful ways to spend, it runs the risk of not making sufficient resources available to the public sector. And rather than the state's being simply the instrument of the dominant class, it also caters to labor interests in carrying out its legitimation function. Nevertheless, the same flaws in psychology and in political analysis that vitiate the unmanageable surplus argument also afflict the case for a fiscal crisis. O'Connor cannot persuasively argue why the capitalists (or indeed the general population) cannot pay more taxes either directly or through inflation. Nor does he expose the political mechanisms that determine whether the accumulation or legitimation function of the state takes precedence, thus allowing the welfare statist to retain the conviction that the social welfare policies characteristic of the legitimation function might eventually overwhelm the activity of accumulation.[29]

O'Connor's case suffers from further defects of its own. Despite his perceptive insights into the general structure and operation of modern capitalist economies, O'Connor fails to present a convincing case for his central thesis of a fiscal crisis. He ignores the possibility of more efficient and therefore relatively less expensive government. He provides little evidence that the prospects of a tax revolt prevent higher taxes, while acknowledging that European countries have sharply higher tax rates. Finally, he neglects to consider that the period of the late 1960s and early 1970s that provides the evidence for his arguments may have been an aberration in its rapid expansion of both domestic and military spending. It is a curious irony that both of the major Marxist versions of the structuralist argument suffer from an ahistorical approach, Baran's from overemphasis on the stagnation of the 1950s and O'Connor's from overemphasis on the inflationary Johnson-Nixon years.

A second fundamental criticism of the welfare state on structural grounds is that it must eventually fail to satisfy egalitarian criteria because of its meritocratic foundations. The classic presentation of this argument is Michael Young's marvelous satire, *The Rise of the Meritocracy*. The meritocracy is a society based on the principle of equality of opportunity; it thus carries to a logical conclusion the moderate Labour party programs of the mid-1950s. All hereditary and institutional obstacles to talent and initiative are eliminated; a person's place in the social hierarchy is determined solely by "merit," defined as intelligence plus effort.

> Since the country is dedicated to the one overriding purpose of economic expansion, people are judged according to the single

test of how much they increase production, or the knowledge that will, directly or indirectly, lead to that consummation. . . . The ability to raise production, directly or indirectly, is known as "intelligence"; this iron measure is the judgment of society upon its members.[30]

Equality of opportunity thus means equality of opportunity to be unequal. Since not all persons make equal contributions to the gross national product, they receive unequal rewards and esteem—so unequal in fact that a demeaning new system of stratification results, in which "the inferior man has no ready buttress for his self-regard" because the only explanation of his low status is his personal lack of "meritorious" qualities.[31] The notion of a fundamental human equality virtually disappears, for the meritocrats "can hardly conceive of a society built upon consideration for the individual regardless of his merit, regardless of the needs of society as a whole."[32]

Young's meritocracy is, of course, an ideal type, a rationalist projection of the consequences of the principle of equality of opportunity. The satire gets its bite from the fact that it illuminates existing proposals and institutions. Indeed, such a discerning student of social inequality as Frank Parkin has appropriated the term "meritocratic socialism" to describe the program of Western European Social Democracy. Meritocratic reforms that increase equality of opportunity "bring about relatively little disturbance of the stratification system," he argues; they are "perfectly compatible with a modern capitalist order" and only perpetuate the chronic inequality of capitalist society.[33]

These criticisms of meritocratic welfare statism apply, however, only to the social security state. There substantial inequality beyond the social minimum (the "Equal" of Young's meritocracy) may flourish, and depending upon one's evaluation of egalitarian principles, this inequality may be legitimate or illegitimate. The meritocratic argument does not apply to the social welfare state, which aims to supersede the principle of equality of opportunity with a more thorough-going equalization of rewards and esteem. The social welfare state is not a meritocracy; indeed, conceding the force of Young's case, the social welfare state rejects the legitimacy of meritocratic considerations.

Young's satire presumes the possibility of an egalitarian social order, but a more stringent form of criticism argues that, definitions aside, welfare states must be meritocratic: Any society that gives such a high preference to enhancing the material welfare of its citizenry must select and reward those persons who can make unusually large contributions to the society's production. Proponents of the welfare state cannot yet offer a convincing rebuttal to this argument. They can point out, however, that this principle rests on a currently widely accepted but questionable assumption that persons deserve to be rewarded for relatively greater "natural" capacities. If this assumption, now under attack from liberal as well as social democratic writers, were undermined, the legitimacy of meritocratic inequality would decline.[34] Alternatively, were welfare states to place less emphasis upon material production, the presumed need for "merit" would also decline. In either case:

> The Social Democrat's view of equality means that, where Nature has created great and fundamental differences in abilities, these must *not* be allowed to determine the individual's chances in life, but rather that society should intervene to "restore the balance." These differences, in the form of physical or intellectual handicaps, can never be eliminated, but they can be reduced in a generous social climate, and one can work against their leading to social discrimination. Disadvantages inflicted by Nature should not be accepted as something we can do nothing about.[35]

Meritocratic bias, like the "unmanageable" social surplus, is not an inevitable flaw in the welfare state, but a shortcoming that the social welfare state attempts to remedy by specific measures designed to redress "the arbitrariness found in nature."[36]

A third argument asserts that the welfare state contains inherent defects in its political structure. This argument holds that the welfare state's reliance on representative government means that it is not sufficiently democratic. Representative institutions prevent the individual from participating personally in critical social decisions and skew politics in favor of vested private interests. This form of political organization, André Gorz maintains, offers only a restricted and inadequate set of liberties:

> The liberty of the citizen consists in his right to vote from time to time, to choose between newspapers generally controlled by

monopolies, to listen to radio and television controlled by the same monopolies, when they are not run by the state, and to choose between the varieties of branded goods competing for his custom. The citizen is free in matters of secondary importance and powerless in matters that count. He has no say in the organization, orientation and priorities of production; in the creation of employment; in the organization, content and methods of education; in the geographical distribution of investments, their amount, etc. All these decisions affecting the meaning and quality of society come within the sphere of the ruling capitalist groups and the state that serves their general interests; they are made in response to financial and commercial considerations unrelated, in any major sense, to any kind of economic, social, or human optimum.[37]

By limiting politics to a narrow set of "political" issues and to a small number of politicians and lobbyists, present-day representative institutions frustrate popular aspirations.

The first part of this argument requires only modest attention. While it is true that the parliamentary agendas of most modern welfare states are largely confined to "political" issues and usually skirt issues like the organization of production and the direction of investment, there is no reason for representative bodies to be so restricted. Modern legislatures (like Sweden's) do consider and pass measures dealing with the work environment and job safety, "public" representatives on corporate boards, and incentives for socially beneficial types of investment. A national assembly would be an unlikely body to determine the precise location, timing, and character of most of a society's investment, but together with local representative bodies it could exercise both general and specific supervision of investment.

The second part of the argument, the contention that representative government is necessarily undemocratic, demands closer scrutiny. The strongest case for this position still comes from G. D. H. Cole's *Guild Socialism Restated*. In addition to the argument just considered Cole has two major complaints against representative government. First, it almost completely substitutes the representative for the represented: ". . . the elector retains practically no control over his representative, has only the power to change him at very infrequent intervals, and has in fact only a very limited range of choice." Second, the representative must represent his elector on too wide a range of positions. The legislator elected to fulfill a vast number of disparate purposes "ceases to have any real representative relations to those who elect him."[38] The voter does not have a representative who can present his view on all the various issues.

These complaints do strike at inherent structural features of representative government. Representative government is not participatory democracy; consequently, for those who favor the individual's participation in major social decisions that affect his life, representative government can never be entirely satisfactory, even if the exigencies of large-scale political organization make it necessary. This necessity is, of course, the first counter to Cole's argument. Regrettably, the need for national defense requires political units of a size that make direct participation in much national business extremely difficult, if not totally unfeasible.

Another rebuttal is open to the defender of the welfare state. While admitting the force of much of Cole's argument, he can contend that much of the public business can devolve to local governments and workplace organizations which permit and encourage individual participation. The program of the social welfare state puts strong emphasis on the individual's having a say in the organization of his work, the policy of his work unit, the alteration of his living environment, and the conduct of his local government.[39] The expansion of local participatory institutions would not eliminate the need for representative government, but it would extend the sphere of direct democracy sufficiently so that complaints about "lack of participation" would look suspiciously utopian.

These charges that the welfare state possesses inherent structural defects constitute a powerful challenge to existing positive states and social security states which do indeed rely heavily upon private capital, meritocratic motivation, and representative institutions. The structuralist critique rests on compelling values: the humane use of the social product; the right of all human beings, regardless of their innate abilities, to life full and satisfying lives; and a wide extension of democratic participation. By exposing such shortcomings of contemporary welfare states as wasteful consumption, status-seeking, and oligarchic politics, this critique challenges the capacity of welfare-statist means to create a democratic and classless society. The structuralist critique goes wrong, however, in assuming that governmental interven-

86

tion can produce nothing more than a positive state or a social security state. It fails to distinguish the social welfare state as a separate species of welfare state, one that can make private capital subserve public interests, mute the impact of meritocratic striving, and extend democratic participation. Since no fully developed social welfare state currently exists, this omission is understandable. Less defensible are implications or overt assertions that a social welfare state is impossible, for not only do social welfare-statist means have the theoretical capacity to meet these radical objections, but advanced welfare states such as Sweden have demonstrated the practical possibilities of these means (see Chapter Six).

New Leftist Critiques

The empiricist critique censures the fragmentary accomplishment of welfare statist aims. The structuralist indictment claims further that welfare statist means are inherently incapable of achieving these objectives. New leftist criticisms, however, maintain that even complete success in obtaining welfare statist objectives would be unsatisfactory, since the objectives themselves are misconceived. Through the colorful and polymorphous new leftist criticism of the welfare state there runs a common theme: The conception of human welfare that underlies the social policy of the welfare state is fundamentally flawed. The specific complaints that the new left brings simply constitute variations on this basic objection. The welfare state refuses to give up the bourgeois values of "consumerism, suburbia, and a bookkeeping conception of life" for the virtues of spontaneity, sensuality, community, an unalienated existence, and an unravaged environment.[40] Thus, even if the welfare state were to carry out its program in its entirety, immense discomfort and uneasiness, primarily of a psychological nature, would remain. Stress and tension would result not only from the structural imperfections of the welfare state, but also from the misdirected social consciousness of its citizens.

Not all forms of this argument exert an immediate appeal. Murray Bookchin, in appealing for the emergence of a new revolutionary mentality, bestows his blessing on an unpromising prospect for a utopian citizen:

87

The most promising development in the factories today is the emergence of young workers who smoke pot, fuck-off on their jobs, drift into and out of factories, grow long or longish hair, demand more leisure time rather than more pay, steal, harass all authority figures, go on wildcats, and turn on their fellow workers.[41]

In a similar vein the situationist students at the University of Strasbourg argued for "the infinite multiplication of *real desires* and their gratification" and took as the rule of their new game "to live instead of devising a lingering death, and to indulge untrammeled desire."[42] This radical formulation expresses a hostility to reasoned conduct and presumes an innocence of desire that is unlikely in the extreme.

There is, however, a more restrained version of this view. Another of Bookchin's models are the rebellious young Americans of the late 1960s and early 1970s, whom he credits with the production of "invaluable forms of libertarian and utopian affirmation: the right to make love without restriction, the goal of community, the disavowal of money and commodities, the belief in mutual aid, a new respect for spontaneity."[43] These values bring into question the necessity of hierarchy, power, and manipulation and undermine the notion that material gratification constitutes the prime satisfaction in life. They contain the major indictments of the welfare state model and hence merit closer examination.

First the new left criticizes the welfare state's conception of welfare as excessively material.[44] "Commodity fetishism" still prevails; individuals continue to conceive of themselves as obtaining satisfaction above all through the consumption of marketable goods and services. They work not for the intrinsic satisfaction labor provides, but to earn money to purchase consumer goods. As Herbert Gintis observes, these attitudes have the sanction of academic orthodoxy:

> Neo-classical welfare theory
> . . . views individual welfare
> As predicated on physical-organic unit-objects
> Alone —
> And marketable physical goods and services
> In particular. . . .[45]

Yet this view of welfare is surely false, as Gintis rightly argues. Welfare does include such intangibles as job satisfaction and familial affection. Furthermore, one's enjoyment of material objects (e.g., a statue) is not a constant, but depends upon one's capacity to appreciate the object, an ability which varies with individual development: "Welfare depends not only on what an individual has / But what he is."[46]

Gintis' criticisms are shrewd and well-taken, but the welfare state need not be addicted to commodity fetishism. It seeks to provide cultural goods outside the market. It places a high premium on education, including education in the arts and humanities. It endorses efforts at "job enrichment." Through taxes and regulation of private advertising it could moderate the stimuli for material gratification. In short, while this criticism exposes unattractive phenomena in contemporary welfare states, there is no reason why such "commodity fetishism" must continue.

A second new leftist criticism is that welfare states place insufficient emphasis on "community." The models of community are many and varied. For Raymond Williams the English working-class community is its archetype:

> There is a distinct working-class way of life, which ... with its emphases of neighbourhood, mutual obligation, and common betterment, as expressed in the great working-class political and industrial institutions, is in fact the best basis for any future English society.[47]

For Martin Buber a proper community

> must be built up of little societies on the basis of communal life and of the associations of these societies; and the mutual relations of the societies and their associations must be determined to the greatest possible extent by the social principle—the principle of inner cohesion, collaboration and mutual stimulation.[48]

For others community is characterized by the intimacy that characterizes a group of school friends, by familial affections, or by reciprocity of awareness. In every case a sense of common interest overrides individual competitiveness.

The boldest statement of the communitarian position occurs in the Cohn-Bendit brothers' *Obsolete Communism*.[49] The Cohn-Bendits declare that not merely competitiveness but all social hierarchy and the division of labor itself stand in the way of community. Their proposal is an anti-bureaucratic utopia. It requires putting an end "to the division of labor and of knowledge, which only serves to isolate people one from the others"; making "all those in whom any authority is vested permanently responsible to the people"; and taking "collective responsibility for one's own affairs."[50] Organization of the Leninist variety, and perhaps even organization per se, is destructive of human relationships.

The proponent of the welfare state appreciates the value of community, for he sees mutual aid and solidarity at the core of his program. Like former Swedish prime minister Per-Albin Hansson, he can conceive of the welfare state as the "people's home." Bureaucracy he regards as unpleasantly hierarchical and potentially destructive of personal privacy, but nonetheless essential. The redistribution of vast sums of money through taxes and transfer payments and the public provision of education, health care, and other services require elaborate large-scale organization; furthermore, the administration of these activities must proceed expeditiously and equitably. Public agencies must eschew favoritism and incompetence if the canons of equality and efficiency are to be served and public support maintained. Precisely the values that Max Weber attributed to bureaucracy—efficiency, rationality, and impersonality—make it indispensable for operating the various fiscal programs, public services, and social insurance arrangements.

The size of this organization inevitably produces occasional mistreatment and injustice. For this reason welfare statists support administrative remedies as an essential complement to bureaucratic structures. Perhaps the best known of these correctives is the institution of the ombudsman, an official empowered with independent authority to seek redress for administrative error. His efforts to minimize incompetence and abuse can never infuse bureaucratic relations with a sense of community—this point the welfare statist must concede, noting meanwhile that his social arrangements offer numerous other arenas (the neighborhood, the work-place, the voluntary organization) where the spirit of fraternity and solidarity may flourish.

Closely related to the communitarian criticism is a third new leftist objection—that the welfare state does not eliminate alienation. One essential facet of alienation is, of course, the individual's isolation from his fellow workers and fellow citizens. Another is the unsatisfying character of labor. For Iris Murdoch the latter element is fundamental:

> The Socialist movement should most explicitly bring back into the centre of its thinking its original great source of inspiration and reflection, the problem of labour: the problem, that is, of the transformation of labour from something senseless which forms no real part of the personality of the labourer into something creative and significant.[51]

The welfare state does have resources with which it can combat alienation. It can encourage improvement of work environments so as to increase the worker's autonomy and satisfaction. Most Marxists, however, argue that such efforts must fail because wage labor is the basis of alienation and wage labor persists. This argument is invalid, for it assumes that in the wage bargain the laborer cedes his autonomy altogether, whereas the welfare state can encourage or even compel labor contracts that recognize his autonomy. Similarly, charges that the labor contract itself treats the laborer as a "commodity," and thus in a demeaning and inhuman fashion, lose their force in a society where only a portion of one's income comes in the form of a wage, where few potential workers can be parasites upon the labor of others, and where general equality and security prevail.

Alain Touraine has suggested that a different and novel type of alienation may present a more serious challenge to modern industrial societies. For him it is not the differential control of wealth and property, but of knowledge and information that produces alienation. The new class division in advanced industrial societies separates those who have the power to manage change ("technocrats, bureaucrats, and rationalizers") from those who lack such power, and what bestows power is information. "Lack of information (hence of participation in the systems of decision and organization) defines alienation."[52] The members of a declining rural community, the worker whose employment disappears through automation, the aging worker prematurely retired all suffer alienation. This argument recalls the Cohn-

Bendits' appeal to break the bourgeoisie's monopoly of socially critical knowledge. The danger Touraine and the Cohn-Bendits cite is a real peril for the welfare state. Impulses toward technocracy must be resisted, and the principal defense mechanisms must be the extension of education and of local and workplace democracy and the open confrontation of proposals for social change rather than their clandestine bureaucratic processing.

Fourth, new leftist critics charge the welfare state with offenses against the physical environment: pollution of air, water, and soil; destruction of natural beauty; compulsive exploitation of natural resources; and corruption of the body itself. The precise causes of this damage are traced to the inherently expansive tendencies of capitalist production and the bourgeois compulsion to dominate and subdue the natural world. In fact, these objections apply to any modern industrial system, not just those organized on welfare statist lines. They pertain to the welfare state only insofar as it requires economic growth to carry out its program. How much growth is necessary is debatable. Certainly, as Adler-Karlsson contends, it is easier to redistribute wealth and income when the growth of the national product makes it unnecessary to deprive anyone of his previous benefits.[53] One can argue, however, that a social welfare state might deemphasize material consumption and establish a "zero-growth" economy with less difficulty than alternative forms of social organization. Its range of regulatory and fiscal tools allow it to stimulate and restrict economic activity with great flexibility; it can, for example, readily tax or prohibit noxious effluents and use tax revenues to stimulate research on new forms of energy.

Summary

The radical criticisms of the welfare state cover a broad spectrum, from empirically based denunciations of persistent inequalities to visionary formulations of human welfare based on spontaneity and sensuality. The breadth of these objections complicates the task of responding. The social welfare statist acknowledges the force of the empiricists' criticisms and shares the concerns of the structural critics. He may even dream of a society based on new psychological foundations, though he regards announcements of its impending arrival as decidedly premature. Above all, however, he wants to emphasize the possibility of creating a classless social democracy through peaceful reformist efforts—to employ advanced economic and social welfare policy not to shore up a faltering society, but to create a new one.

Throughout this chapter the rebuttal of the radical case has centered on the welfare state's *potential* to meet the more compelling radical objections without revolutionary violence and wholesale socialization of the means of production. The radical critics can show the defects that result from the persistence of capitalist features in modern interventionist states, but they cannot demonstrate the inevitability of these flaws. Accordingly, our stress has fallen on what the welfare state (and particularly the social welfare state) *can* do to achieve attractive radical objectives. The rebuttal is not couched in terms of prediction or necessity, for the political future is to a great degree open; it depends upon human choice. In a democratic society it depends upon the choice of all voters, not just a capitalist class with its hands upon the levers of the state. The voters' choices reflect in many instances the effects of the capitalist propaganda apparatus, but they also display the influence of progressive opinion. If they did not, there would be little hope for the Social Democrat and still less for more radical politicians. This, then, is our conviction: That a democratic majority, backed by a committed labor movement, can capture and employ political power to create a more decent society along the lines of a social welfare state. To provide a stronger empirical basis for this conviction and to show that the more fully a welfare state is developed, the less the radical criticisms apply, we now turn our attention to actual achievements of government intervention in Great Britain, Sweden, and the United States.

5

The British Social
Security State

For anyone concerned with social welfare policy, the British experience is of major importance. Not only have British policy makers originated a number of widely studied specific policies (the "workhouse," the National Health Service, social insurance partially underwritten by general taxation), but they have often based these policies on well-articulated general principles. The number of phrases drawn from policy debates that have passed into general parlance—"security from the cradle to the grave," "least eligibility," "national minimum," and the words "welfare state" itself—indicates the transnational scope of these principles. Moreover, these principles have been explicitly founded on either contemporary economic doctrine or on the output of empirical social research, a boon to students of social history, policy studies, and applied economics. Nor does this list exhaust the potential benefits to be derived from the study of the British case. British influence on American policy, at least up until World War II, has been so pervasive that an understanding of American developments is very difficult unless one considers "diffusion" from Britain.[1] And finally, the British experience raises a number of normative issues—for example, the reconciliation of "liberalist" with collective social security provisions—which bear directly on the "future of the welfare state."

Since we cannot hope to give adequate coverage to all these diverse areas in one chapter, we shall concentrate on particular themes of value for the purposes of this book. We begin by tracing the development of current welfare policies emphasizing (1), for later comparisons with the United States, the manner of decision making, and (2), the tension in policy output between the coherence and simplicity of the logic behind the policies and the increasing complexity of social reality. Next, we consider the Beveridge Plan both as a case study of the above and as a concrete manifestation of the strengths and weaknesses of the social security state model developed in Chapter One. We are then in a position to make more sense of the present state of British welfare, which we describe as a series of attempts (of varying success) to break the strait jacket of the Beveridge Plan in policy and in defining underlying values. Finally, we look briefly at the charge that the British welfare state is somehow "responsible" for Britain's poor economic performance since the war, a charge that enables us to consider the Conservative critique in a more concrete fashion.

Four Waves of Reform

The British government has long been concerned with the well-being and well-ordering of its population. Attempts to realize this aim have taken four forms: the Elizabethan Poor Law (1601–1834), the New Poor Law (1834–1908), what might be termed Three-Tiered Reform (1908–1939), and the Beveridge Plan and associated policies (1944–   ). Each, of course, left residual policy and attitudinal biases developed from the perceived failures of the earlier attempt ("failure" generally being defined in terms of large public expenditures). Nevertheless, the premises on which the four have been based are sufficiently differentiated to permit individual treatment.

The Elizabethan Poor Law

The Elizabethan Poor Law, effectively launched with the Act of 1601, can best be seen as the codification of medieval social doctrine in secular form.[2] At its base stood the three traditional categories of the poor: the vagrant and "sturdy beggar," who must be ruthlessly repressed; the "impotent poor" (the aged, the blind, and the infirm), who were to be maintained in almshouses or "poor houses"; and the able-bodied paupers willing to work, who were to be given productive labor at public charge. This scheme was to be administered locally, each parish being responsible for the appropriate ordering of its own poor. Sustaining this whole program were the powerfully developed sense of community and the vital force of Christian charity. Parishes which themselves were not far from subsistence level could hope to support poor relief on this scale only if most of the land was tilled in common, if wages were "fairly" determined, and if at least some of the better-off agreed with Aquinas' conclusion that not to give alms when required (which under the circumstances was perpetually) was a mortal sin.[3]

The social and attitudinal prerequisites for the effective functioning of the Poor Law underline the tenuousness of the relief system. And indeed it was not widely maintained beyond the Civil War and Restoration. The weakening of central authority made the enforcement of rates, prices, and land use politically unfeasible; with the capture of central institutions (Parliament) by groups favoring enclosure, free wage rates, and labor mobility, noncompliance became almost total. Moreover, even had the political will to enforce the statute been stronger, it is hard to see how it could have been reconciled with the changing social and economic patterns that broke the autonomy of village life, promoted "scientific" farming, necessitated large movements of labor to new industrial and commercial centers, and based continued economic advance on investment of profits in infrastructure and machines. No wonder the strictures of the Poor Law were viewed with scorn by men of affairs.

Nor did religious doctrine remain unaltered. Not only did there develop a debased form of Calvinism in which monetary success was seen as a mark of God's favor, more importantly there arose the distinction between worldly and unworldly affairs with the writ of religion strictly limited to the latter. In terms of social policy, the void was filled by a somewhat uneasy mixture of liberalism and mercantilism—each man had an absolute right to dispose of his property as he saw fit, and since the average worker was by nature inherently slothful, the only way to keep him diligent was to force him to fend for himself.[4] Not surprisingly, as a coherent national social policy the Elizabethan Poor Law soon became moribund, replaced by a welter of ad hoc repressions, alms giving, and works projects, the mixture varying from locality to locality and within each locality across time.[5] No wonder disputes over which parish had to take care of which poor soon replaced (as it did later in the United States) considerations of what relief was appropriate.

What finally terminated the Poor Law de jure was the advent of the Napoleonic War. The war had a double impact on poor relief. Its dislocation and the perceived need for social peace during this time of national peril first greatly increased the cost and scope of public largess, with the principle of granting "outdoor relief" (paid outside the workhouse) ratified formally by Parliament in 1796.[6] But its termination not only gave rise to complaints over the new "burdensome" rates, it also ushered in a period of reform. It was considered high time to reorient political and social affairs around new principles; one of the obvious relics of the past was the Elizabethan Poor Law.

The New Poor Law

The Elizabethan Poor Law can be conceived as the secular expression of medieval doctrine; its difficulties began with the dissolution of medieval values and social structures. The New Poor Law was an even clearer legislative expression of the doctrine of capitalist accumulation. In the field of poor relief this doctrine rested on the political economy of David Ricardo and the administrative plans of Jeremy Bentham, translated directly into policy via the Royal Commission Poor Law Report of 1832 co-authored by Nassau Senior (a practitioner of political economy) and Edwin Chadwick (Bentham's former secretary).

The position of these interpreters of political economy on the place of poor relief is clear. First, following the work of Malthus on population, any assistance to the improvident was deemed merely to increase their propensity to breed and thus would help upset the always delicate balance between population and resources. Second, since there was said to exist at any one time only a finite "wages fund" available for distribution, to relieve the poor directly would reduce the amount for others; thus, according to

Ricardo, the old poor laws, rather than "making the poor rich, are calculated to make the rich poor."[7]

Given these two premises, it would seem logical to abolish poor relief altogether. This opinion was indeed adhered to by Ricardo and Malthus and was even supported by such notable divines as Dr. Thomas Chalmers:

> The system of legal charity is replete with all sorts of mischief. . . . Not alone by the imprudence it has generated; as may be seen in the reckless marriages, and in the relaxed industry and economy of the people. But also in the vice which it has generated; the low and loathsome dissipation; the profligacy of both sexes; with all the mischief which proceeds from idleness, and through which the pauperism of England has become so deeply responsible for its immoralities and its crimes. . . . The virtue of humanity ought never to have been legalized, but left to the spontaneous workings of man's own willing and compassionate nature.[8]

In practice it was felt politically unpractical to carry the logic of political economy this far. What was needed was a new poor law based on conceptual and administrative principles that insofar as possible would limit the ill effects of any form of public relief.[9] These principles, often drawn from the writings of Bentham, were:

1. The termination of "outdoor relief" to able-bodied persons who could only be relieved in "well-regulated workhouses."
2. Public conception of the penal nature of these public institutions. The offer of public assistance was not intended to be accepted, and every effort was made to attach stigmas to its use. As one member of the Poor Law Commission commented, "I wish to see the Poor House looked to with dread by our labouring class, and the reproach for being an inmate in it extend downwards from father to son. . . ."[10]
3. The notion, in Bentham's phrase, of "least eligibility." No one was to be maintained at a standard of living "really or apparently so eligible as the situation of the independent laborer of the lowest class."
4. Centralized administration that would insure uniformity, sponsor unions of parishes to foster economies of scale, and

properly differentiate and segregate the elderly, the children, and the able-bodied, the sick.

5. Reduced expenditures for poor relief considered essential because, it was solemnly declared, "If the expenditure on the poor . . . were to go on at the rate at which it has increased for the last thirty years, it would ultimately throw the land out of cultivation, and destroy by famine or pestilence all who had not the means of emigration."[11]

In many respects these goals, legislated in the Poor Law Amendment Act of 1832, were not in practice achieved. The Act was greeted with such opposition, particularly in Northern England, that the Poor Law Commissioners found it expedient to delay the effective prohibition of assistance outside the Poor House (outdoor relief).[12] This expediency was perpetuated; never in the course of the Act were fewer than fifty percent of aided individuals given outdoor relief.[13] Central control, weakened even during the original enactment, became progressively less compelling. Partly in consequence, many of the structural reforms, such as the isolation of certain categories of people, were rarely undertaken. The Webbs could claim with justice that the New Poor Law in fact continued the previous evils of the "Mixed Work House" against which Senior and Chadwick had spoken so eloquently.[14]

Despite these apparently major difficulties, the act was for years declared a success: "Few measures have in their origin so fully occupied public attention or been productive of such important benefits in their results."[15] The reasons for this assessment are not hard to find. Foremost, there was an immediate saving of money, with expenditures for poor relief falling from over seven million pounds in 1832 to four million in 1837. It would be forty years before expenditures reached their earlier level. Some savings may have accrued from administrative reforms; most, however, resulted from the effectiveness of deterrence. The workhouses rapidly acquired the name "Bastilles," with stigmas that lingered at least through the 1930s. Those who could attempted to make collective provisions through Friendly Societies; those who could not (for example, widows and orphans) were often willing to undergo almost any deprivation rather than turn to public assistance. And this, from the standpoint of contemporary political economy, was as it should be. This treatment of the poor underscored the "liberal" intent of public policy that would tolerate no impediments to the process of capitalist accumulation and that based its public philosophy on the moral code of Samuel Smiles.

The New Poor Law Challenged

The (non) policy of the New Poor Law came under attack at the latter part of the nineteenth century from a number of directions. There arose for the first time a group of reformers ("socially unattached intelligentsia," to employ Karl Mannheim's phrase) concerned with social issues and able to carry out their work with the support of charitable, religious, and educational institutions not established a generation earlier.[16] These women and men had a markedly different approach from that governing the political economists who inspired the poor law, policy deduced from theoretical principles. The aim now was first to discover the "facts" and then to devise policies to change them. This effort, it should be emphasized, rarely entailed identification with the poor and their problems. The elitism of the new group of reformers was just as strong as that of Senior and Chadwick—the poor were to have things done to them as much as for them.[17]

This methodological approach—completely atheoretical, however much Beveridge might label it a crucial illustration of the power of science—was to produce problems later. At the time, however, it proved a powerful critique of the existing Poor Law because it revealed an empirical situation at odds with the premises of the earlier political economists. Briefly, it was found that the New Poor Law was totally inappropriate for the era of developed heavy industry.[18] Of trade cycles, to cite but one example, early political economy was blissfully unaware; indeed, according to Say, they were inconceivable since supply had by definition to equal demand at any given point. Nevertheless, they occurred. Workers were thrown out of work periodically, hardly through their own failings. What they needed was not the discipline of the poor law, but support until the cycle turned up. Moreover, even apart from considerations of macro-economic change, it was discovered (and the idea was developed by B. Seebohm Rowntree)[19] that families tended to go through a cycle of poverty. In old age, problems were particularly acute, primarily because of the inability of the industrial working class to accumulate sufficient property (assets) to support themselves. Finally, the discovery of a vast group of casual fringe workers (Booth's classes A, B, and C) particularly aroused the zeal of the reformers—this group, many contended, must be organized, regimented, put to work. If they refused, the Webbs recommended "they would be liable to be proceeded against as rogues and vagabonds, and they could be committed to the penal settlement or to prison."[20]

How were these "facts" to be overcome? Again, experience provided both negative and positive answers. The former revolved around charity. Random distribution of alms produced no permanent change in the lifestyle of the recipient; indeed it probably removed incentives to change it.[21] As for "scientific charity" (a major social development of the later nineteenth century in both Britain and the United States, founded on individual case work), it ignored the social causes of poverty, continued to distribute money randomly, and had of necessity high administrative costs.[22] Two types of action did seem worth taking: public labor exchanges to further the "decasualization of labor" and rationalize the labor market in general (a policy adopted from Germany and pushed in countless statements and articles by William Beveridge); and social insurance to spread liabilities and thus even out individual cycles of poverty. What was needed was to impress political decision-makers with the value of these policies.

With the advent of the Liberal Government in 1906, the "political climate" became favorable. To be sure, the disparate collection of individuals constituting the Liberal administration had no program of their own,[23] and a number of figures (especially Gladstone's biographer Morley) had a horror of any social experimentation. Nevertheless, opportunities for influence abounded. In the first place, the hand of Gladstone had finally (after forty years) been removed from Liberal Party policy; there was a need to supersede "Peace, Retrenchment and [political] Reform" as a policy guide. Social policy, in a diffuse way, seemed to be the answer. As Balfour remarked, "their fundamental difficulty is that they came in on the vague expectation that they were going to carry out great schemes of social reform."[24] This was termed a "difficulty" because the first two years of the Liberal regime had produced nothing of note except the death of the

Prime Minister, Campbell-Bannerman. Unless some action were taken soon, it was widely predicted the government would dissolve. An additional political impetus toward social reform was the presence in the cabinet of two dynamic, competitive individuals, Lloyd George and Winston Churchill, each determined to make his distinctive mark on political life and each receptive to ideas for social change.[25]

Finally, we must mention the rather crass, and perhaps for this reason often slighted, consideration of money. The cost of the British system of public poor relief declined with the introduction of the New Poor Law and stabilized thereafter . . . until the 1880s when it began inexorably to rise, reaching £13.4 million in 1904, almost twice the level found so unacceptable in the 1830s. Moreover, unemployment demonstrations, ad hoc political pressure, were pushing local costs much higher as "make work" projects outside the Poor Law became more prevalent.[26] Once again complaints arose over onerous rates; hope was expressed that insurance (not paid for in large part by the state) would reduce Poor Law expenditures.[27]

Once the political commitment had been made to embark on measures of social reform, legislation followed rapidly.[28] The Labour Exchange Act was passed in 1908; the National Insurance Act followed in 1911. The latter, with its coverage broadened in 1920, extended health and unemployment insurance to selected categories of workers, including those who were victims of cyclical unemployment. From the outset two-ninths of the contributions came from general revenues. A pension bill was enacted in 1908 giving 5 shillings per week to anyone over seventy years of age having less than a designated income. This measure, an anomaly in that it was not based on insurance principles,[29] was followed by the 1925 Contributory Pensions Act which lowered the benefit age to sixty-five and placed funding in the familiar employer-employee-state pattern. Thus by the mid-1920s Britain had a social insurance system covering health, old age and unemployment, based broadly on the prescriptions of social reformers. Only in one major respect did the plans differ: It was decided from the outset *not* to use social insurance as a device for social regulation, not "to let the State use its power over those in distress for any purpose except to relieve distress."[30] This decision put

British social reform on a secure "liberal" basis, a basis never challenged in subsequent legislation.

A Three-Tiered System

These reforms placed Britain in the forefront of nations attempting to relieve individual distress by social insurance (in some areas, particularly health insurance, their scope exceeded that which the United States has yet to achieve). That they soon proved unsatisfactory even in their own terms, less and less able to meet their professed goals, is a consequence of two major factors. First, in a pattern presaging that of the United States in the 1930s, their political base of support was narrow. With the decline of the Liberal Party after World War I, social insurance lacked coherent, Parliamentary support. Second, organized interests meanwhile either held aloof (the Trades Union Congress) or were latently hostile (Friendly Societies). Attempts to placate the latter were in large measure responsible for the unwieldy and costly structure of legislation, particularly evident in the area of health care.

Perhaps even more important was the previously mentioned atheoretical basis of the reform movement. The absence of new conceptual thinking had a number of deleterious effects. First, benefit levels were not set according to any coherent scheme; they were based neither on a relationship to past earnings as was the case in most of Europe,[31] nor on a determination of minimum needs. Levels instead were determined by an interplay of political and internal actuarial principles resulting in a random raising and lowering of benefits. Second, when a policy did not perform as expected, there was no provision for a sustained critique. From the outset, for example, the Labour Exchanges failed in their aim of effecting a transformation of the labor market. Some of the causes could easily be attributed to poor staffing and the depressing ambiance of most of the establishments. But what reason had one to expect that the (costly) resolution of these problems would lead to fundamental improvement? No definitive answer was, or could be, offered.

Third, social reforms were instituted quite apart from overall macroeconomic policy. The relation between the two was indeed never grasped by policy makers, and thus policies like the 1925 return to the gold standard, which had as their outcome a sharp increase in the rate of unemployment and a renewed bitterness in industrial relations, were carried out under the aegis of the former Liberal reformer, Winston Churchill. Finally, and most importantly, there was never a challenge to the orthodox economics of Ricardo updated by Marshall. The New Poor Law might be undercut, but the thinking that lay behind it was still there.[32] It was not until World War II that social reformers were to come to grips with Keynes.

The end result of these problems was to produce a poorly articulated three-tiered structure. At the "top" those with high incomes or middle-class occupations continued to provide for themselves. In the middle, a group consisting mostly of skilled or highly organized workers were covered by various insurance plans. At the bottom, marginal workers, family members of insured workers, many widows (in sum, the "poor") continued to be relieved ad hoc by public hospital wards and local relief boards. This "system" was not to last the depression. The 1911 unemployment scheme (devised for cyclical, not prolonged, unemployment) soon collapsed;[33] hospitals were thrown into financial crisis; after all the brave talk of breaking up the "nasty old poor law" individuals were thrown back on "the dole." Policy thinking, it seemed, had not gone much past Malthus; the old solution, emigration, was once again deemed a "definite economic advantage to the state" in reducing unemployment.[34]

The "Beveridge Plan"

By 1939, the Three-Tiered System had proven to be a failure. World War II, with its aura and practice of social solidarity, its disruption of traditional work and consumption patterns, and its increased scope for government intervention and control, provided the dynamizing force to reconsider social reform. The new spirit was well captured by William Beveridge in the first draft of his famous report.

> The time has now come to consider social insurance as a whole; as a contribution to a better new world after the war. How would one plan social insurance now if one had a clear field, that is to say, if one could plan an ideal scheme, using all the experience gained in the past, but without being hampered by regard for vested interests of any kind? The first step is to outline the ideal scheme; the next step is to consider the practi-

cal possibilities of realising the ideal and the changes of existing machinery that would be required.[35]

This "ideal scheme" as it developed in a series of White Papers and subsequent legislative enactments consisted of the five major elements.

1. "All-In Insurance." Comprehensive insurance for the entire population had been an articulated goal of reformers and many politicians since the 1920s, always to flounder on a double difficulty—to bring in the "bottom tier" would be financially unwise, and the top tier could see no reason or benefit in joining. In uniting the nation in one plan Britain confirmed its break with continental practice.

2. Flat-rate contributions and flat-rate benefits at determined subsistence standards, centrally administered. These benefits were to be given as long as necessary and were to be available *as of right.* Thus both local responsibility and the "dole" were finally to be interred. This system, which by making benefits totally unrelated to previous earnings again differentiated Britain from the continent, finally brought the realization of the "Minimum Standard" that Churchill some forty years before had perceived "dimly across the gulfs of ignorance."[36]

3. A system of children's allowances to deal with the problem of family poverty, even when the head of the household was fully employed and therefore ineligible for insurance benefits.

4. State provision of basic services. Of primary importance was a free and comprehensive health service available to all, and free education up to school-leaving age (raised to fifteen).

5. A merger (at last) with contemporary economic doctrine based on the possibility and necessity of a full employment policy.

The system marked the full realization of what we described earlier as a social security state: the establishment of a "safety net" below which no one would be allowed to fall and the assurance that lack of money would not of itself be an impediment to medical or educational services. Beyond this establishment of a national minimum the state had neither the responsibility nor the right to go. Thus, despite statements in the contemporary American press that the Beveridge Plan and associated reforms had somehow taken Britain "half way to Moscow,"[37] the British social security state more closely resembled a modern version of the liberal idea that while all should be given a roughly equal chance in life's race, the winners of the race would continue to be the swift. As Beveridge later wrote, "The Beveridge Plan is essentially liberal, designed to combine basic security (enough to live on at all times) with freedom of the citizen to manage his own life and that of his dependents and the responsibility for doing so."[38] This sentiment, not merely piously avowed but rigorously developed, can be labeled with justice a noble social expression of the liberal ideal. The failure of the plan to turn out as hoped forms the backdrop against which current British welfare policy must be viewed.

The British Social Security State

Legislation enacted in the immediate postwar period that embodied the principles outlined above continues to form the fundamental prop of the British social security state. While we shall soon consider the difficulties posed by their operation, it would be amiss not to take note of their successes, whether measured by past practice, by comparison to the social security state model, or by comparison with the United States. Wealth is not the governing factor in according access to medical care; educational opportunities have been broadened; there has been an almost total upgrading of life to minimum standards; the administrative structure still operates at a fair level of efficiency. These benefits are conspicuous when we look at the much maligned National Health Service.

The National Health Service, in terms of size, expenditure, and social impact, is the largest and most important undertaking of the central government, encompassing the services of over 60,000 doctors and 280,000 nurses, spending close to six percent of total national income, and providing an essential, and usually free, service to over 95 percent of the population (the remainder voluntarily make private provisions). About 85 percent of the cost comes from general taxation revenues, ten percent from "insurance" contributions (in effect a flat rate tax), and five percent from special charges to individuals.

Any foreign visitor—particularly one from the United States—who happens to fall ill or have an accident must be impressed by the British system. No demands for pre-payment greet one at the hospital door; no "family doctor" hovers by the hospital bed in order to collect a later fee; no agonizing choices arise over whether one is actually so sick that seeing a doctor is worth the financial expense. In addition to these achievements, the National Health Service has sponsored important structural changes. The old duality between public and private hospitals has been ended; money has been provided for new construction; planning the spatial distribution of physicians has been undertaken; and special, less "popular" services (especially mental hospitals) have been incorporated within a unified system.

Furthermore, all this has been accomplished without exorbitant costs, coercion, "labor direction," or other evils hypothesized by critics at the time of the establishment of the service. As a percentage of gross national product, health expenditures are below those found in most other advanced Western countries, including the United States. Administrative costs are about 2.5 percent of expenditures, one fourth of the estimated total in countries such as Sweden with insurance-based health services.[39] Only two percent of physicians have administrative work as their primary activity compared with nine percent in Sweden and seven percent in the United States.[40] And although comparative health statistics are notoriously difficult to handle, most indicators place Britain slightly ahead of the United States (and distinctly behind Sweden).[41]

In sum, when compared to the health care delivery "system" in the United States, the National Health Service comprises a lower proportion of National Income, eliminates financial worries, is unencumbered by excessive bureaucracy, and produces a "national health profile" at least as good as the American. Nevertheless, the Health Service in particular and the whole welfare system in general is conceived to be in a period of crisis, more and more difficult to operate, afflicted with ideological disputes, and in need of major reforms. It is important to explore the reasons for this general impression, not only to understand the actual limitations of British welfare policy but also to illuminate the strengths and weaknesses of the social security state model in practice.

One of the reasons often given for the shortcomings of the British Welfare State is the early political tampering with the principles as set forth by Beveridge for the field of social insurance and Butler for education. In social insurance, children's allowances (never a popular program) were put at a level inadequate to eliminate family poverty even when the head of household was fully employed. The situation has not changed since. In 1972, allowances for a family with three children amounted to 5.2 percent of average industrial earnings, a sum hardly sufficient to overcome any extensive earnings shortfall. In contrast, similar programs in France and Belgium were providing benefits equal to approximately 20 percent average industrial earnings.[42] After a seven-year hiatus family allowances were finally raised in 1975 from £0.90 a week for the second and £1.00 for each additional child to £1.50 for the second and subsequent children. Even this modest increase, however, has been offset by inflation and by a decision not to raise child tax allowances. It is doubtful whether the relationship between allowances and average earnings has greatly changed.

Pensions have likewise experienced continual political intervention. In order to build up a sufficient reserve, Beveridge had envisioned a twenty-year transition period before full benefits were to be paid. This hiatus, however, proved politically unacceptable; some groups were accorded full pension benefits immediately, and full rights for all were declared in 1958.[43] Unfortunately, "declared" is the appropriate word, since adequate funding for these extra costs was nowhere provided. This gap has been filled from two directions: (1) the retention of various forms of means tested public assistance (a category the Beveridge Plan was supposed to eliminate but which still aids approximately 20 percent of all pensioners); and (2) graduated contributions for old-age beneficiaries implemented in 1961 and extended in 1966 (in direct opposition to the dogma of flat rate contributions–flat rate benefits).

The presumed intentions of the 1943 White Paper on Education and the subsequent Education Act of 1944 have been similarly distorted. The Education Act, as previously mentioned, abolished fee paying for public secondary schools and raised the minimum leaving age to fifteen. It also envisaged a system of primary and county colleges for part-time education.[44] While the act did charge the local education authorities to provide secondary education "offering such variety of instruction and training as may be desirable in view of their [the pupils'] different ages, and abilities," it also prescribed the "governing principle that, insofar as compatible with the provision of efficient instruction. . . , pupils are to be educated in accordance with the wishes of their parents."[45] It is not unreasonable to assume that one of the goals of the Education Act was the weakening of a vital prop of the British class structure: The early identification, segregation, and separate educational development of a minority of students in "grammar schools," which, if parental desires were considered, would have to be altered beyond the abolition of fees. This outcome, in any event, seems to have been the expectation of R. A. Butler, chief architect of the Act and Minister of Education, when he stated in the House of Commons debate on the measure that he expected local education authorities to take "full regard" to the wishes of parents in planning the student's educational future.[46]

And yet, despite these hopes, educational provision has not been reoriented around a social security state–equal opportunity model. Budgeting difficulties have prevented the anticipated launching of county colleges and have allowed too few nursery schools to be built. Competitive examinations continue largely to determine one's educational fate. The battle over comprehensive schooling goes on. That the end result is a perpetuation of ascriptive educational philosophy seems not to be lost on the British. This is a permissible interpretation of a recent study of Swedish and British workers (to which we shall refer again in our final section). Respondents were asked the major factor determining a person's class. Whereas 38.1 percent of the Swedes mentioned "educational qualifications and experiences," only 13.5 percent of the British did so.[47] Education is still not considered a good means for an individual to "get ahead."

Difficulties with the Principles Themselves

With the advantage of hindsight, Britain in the immediate postwar years can be seen as a land well suited to the introduction of a social security state, Beveridge style. The feeling of national identity was high; the exercise of government authority was rarely questioned; there was a widespread belief (even among people and groups unsympathetic to major changes) that social reform was proper and inevitable.[48] In addition, a number of structural variables were hospitable to the establishment of a social security state. The population was heavily industrialized; sectors harder to accommodate within the system (e.g., farm laborers) were relatively underrepresented. The tradition of centralized administration further diminished the chances of territorial "anomalies." The social structure was supportive. There were few divorces, few unwed mothers—few cases, that is, that were likely to cause welfare administration problems. Finally, the economic setting was favorable. On the one hand, there was more than sufficient surplus from average wages to finance the needed transfer payments (without this condition, the "national minimum" becomes either an aspiration or a political weapon with which to expropriate the rich, or both). On the other hand, average wages did not yield a life style so above the national minimum that a descent to that level (whether by sickness, unemployment or retirement) could be perceived as an intolerable loss of income and status.[49]

Since the late 1940s, however, most of these conditions have changed. No longer do the principles of the social security state fit so amenably into social and economic life. Pensions, accounting for nearly 50 percent of social security expenditures, are one important example. Since 1948, pension benefits have increased at relatively the same rate as average gross earnings, a situation that at first glance appears stable. But because both have grown faster than the retail price index, the gap between average earnings and pension benefits in real terms has become a chasm. This chasm has been bridged more and more frequently by the introduction of private and corporate pension plans that perform the same "supplemental" function as those in the United States (to be described in Chapter Seven). The outcome has been the de facto tendency to reestablish a two-tiered system, the demerits of which the Beveridge Plan was supposed to overcome. Efforts by successive governments to inject an attractive earnings-related component into the plan and to achieve a useful relationship with the private occupational schemes have so far not yielded major results. The latest attempt passed Parliament in August 1975 with implementation scheduled for April 1978. The measure introduces an earnings-related benefit on top of the flat-rate amount, both of which are financed by a graduated payroll tax in effect since April 1975. Whether this plan will resolve the difficulties (or even, given Britain's economic trials, whether the fund will be self-sustaining) remains to be seen.

While successive governments attempt to make the pension scheme more in tune with the needs of the "affluent worker," many social critics point to the previously discussed gap between flat-rate benefits and the national minimum (defined as the Supplementary Benefits Level) to argue that the goal of eliminating "poverty" should take precedence over all else. This opinion is encapsulated in the title of a recent article by A. B. Atkinson, one of the most insightful, and prolific, social commentators: "Social Security: Poverty is the Test of Policy."[50] Taken literally (which Atkinson here often does), one can only infer that the abolition of poverty is *the* legitimate focus of social policy, a viewpoint that leads to the splitting of the "natural" welfare state constituency in an unproductive way. The Beveridge Plan was geared at a minimum to the needs of the employed wage earner, the vast majority of the population. And although estimates of the number of people below a "poverty line" are notoriously diverse, none puts the percentage of the population above fifteen.[51] If, therefore, welfare reform is to be concentrated on this segment, there seems little in it for the average worker (union member) except higher taxes.[52]

This consideration bears directly on the potential "erosion" of the social security state. If the average industrial worker has a reasonable expectation that he will receive social security benefits at some time during his life, he will more likely support policies making those benefits adequate in amount and in time. In this connection, the actuarial myth of social insurance, which underpins the social security state, is also valuable—benefits are to be received as of right because each beneficiary has helped pay for them; and because each individual is a potential recipient, the charges and taxes are paid less grudgingly. But if social security is seen as restricted to a special group, political support understandably wanes. And if the special group tends to fall outside the funding mechanism of social insurance, political problems are compounded. Finally, it is difficult for the social security state to adjust to the new situation, because it is limited *in principle* to

sustaining individuals at a national minimum. For those who live
their lives above the national minimum it has little that is concrete
to offer and nothing coherent to say.

Problems with the Postwar British Economy

Beveridge based his cost assumptions (not unreasonably, given
the fairly static price level before World War II) on an insignifi-
cant rate of inflation, and he budgeted Treasury (general taxation) contributions accordingly. This assumption has obviously
been proved inaccurate, with unfortunate consequences for his
plan. Inflation has augmented the problems of the elderly and all
those on fixed incomes, it has hindered the introduction of rational cost controls, it has brought the issue of proper benefit
levels into constant political contention, and it makes a determination of the market value of various services more difficult.

This last point should be emphasized. A major problem with
providing "free" public goods and services is the determination of
whether the cost (in taxes) bears any relationship to what, either
individually or in the aggregate, citizens would pay in the "market." The issue becomes particularly complex if we recognize that
almost all government policies concern goods that are both
"public" and "private"—as it is sometimes said in the public choice
literature, gravity is the only pure example of a public good.
It is this mix of private and public components that make the
various "market" solutions to welfare provision of the type proposed in Chapter Three seem naive; the "publicness" of housing,
education, health—their relative absence of exclusivity and joint-
ness of use—preclude straight market solutions.

On the other hand, these goods have a vital "private" component that argues strongly for their being brought into some
harmony with individual preferences. The problem here often is
not (as most Conservative critics contend) that public authorities
will "overspend" on services, thus inordinately taxing the population. Governments, in the interest of dampening balance of
payments crises, or refuting charges of "big spending," or in the
service of some other extraneous goal, can as logically squeeze
services more that the population would prefer. This tendency
has been encouraged in Britain, as it has not in Sweden, by a
combination of inflation and slow economic growth and by the
absence of a continuing government commitment to upgrade

welfare services. As a result, there has never seemed to be a surplus available for a qualitative advance in welfare provision; on the contrary, it has seemed a major accomplishment just to maintain past allocations. This continual inattention is particularly evident in the National Health Service and has added to the concern that the welfare state is being eroded. Funding for new hospital construction, medical facilities, and community health centers has been too low—as witnessed by the much lower percentage of GNP devoted to health care than in Sweden or the United States.[53] Indeed, the whole service has taken on a certain seediness: overcrowding in hospitals has worsened, waiting time for operations has lengthened, facilities themselves are wearing out. And, as might be expected, with these troubles has come "political" controversy with doctors threatening to spend more time with private, fee-paying patients, with ministers threatening to eliminate private beds. Demoralization in general and emigration in particular are growing concerns. These gloomy findings are being detailed at the ongoing deliberations of the Royal Commission on the National Health Service. More money is clearly a major answer. Where it is to be procured no one has been able to say.

New Social Developments

As we stated earlier, the original British social security plan was geared to the needs of the industrial wage earner and his family considered as a unit. The continuing atomization of the nuclear family has added greatly to the administrative problems, seen concretely in the rise of one-parent families. As of July 1975, there were approximately 200,000 one-parent families with over 1,000,000 children under sixteen years of age. Almost half of the families were in need of public assistance for which the committee recommended the introduction of a special social security benefit. Since the government, however, has deemed this idea politically unsound (at least until 1980—here we see a specific instance of the difficulties involved in an exclusive focus on "poverty"), the group has been thrown back on the tender mercies of means-tested national assistance (now called Supplemental Benefits), a recourse the Beveridge Plan was intended to make unnecessary.[54]

"Supplemental Benefits" are less than an ideal mechanism to

those falling through the safety net set by social insurance. One difficulty, also found in the United States, has been the "take-up rate." The great attractiveness of the insurance scheme was that benefits would be delivered automatically as of right. Now that benefits have to be applied for, the chance of people falling through the safety net is greatly increased, more so because of the seemingly perpetual association of application for means-tested aid with official investigation, social stigma, and the work house.[55] It is estimated, for example, that over 30 percent of all pensioners do not claim entitled benefits. Recently, there have been troubles in the other direction: Claimants (in a pattern paralleling that found in the United States, and for the same reasons) have been "demanding" money, staging sit-ins (especially in London), and in general displaying far from deferential, grateful behavior. This new pattern of client activity has led to the demoralization and inefficiency of the staff administering Supplementary Benefits that, in turn, has increased administrative costs. The cost of administering the pension plan, for example, amounts to only one percent of expended funds. The figure rises to 5.5 percent for sickness benefits, 10 percent for unemployment insurance. With Supplementary Benefits, however, administrative expenses account for 24 percent of total expenditures.[56]

In sum, we might conceive of the British welfare state as a machine, a far different one from the jerrybuilt structure we shall encounter when we deal with the United States. The British machine can be said to resemble an ancient, carefully constructed automobile, an old M.G. or Jaguar, well suited to provide noble grounds for the noble emotions. But, alas, the engine is not what it was; slowly efficiency is being lost, troubles mount, and strange internal sounds are heard. This decline has not passed unnoticed: Swarms of mechanics surround the machine squabbling among themselves and tinkering in random fashion with various parts. Their ministrations, however, do not seem to do much good; indeed, the replacements seem distinctly inferior to the original. Some spectators, viewing the scene, have concluded that the machine, as great as it once was, must now be jettisoned in favor of a new model. But with no consensus as to the principles that are to be followed in constructing this new model, the old machine lumbers on.

The British Welfare State and the
British Economy

Ever since the publication of the Beveridge Plan, conservative critics have not been slow to attribute the ills of British society and the faltering state of its economy to the sloth and torpor supposedly engineered by the institutionalization of a national minimum. The general critique has not usually gone as far as that of one writer who maintained in an early "refutation" of the Beveridge Plan that a universal scheme of social security was in direct contradiction to "nature's primal law of the 'Survival of the Fittest' " and by putting "a premium on improvidence" it foretold imminent social and moral collapse.[57] But even the most restrained critics have maintained that the success of the welfare state depends on what the *Economist* in 1946 termed Assumption D: "that the country will accept the doctrine of hard work. . . . Without it, the economic machine of the country will break down under the weight of the passengers it is being asked to carry."[58]

A main thrust of the critique has been that the economic machine has indeed collapsed. Enterprise has been dampened, initiative thwarted, freeloaders succored, and the frugal expropriated. This is not to imply that the truly needy should not be cared for, say these critics, but first things must come first. As Winston Churchill declared, "Many years ago I used the phrase 'bring the rearguard in' . . . But now we have the new Socialist doctrine. It is no longer, 'Bring the rearguard in,' but "Keep the vanguard back.' There is no means by which this island can support its present population except by allowing its native genius to flourish and fructify."[59] In other words, the first duty is to the generation, not the distribution, of economic wealth. This last point, with the publication of the party document, *The Right Approach,* seems to have become the rallying cry of the Conservative Party led by Margaret Thatcher and inspired by the "monetarist" exhortations of Keith Joseph.

The same stance has been assumed with increasing stridency on the other side of the Atlantic. The notion that "it can happen here," that the horrors of foreign experience can be visited upon our shores unless we display firm vigilance and adhere strictly to our true principles, has long been a major theme in American

115

political discourse. Now the "it," which used to be some form of "totalitarianism" or religious belief, is being focused on the poor British welfare state. From the popular pen of Paul Harvey to the sober editorial page of the *Wall Street Journal* the same alarm is sounded. First, Paul Harvey:

> You and I have been the victims of grievance-mongers.
> These are the people who believe that government can and must engineer a socially just society; that government must provide housing, health care, education and income redistribution.
> But the more we and other nations have trusted government to improve the quality of life, the more we have of crime, laziness and urban decay.
>
>   *   *   *
>
> Britain is a horrible example of the direction in which the United States is headed. In socialist Britain, government provisions for health, education and welfare have caused these services to deteriorate while the nation itself, after years of hemorrhaging red ink, is dying!
>
>   *   *   *
>
> They and we have been sharing wealth when we should have been producing wealth. That takes everybody's sweat.[60]

Mr. Royster gives the same message to the American "elite" without, it may be noted, much increase in sophistication:

> Britain, for those who would learn from it, offers a model study in how to bring to ruin a once vigorous nation.
>
>   *   *   *
>
> Spend and spend, tax and tax, inflate and inflate. It's not only a clear formula for wrecking an economy but also for assuring that out of the wreckage comes a total socialist state. Reduce people to the point where they cannot care for their own needs, the state must. Reduce industry to the point where it cannot provide its own capital, the state must.
>
>   *   *   *
>
> [Intended or not,] Britain today offers a text book case on how to ruin a country—a sobering model, too, for any visitor who tarries there awhile and returns home wondering if he has seen the future.[61]

This image of the functioning of the social security state is far different from the one presented in this chapter and in this book (although it has direct parallels with the conservative critique described in Chapter Three). We criticize British welfare institutions for their inability to expand *beyond* the Beveridge model, and we shall argue for the establishment of a national minimum in the United States as an important *but still not sufficient reform.* We advocate more than that the United States adopt the British "model," we attribute many of Britain's difficulties to the failure to take the welfare state far enough, and thus we advise going beyond the social security state and toward the social welfare state. Is this advocacy the road to economic ruin?

A question like this can obviously never be answered with total certainty. We approach a negative response from three directions which, we hope, are mutually reinforcing. In the first place, it is one thing to speak in somewhat lofty tones of the "erosion" of the welfare state, when it is a goal of public policy to achieve greater equality beyond a national minimum. It is quite another when a commitment to a national minimum has not even been made. This is the situation in the United States. Talk of erosion is a bit premature when the structure is not constructed. Secondly, there is no need for the United States to suffer the particular British disabilities. As we have reiterated, the social security state is basically parasitic. It does not correct economic ills; neither does it compound them. Our society is not burdened by an excess of traditional class feeling; our interest in industrial efficiency is high.

This latter point—that the association between the advent of the British welfare state and the onslaught of economic troubles ought not to be blithely generalized—is strengthened when we note, thirdly, that a comparison of British welfare expenditures with those of her European neighbors yields no evidence that the British are uniquely overburdened. Indeed, a recent Political and Economic Planning Study, *Social Security in the European Community,* shows that, except for the Republic of Ireland, Britain has the lowest level of benefits in the Community and spends the least percentage of her national income on social security, health, and welfare.[62] Moreover, in the effort to stem inflation and to restore business confidence, the Labour government has reconciled itself to at least 1½ million unemployed, has eliminated or greatly reduced subsidies on basic foods, and has looked benignly at the spiraling cost of public services. "Welfare," in short, has reaped no profits from the economic troubles of the 1970s. These data support our previous argument that British welfare provisions have not been sufficiently advanced. They fail to confirm the notion that the level of benefits has ruined the economy, since if this was the case, the economic performance of the other members of the Community should (because of their higher burdens) be worse, whereas in fact it has been distinctly better. Given these data, any dampening of the initiative of the average British workers might more logically be attributed to some defect in national character than to the onerous burden of the welfare state. This was indeed the position of many seventeenth and early eighteenth century mercantilist writers,[63] and echoes are still heard in much of the "State of England" literature. But concrete evidence beyond the level of anecdotes about the inefficiency of railway porters would be hard to muster.

Can we then "absolve" the British welfare state from all responsibility for Britain's sagging economic fortunes? As with our earlier question, even a preliminary answer is more complex than it might at first appear. For while a direct link between welfare spending and economic troubles is hard to sustain on the basis of comparative economic statistics, at another level the structure of British welfare institutions *may* have helped to retard economic enterprise. The social security state, as described abstractly in Chapter One and more concretely here, is essentially parasitic. It can be grafted onto any economic system provided that system produces a surplus sufficient for redistribution. Now it is generally agreed that the British economic order, while yielding the necessary surplus, was and is notoriously inefficient and in need of remodernization both in terms of industrial plant and of industrial attitudes. This remodernization since the war has proceeded only fitfully, and there has been nothing in the operation of the welfare institutions to advance the process. Indeed, it can be argued that the closed nature of the British welfare state has discouraged participation and has not directly challenged the traditional picture of class divisions, a picture that, by encouraging dilettantism at the top and irresponsibility at the bottom, is often given as a reason for the slow pace of modernization.

To treat the issue more directly, the transformation of the industrial plant would be greatly facilitated by a coherent national economic and labor policy, and industrial attitudes might be shaken up by an old-fashioned circulation of elites. All this is beyond the purview of the social security state, which is oriented toward relieving the distress of the casualties of the economic order, not toward making the order more efficient, and still less toward altering its fundamental basis.[64] The manner in which the social security state was introduced further removed welfare from production and participation. It was, as we have described, animated by individuals best described politically as Liberal and imposed administratively from the top. Neither major party was greatly involved either in the intellectual construct or in the establishment of administrative procedures. Under a social welfare state the divorce between politics and administration would be harder to sustain. The social welfare state is based on public direction of industry and on an active labor market policy. It emphasizes participation in public and private enterprise. And it attempts to instill into economic affairs the value of equality rather than of security alone. It is not as easy to imagine, for example, national unions attempting to secure their position by inflationary settlements at the expense, among other groups, of the welfare constituency.

That these differences between the social security and social welfare states have more than abstract significance, is suggested by the following table, taken from the previously mentioned study of British and Swedish working class attitudes. For British workers traditional reasons (family, status, merit, ability) outweigh modern ones, while Swedish workers rarely mention these concerns.

One should not draw the inference from this table that Swedish workers are more content and docile. On the contrary, Swedish workers "were more aware of economic inequalities than the English respondents, and [they] strongly disapproved of them."[65] They also advanced more basic reforms—43 percent of Swedish respondents advocated greater equality, removal of social injustices at work, and a more just society; *two* percent of the English respondents espoused these goals. And these are precisely the reforms tending toward the social welfare state; not coincidentally, they are also the reforms advocated and promoted by the

Why Are There Classes?

Because of	Swedish Workers (%)	English Workers (%)
Birth and family background	1.7 ⎫ 8.5	10.9 ⎫ 48.7
Status and "Snobbery"	5.9 ⎬	12.6 ⎬
"An Inevitable Feature of Life"	0.9 ⎭	25.2 ⎭
"Money, wealth, economic factors"	55.1 ⎫ 75.4	37.1 ⎫ 39.6
Educational qualifications	20.3 ⎬	2.5 ⎬
Other	11.9	6.7
Don't Know	2.5	2.5

Source: Richard Scase, "Images of Inequality in Sweden and Britain," *Human Relations,* 28, 3 (April 1, 1975), p. 264.

Swedish Social Democratic Party but not in any coherent fashion by the British Labour Party. These are the reforms that provide the creative tension furthering the incorporation of the Swedish working class in the *production and distribution* of economic goods.

In conclusion, Britain's present position, while perhaps tenable, is far from satisfactory. The erosion of the social security state is always a potential danger. Geared to the needs of the average industrial worker, it has difficulty responding to new social problems that cannot be met even through the fiction of social insurance; predicated on a life cycle more appropriate to an earlier generation, it has difficulty mobilizing continued political support for programs that do not appear beneficial to the majority. But in Britain, almost constant economic crisis has turned a problem into a quagmire. We argue that Britain cannot arrest this erosion and ameliorate the economic crisis by adopting the policies either of "neo-liberalism" or of "socialism." The former, advanced by elements in the Conservative Party and outlined more fully in Chapter Three, would not encourage the incorporation of the working class in British economic life, nor direct the modernization of industry, nor overcome managerial inefficiency. Indeed, it would probably have the opposite effect. The latter, involving more public ownership and civil service direction of industry, seems to be the policy, insofar as it has one, of the present Labour Government. There is no indication that this policy will be more successful than in the past. We advance a commitment to the social welfare state that has the potential both to involve the majority of the population in welfare provisions and to modernize the industrial structure. How the system might work in practice we discuss in the next chapter.

6

Sweden: Toward the Social Welfare State

For more than a generation Sweden has been both celebrated and condemned as the society most closely approximating the ideals of the welfare state. In 1937 Marquis Childs recommended the Scandinavian "middle way" (and the Swedish experience in particular) as a sane and moderate alternative to Bolshevism and to unregulated capitalism.[1] In 1938 the Fabian Society published the findings of a group of observers it had dispatched to study the activities of the Swedish Social Democratic government; the investigators reported enthusiastically on innovations in such diverse fields as budgetary policy, social services, agriculture, education, and the nationalization of soccer pools.[2] World War II interrupted study of the Swedish experiment, but in recent years a spate of literature on the "Swedish model" has appeared, exalting it as the alluring "prototype of modern society" and condemning it as a proving ground for "the new totalitarians."[3] Estimates of the moral worth of Swedish society clearly vary, but neither enthusiasts nor detractors doubt that Sweden is the archetype of the modern welfare state.

The Swedes themselves conceive of their society as a welfare state. The basic principles upon which the welfare state rests are generally acknowledged; the political parties may argue about the details of financing, coverage, and expansion of services, but that the state has an obligation to secure its citizens against the avoidable distress of sickness, accident, old age, inadequate housing, and loss of income, no party is rash enough to deny. In Denmark and Norway political movements that reject this principle and appeal to taxpayers disgruntled with the high payments that the welfare state requires have recently scored substantial gains, but in Sweden no similar party has yet appeared. Employing the expression of former prime minister Per-Albin Hansson, Swedes sometimes refer to their country as "the people's home" (*Folkhemmet*). This simple and emotive phrase expresses the conviction of an underlying unity of the Swedish people, a unity that implies mutual dependence and responsibility: "The good home is characterized by equality for all, charitableness toward and concern for the well-being of others."[4]

At least four different traditions have nurtured this consensus upon the merits of the welfare state, and each continues to influence the development of social welfare policy, though in varying degrees. First, the paternalist conception, which provided a rationale for the first tentative developments of welfare policy and which still appeals to conservative defenders of the welfare state, stresses the obligation of the well-to-do to succor the unfortunate. Closely related is the tradition of Christian charity, which emphasizes the moral duty to help the disadvantaged. A third, purely secular tradition, the rationalist conception of preventive social policy, stresses the economic advantages of social aid. Originally devised by the Myrdals to provide a nonpartisan justification for social welfare policy, the logic of preventive social policy is that it is more efficient and less costly to prevent the development of social pathology than to cure it once it has emerged. Finally, and historically decisive for the construction of the welfare state, is the tradition of Swedish Social Democracy, a unique mixture of the three previously mentioned traditions with the socialist ideals of liberty, equality, solidarity, democracy, economic efficiency, and personal security. The relative importance of each of these values varies over time and from person to person, but whatever their precise mixture they provide the moral foundation of the welfare state in Sweden.

Sweden's social welfare policy actually differs little from that of the other advanced welfare states. Sweden devotes a high percentage of its gross national product to the provision of social services, but some other nations, including its Scandinavian neighbors, Norway and Denmark, spend comparable percentages. Nor has Sweden always been a pioneer in the development of social welfare policy; for example, its compulsory health insurance program dates from 1955, or seven years after the British National Health Service came into operation. The source of Sweden's reputation as a unique and quintessential welfare society must be sought in the elaborate and impressive "information programs" conducted by the Swedish government; in critics' attempts to portray Sweden as a shocking example of the welfare state's propensity to arouse tendencies to suicide and sexual promiscuity; and in Sweden's remarkable success in maintaining high levels of employment, productivity, and economic growth.

These economic achievements have permitted the Swedish citizen to enjoy a considerably higher standard of living than that found in other welfare states. The Swede's per capita income is now higher than that of the American. Income comparisons, depending as they do upon rather arbitrary values of national currencies, are admittedly tenuous and open to challenge, but the prosperity and comfort of Swedish life are obvious to the most casual visitor. Indeed the statistics probably understate the Swedish standard of living, for they take no account of the relatively more egalitarian distribution of wealth, the absence of slums and primary poverty, and the contributions made to the "quality of life" by enlightened community planning. Clearly Sweden has moved beyond the minimum standards of the social security state.

The Development of Swedish Social Welfare Policy

Modern social welfare policy in Sweden, as in Britain, dates from the early 1900s.[5] The first Swedish legislation, following the pattern of Bismarck's social reforms in Germany and corresponding to Lloyd George's Liberal reforms in Great Britain, established modest programs of industrial accident insurance, old age pensions, and health insurance. The primary sponsor of these programs was the Liberal Party, supported by the smattering of

Social Democrats then in the *Riksdag* and by some Conservative politicians who were both distressed and alarmed by the condition of the Swedish laboring population. In the 1920s welfare policy stagnated; Liberals and Conservatives shrank back before the spectre of an excessively interventionist state, while the Social Democrats lacked the parliamentary strength and a suitable strategy of reform to build on the early Liberal achievements.

The Social Democrats' accession to office in 1932 (the beginning of a tenure in office that extended virtually without interruption until 1976) marked the beginning of "a new era" in social policy.[6] In coalition with the Farmers' Party the Social Democrats expanded the social services and embarked on the construction of a modern welfare state. Through budgetary planning and supplemental public works they pursued an active labor market policy aimed at preventing unemployment. Through fiscal incentives and subsidies they attempted to reduce the incidence of inadequate and overcrowded housing. Finally, through a system of family allowances they tried to raise the declining birth rate and to ensure a minimum standard of care for young children. The distinguished historian of Swedish social policy, Karl Höjer, has briefly summarized the achievements of this period: "Our social policy has a long previous history, but in the period after 1932 it was extended into three large new areas, namely an active labor market policy, a social housing policy, and a family policy."[7]

The Social Democrats, after toying with the possibility of vigorous public intervention in industrial relations, decided to leave labor-management relations in the hands of the private parties. After two and a half years of discussion the Landesorganisationen (LO) and the Swedish Employers' Federation (SAF) concluded the famous Basic Agreement at Saltsjöbaden in 1938. This pact established the boundaries within which labor-management negotiations proceed and has served as the basis for Sweden's remarkably harmonious labor relations. The LO and SAF still bargain within the Saltsjöbaden framework; together they make recommendations on wages, working conditions, and fringe benefits that serve as the basis for contract settlements. The government's role, until recently, has been minimal. In case of extended disagreement it can act as mediator, but there is no Swedish equivalent of the Taft-Hartley act, the minimum wage law, compulsory arbitration statutes, or national wages and prices policies. In recent years, however, the government has consulted with the unions and employers on the impact of the tax structure on the wage bargain.

The governmental initiatives of the 1930s were innovative, but relatively modest in scope and in financing. They alleviated, but by no means eliminated, the problems of unemployment, poor housing, and a low birth rate. During World War II the overriding necessities of national defense and the provision of food and raw materials took precedence, and the Social Democrats were compelled to suspend their initiatives in the field of social policy. As the war drew to a close, however, the Social Democrats looked forward to their *Skördetiden,* the harvest period when the reforms projected in the 1930s would be realized. In 1944 the party adopted "The Twenty-Seven Points," a postwar program stressing three major goals: "full employment," "just distribution," and "efficiency and democracy in industry." The program envisioned some modest nationalization where monopoly or mismanagement occurred; however, "no general socialization of industry was proposed."[8] The emphasis fell upon concrete measures to secure citizens against a decline in living standards because of sickness, old age, unemployment, or large families. Health insurance, increased pensions, children's allowances, and housing subsidies figured conspicuously among the twenty-seven points and constituted the central elements in the postwar reforms. Of these four proposals only the last, the housing policy, failed to be passed by virtually unanimous vote in the *Riksdag.* Wartime increments in taxation permitted these programs to be financed without substantial increases in the overall level of national taxation, although the Social Democrats did impose higher taxes upon large incomes, corporation profits, and estates in an effort to shift a greater portion of the tax burden upon the wealthy.

The near-unanimity that marked the passage of the health insurance program, the national pension scheme, and the children's allowances did not last. The continuation of wartime regulations and rationing, the tax increases directed at the wealthy, the Social Democrats' clumsy handling of an inflated economy, and the spectre of socialization provoked an intense ideological debate culminating in the 1948 election campaign. The Liberal party leader, Bertil Ohlin, and the editor of *Dagens Nyheter,* Herbert Tingsten, coordinated the offensive against governmental planning and socialization. In the balloting the Liberals performed brilliantly, more than doubling their number of votes, but their gains came at the expense of the Conservatives and the Communists, not the Social Democrats, who lost less than one percent of their previous strength. Nonetheless, "the 1948 election marks a turning point in Swedish politics: The socialist harvest period was past and it was a changed, a more pragmatic social democracy that now ruled—to complete the reforms already begun and to retain power."[9]

In the early 1950s the Social Democrats moderated the pace of reform efforts, and another period began for which the term "the politics of compromise" is eminently suitable.[10] In coalition with the Farmers Party, the Social Democrats finally implemented the national health insurance program in 1955; approved in principle by the *Riksdag* in 1946, the introduction of the plan had been scheduled for 1950, but was twice delayed. The next substantial—and controversial—step in the building of the welfare state came in the late 1950s with the introduction of the Social Democrats' supplementary pensions scheme. This proposal for a public, income-related pension plan aroused the most intense debate in Swedish politics in the last twenty years. After a national referendum and a parliamentary crisis the Social Democratic plan was passed by a single vote, with one opposition member abstaining. This victory completed the building of the essential elements of the contemporary Swedish welfare state.

The Social Democrats' most recent initiatives have sought to improve the workers' situation within the enterprise. A 1974 law required larger firms to earmark 20 percent of their net profits for improvements in the workplace environment. A 1976 law eliminated the notorious "clause 32" which permitted employers the sole right to hire and fire and to organize work; the new legislation allows unions to negotiate and to strike for co-determination of a wide range of company policies. Currently under discussion are the "worker funds" proposals elaborated by Rudolf Meidner, the LO's leading strategist. The Meidner proposals call for all companies with at least 50 employees to set aside 20 percent of pre-tax profits, in the form of new shares, into a central "equalization fund." Union representatives will administer this fund on behalf of employees. Eventually workers would have controlling interests in their firms; unlike most capital-sharing plans, however, their equity would be collectively rather than individually held. In accordance with Swedish tradition the Meidner proposals will undergo lengthy public scrutiny before coming to a vote in perhaps 1979 or 1980, should the Social Democrats return to office.

The Complexity of Swedish Welfare Institutions

Perhaps the most valid criticism of the welfare state in Sweden is that its workings are beyond the comprehension of most citizens. Welfare institutions and policies lack a simple symmetrical structure. They are so intricate and complex that, as Joseph Board has observed, "It would scarcely be possible to cover adequately the range and detail of social welfare programs in Sweden."[11] Symptomatic of their complexity is the proliferation of guidebooks describing the benefits to which the Swedish citizen is entitled and the ways in which he can obtain them. Regular editions of *Vår Sociala Förmåner (Our Social Benefits)*, *Vår Trygghet (Our Security)*, and *Socialboken (The Social Book)*, offer several hundred pages of advice, but none pretends to be definitive. For such abstruse matters as the precise calculation of one's supplemental pension, each refers readers to the local social insurance office. At these offices Swedish citizens can investigate any difficulties regarding the provision of their benefits. This centralized information system has improved the average citizen's access to benefits, but much remains to be done to simplify and to streamline the system.

One reason for the complexity of welfare institutions, as the preceding historical sketch indicates, is that they are not the result of coherent planning. Rather, they have grown in an uncoordinated piecemeal fashion, in response to immediate social ills.

A second reason for their complexity is that they exhibit a variety of organizational principles.[12] Some are organized on the principle of *social insurance;* that is, they provide benefits as of right to those who qualify by the payment of specified contributions, either by themselves, or their employers, or both. In this category fall the supplementary pension programs, unemployment insurance, and (in part) the national basic pension and the national health insurance program. The last two programs are also partially *public services;* that is, they provide services as a right, without a means test or contributions, and are financed partially from general taxation. Education is perhaps the purest example of a public service. Family benefits and housing allowances are extremely complicated, but in general children's allowances and a minimum standard of housing are provided on the public service principle. Finally, certain benefits constitute *public assistance,* the provision of aid financed out of general taxation and subject to test of the recipient's need and means. Certain housing supplements and "social help" (public relief or "welfare" for those who fall through the safety nets provided by other programs) operate on this principle. Aid to the handicapped, based solely on need, is an interesting case that only partially fits this category, for in Sweden all handicapped persons have the right to all required assistance and no means test is involved. The system gives the handicapped person the possibility of getting the assistance he needs without an upper limit on costs. Organizationally the arrangements for aid to the handicapped are an unusual mixture of the public assistance and public service principles.

A third reason for the complexity of welfare institutions is the diversity of their objectives. In part these differences are historical in origin. The early social insurance programs, patterned on Bismarck's legislation and on the Webbs' proposals, attempted to ensure a basic minimum standard. They not only redistributed income over a person's life cycle, but they also redistributed the assumption of risks within the society. They required the more fortunate to bear part of the burden of the "poor risks," but the actual redistribution of income among classes accomplished by these programs was minimal. Today, as previously, these social insurance programs make only a modest contribution toward greater equality, nor are they designed to do anything more. The public services, on the other hand, aim to provide for each citizen in accordance with his needs, not in relation to his social insurance payments. Accordingly their effects, especially given the progressive character of the Swedish tax structure, are far more egalitarian.

Finally, there are services organized on the "income security principle," which ensure people against precipitous falls in income. The aim of these services, such as the supplementary pension and the supplementary sickness benefit, is to achieve a secure standard of living, one relatively impervious to loss of earnings through unemployment, age, or illness. The effect of such programs is to recognize and in large measure to endorse the structure of incomes established in the labor market. Since these market-determined incomes are unequal, income security programs preserve the disparities of the market. Were the solidaristic wage policy of the Landesorganisationen, the nation's largest trade union federation, to succeed in leveling the uneven distribution of pre-tax incomes, then the social services organized on the income security principle would confirm and reinforce the new egalitarianism of the wage structure. In short, the income security programs have little redistributive effect; they consolidate the market-determined income structure rather than altering it.

Swedish welfare institutions thus contain programs with fundamentally different principles and objectives. The public services are radically egalitarian in their conception, but the programs based on the idea of a minimum standard or an assured standard allow a wide and persistent range of inequality. The importance of the minimum standard has declined, but what lies beyond it is unclear. Social Democratic governments have found no consistent strategy to replace it; instead, they waver ambivalently between the principles of equality and income security.

Current Social Welfare Provisions

The popular phrase "security from the cradle to the grave" slightly understates the scope of social welfare policy in Sweden. An expectant mother receives free pre- and post-natal care and free delivery in the hospital. In addition she receives a maternity benefit of 1080 kronor (about $275) for childbirth and 180 days leave from work. Provided that she has been properly insured, she is entitled to a supplementary loss of income benefit during her absence from work. Under provisions that took effect January 1, 1974, parents are free to decide for themselves which of them is to stay at home and care for the baby during these six months—or they may choose to divide the leave between them. (Some lingering inequalities in the payment of female workers make it advantageous for families to decide that the mother should be the one to stay with the child; in 1974 only a couple dozen fathers took the opportunity for child-leave.)

For each child under 16 the family allowance system provides 1800 kronor (about $450) a year, tax-free, regardless of the family's income. If the child proceeds to advanced schooling, the allowance is continued. A working mother may send her children to publicly supported nursery schools or play centers—if space is available. At the local child welfare center her child receives free medical supervision, including a thorough medical examination at age four. When the child reaches school age, he or she receives free lunches and free dental and medical care.[13]

Housing policy is similarly designed to ensure insofar as is possible a healthy environment for the growing child. Families with incomes of less than 8000 kronor (about $2000) per year receive income supplements sufficient to cover their housing needs. Low-income families with numerous children also receive housing subsidies according to a sliding scale that takes into consideration both size of income and number of children. Beyond these measures the government intervenes directly in the building market, through the provision of loans and subsidies for housing construction. This aid is conditioned upon the builder's adherence to standards regarding planning, materials, amenities, and the like. Because about 90 percent of all dwellings are constructed with such loans, the government exerts a powerful influence on the quality of housing. Furthermore, local communities are empowered to purchase land and to establish stringent regulations concerning its development.

The child who grows up in this environment has access to an educational system designed to democratize educational opportunity and to inculcate the values of equality and solidarity. In 1962, the Riksdag passed legislation establishing nine years attendance at a comprehensive school as the norm. The comprehensive school greatly reduces the former rigid distinction between the elite *gymnasium* (now defunct) for a select minority of students and mass educational institutions for the vast majority, a system which confirmed and preserved class differences in education. The new system does little "streaming" according to ability until the ninth year and requires each pupil to obtain three weeks of practical work experience during the eighth year. Despite university expansion and free tuition, however, access to higher education remains limited; both popular attitudes and still restricted facilities retard educational reform.

The national health program covers expenses for hospital treatment, doctors' fees, drugs, and in some cases travel costs. Since January 1, 1974, a national dental insurance scheme has refunded half the cost of dental care. The health care system imposes nominal charges for the use of services. Patients are free to choose their own doctors. Medicines essential for the treatment of chronic illness, such as insulin, are provided free of charge if prescribed by a physician. Reimbursement for charges in connection with physiotherapy or convalescent care amounts to three-quarters of actual expenditure. Besides paying the costs of medical care the Swedish system also provides partial (and taxable) compensation for loss of income due to illness. In most cases, provided that the patient reports his illness promptly, he receives about 80 percent of his lost income.

Security against loss of earnings from unemployment has long been a central focus of Swedish social welfare policy. The general strategy has been to concentrate on assuring employment rather than compensating for unemployment.[14] Consequently, the development of Sweden's unemployment insurance system has lagged behind other welfare measures. The present scheme is not a compulsory national program, but operates through individual unions. Unemployment insurance covers about 2.2 million workers, but at any one time a substantial proportion of the unemployed may lack coverage. During the summer of 1973 fully 11,200 of the 46,700 unemployed, or about 24 percent, were uninsured.[15] These persons may receive aid in some other form, but it is clear that the unemployment insurance program per se falls well short of being comprehensive.

The Swedish pension scheme is a complicated compound of the basic national pension (the *folkpension*) and the supplementary pension (*allmänna tilläggspensionen,* or ATP). Every Swedish citizen who has lived in Sweden for the six years preceding age 63 is eligible for the basic pension, which in 1976, when supplemented by a municipal housing allowance, ensured a retirement income of 11,250 kronor per year for single persons and 19,100 kronor per year for couples. Both the supplementary pension and the basic pension are tied to the cost of living and adjusted for inflation. Normally the pensioner begins receiving his payments at age

132

65, but it is possible to receive a reduced amount as early as age 60. A person who has had a working income above a certain minimum level for at least three years is eligible to receive a supplementary pension; to receive a full supplementary pension it is necessary to have earned more than the minimum level for thirty years. The size of the pension is calculated according to an exceedingly complicated point system based on the amount paid into the program; in fact, upon retiring, the pensioner ordinarily receives a total pension amounting to roughly two-thirds of his income during his fifteen best years of earnings—unless he had an income over 60,000 kronor (about $15,000), in which case he receives a smaller percentage of his former income.

For those unfortunate enough to slip through the safety nets extended by these social services and insurance programs a generalized form of assistance known as "social help" is mandated. The provision of social help is a local responsibility; indeed, the local commune is legally obligated to extend assistance to those who require it. The aid extended may include economic assistance, health care, personal counseling, and possibly even the provision of a small "stake" to establish the recipient in a modest business undertaking. As a general rule, however, no one on social help is to receive more than a low-income person who provides for himself.

These programs do not exhaust the range of social policy measures; no consideration has been given to widows' and survivors' benefits, industrial accident insurance, disability pensions, legal assistance, home help, holidays for disadvantaged children, rent regulations, family planning services, or the statutory five-week vacation with pay. But the programs considered above constitute the essential core of the system, the ones most often utilized by Swedish citizens and the ones that have established Sweden's reputation as a model welfare state.

These social programs are expensive. The Swedish tax burden is among the highest in the world. In 1970 social security contributions together with direct and indirect taxes on individuals and corporations amounted to 40.8 percent of the gross national product, slightly behind Norway's 40.9 percent and well above the United State's 29.9 percent.[16] The financing of the individual programs is varied and complex; the accompanying table provides an overview of the cost burden of five major programs. The family allowance program and the housing programs are financed from general tax revenues.

The mere detailing of legislative enactments and financing arrangements, of course, cannot constitute an adequate description of welfare policy. Between legal stipulation and the actual provision of services lies the functioning of an administrative apparatus that can in certain national settings frustrate, demean, and exclude clients. In Sweden, however, social welfare institutions have functioned with remarkable honesty and efficiency.

Economic Policy

Foreigners sometimes believe that Sweden is a socialist economy with a large nationalized sector and that the high standard of Swedish living results almost entirely from governmental programs, but this impression is false. The Swedish system relies heavily upon the private sector; the public sector generates only 15 percent of total goods and services. Ownership of the means of production remains overwhelmingly in private hands. The public sector does include substantial holdings of critical national resources—about one-fourth of the nation's forests, about 85 percent of the iron ore, and half the water power—in addition to Swedish Railways, a public bank, and liquor and tobacco monopolies; however, the essential task of keeping Swedish products competitive in world trade, a sine qua non for the flourishing of the welfare state, falls largely to private industry. Without the contribution made by private capitalists Sweden would be a far less affluent society.

Social Democratic economic policy has aimed not to nationalize economic activity so much as to make it proceed efficiently and equitably. The central thrust of policy has been maximalist full employment. As long ago as 1919 the influential Social Democratic theorist, Ernst Wigforss (Minister of Finance, 1932–1949) advocated this approach in his unofficial "Gothenburg Program":

> *Right to work for all members of society to be recognized.* Thus, security against unemployment ought to be provided in the first place through society's furnishing work for the unemployed at the wage rates prevailing within the profession. Only secondar-

Costs Within Five Social Insurance Areas 1970
(in millions of crowns)

	Health Insurance	Industrial Accident Insurance	Unemployment Insurance	Basic Pension	ATP
National Tax Revenues	565	9	311	4705	—
Local Government Contributions	—	—	5	849	—
Employers' Contributions	2433	198	—	—	5760
Insureds' Contributions	1814	—	102	2294	340
Other	76	48	41	69	2259
Totals	4888	255	459	7917	8359

Source: Vår Trygghet, Stockholm, 1971, p. 90. (Employees no longer contribute to the basic pension and health insurance programs.)

ily should there be resort to public assistance for those willing to work but unable to find employment.[17]

This policy has been so successful that in recent years the full employment target has undergone a qualitative change. No longer is the goal simply to maintain a high level of employment, but to provide every citizen desiring employment with freely chosen, satisfying, and remunerative work. To meet this objective a battery of new programs has emerged to enhance career choices, to allow for retraining even when one has not lost employment, to ease women's entry into the labor force, and to improve the work environment.

The danger of full employment policy is that it will stimulate inflation, which in turn will endanger economic stability and income gains. The LO recognized this danger in the early 1950s and devised a policy to combat inflation by stimulating efficiency and structural change within the economy. Recognizing Sweden's need to retain a competitive position in international trade, the LO has consciously demanded wage increases that have the effect of driving inefficient marginal firms out of business. Rather than tolerate "featherbedding" in the name of traditional work rules or struggle to maintain the low-wage jobs associated with declining industries, the LO has actively sought to eliminate such jobs.

Why have Swedish unions been able to pursue this policy of economic efficiency, a line strikingly different from that of British or even American unions? It is because the newly unemployed worker need not fear for his livelihood. Swedish society eases his adjustment by pursuing an "active labor market policy." An active labor market policy involves Keynesian budgetary planning for full employment; a system of state investment funds to stimulate the economy in periods of recession and to promote growth in regions with relatively high unemployment; a state employment service that registers job openings; retraining programs; mobility allowances; and, obviously, the cooperation of the private sector. While it stops well short of Soviet central planning, it is clearly more ambitious than the modest counter-cyclical planning characteristic of the American economy. Marginal planning, the determination of the mixture of factors of production and of the level of output, is left to the individual firm; however, certain traditional prerogatives of private enterprise, such as the timing and location of investment projects, are subject to a considerable degree of public supervision and tutelage.

The LO's economic policy envisions not only economic efficiency and rapid growth, but an equitable distribution of rewards. A major instrument for redressing market-determined inequality of incomes is "solidaristic wage policy." The essence of solidaristic wage policy is the pursuit of wage settlements that minimize the differentials among various wage and salary earners by raising the position of the lowest wage earners. Unlike American unions, the LO does not attempt to legislate a minimum wage or to maintain existing wage contours (the relative positions of different wage earning groups), but strives to reduce the gaps among wage rates. In short, the LO attempts to make pre-tax incomes more equal and has succeeded in doing so, though in recent years it has encountered growing white-collar opposition.

The LO has also pressured the government to exert greater public control over the investment decisions that determine the nation's economic priorities. Private business still undertakes about 60 percent of gross investment, but the state has usurped a substantial portion of private industry's power to decide when, where, and what society produces. It has extended its control over the capital market primarily through the leverage afforded by the national pension funds and the national development bank. These funds were originally used primarily to finance housing and to support existing private firms, but the Social Democrat's commitment to build a large new steel mill in Luleå suggests that they may adopt a more aggressive posture in undertaking investments shunned by private industry. (Whether these investments will prove profitable is still an open question.) The state has also intervened directly in the determination of private investment. In 1974, as noted earlier, the government mandated that certain industries devote 20 percent of their net profits to improving the workplace environment. Such governmental intervention in the capital market not only promotes full employment, but also imparts a public and democratic character to the investment decisions that determine the nation's economic future.

Sweden's successes in economic policy have created new problems, of which two require discussions here. First, basing wages on the principles of equality and solidarity rather than upon a firm's ability to pay alters the profitability of firms in ways that endanger policy objectives. Inefficient low-wage firms that cannot pay the higher wages demanded face two unattractive choices: They may close and cause unemployment or they may raise prices and contribute to inflationary pressures. Full employment policy is required to cope with the first outcome, and measures to promote competition and rationalization to cope with the second. A still trickier problem arises with the "super-profits" of the efficient firms who benefit from wages lower than they are able to pay. In recent years the LO has demanded (successfully) that the government require such firms to set aside a portion of their profits for socially determined investment objectives. It has also advanced the Meidner proposals for "worker funds" to ensure that workers as a whole benefit from increased rewards to capital.

A second policy problem arises from the fact that because of heavy tax pressures and inflation, trade unions find it extremely difficult to raise the real wages of their members. Inflation not only takes its bite of wage increases, but pushes workers into more progressive tax brackets. To gain modest increases of a few percentage points in real wages, unions may have to demand increases in money wages of more than twenty percent. Such increases naturally jeopardize Sweden's competitive position in international trade. As a result the government has arranged a series of discussions between government, labor, and business (the "Haga conferences"—named for the ancient castle in which they are held) and has concluded deals describing the proper "room" for wage increases in exchange for manipulating the tax system in beneficial ways. The public intervention in labor-management bargaining, unprecedented in recent Swedish history, has unnerved the LO by raising the specter of a national incomes policy. It has also failed to restore fully Sweden's competitive status in international trade.

The Impact of Social and Economic Policy

Both quantitative and qualitative indicators testify to the beneficial impact of Swedish programs and economic policies. That the average Swedish citizen currently enjoys a per capita income of about $5,600 is testimony to the achievements of private capital, the effectiveness of governmental budgetary planning, and the active labor market and solidaristic wages policies. The Swedish economy's steady, if not spectacular, growth rate stems in considerable measure from consistently high levels of employment. In 1932 every seventh union member was unemployed; from the end of World War II until very recently unemployment rates above 2 percent were virtually unknown. Sweden's participation rates (i.e., the percentage of the working-age population in the active labor force), currently about 70 percent, are the world's highest. Swedish infant mortality stands out as the world's lowest. Swedish life expectancy figures are consistently the world's highest, or very nearly so. (In both areas Sweden ranks notoriously well above the United States, despite the fact that it probably spends a smaller portion of its gross national product on health care.) Significant improvements in both infant mortality rates and in life expectancy have been recorded during the period in which the welfare state has undergone its most extensive development. From 1931 to 1935 the infant mortality rate per 100 live births was 5.01; from 1961 to 1965 it was 1.48. In the 1920s the average life expectancy was 62.07 years, by the 1950s it had increased to 72.48 years.[19]

All of these indicators testify to the success of Swedish social welfare institutions. They show that in a number of areas Swedish social policy has achieved the preventive effects stressed by the Myrdals as the objective of social policy. Active labor market policy has kept unemployment low. Statistics document that the Swedes are healthier than the citizens of advanced industrial countries like the United States and Great Britain. Death itself has been forced to postpone its inevitable intrusion upon human life. One can also gauge the preventive impact of social policy by surveying the number of recipients of "social help" or public assistance; if the various insurance programs and public services are working effectively, then the beneficiaries should remain relatively few. In fact, the number of "welfare" recipients declined fairly steadily from about 10 percent of the population in 1932 to about 4 percent in the mid-1960s. Then, for reasons that are not clear, the percentage rose to roughly seven percent in the early 1970s.[20]

Another way of measuring the success of Swedish welfare state institutions is to examine the area of social policy that has drawn perhaps the most intense criticism—housing policy. Sweden long suffered from a chronic housing shortage. The housing survey conducted in the mid-1930s found that 51 percent of urban dwellings contained only one room and a kitchen; of those dwellings with three or more rooms and a kitchen, nearly 20 percent sheltered more than two persons to a room. Rural housing offered more space, but lacked modern facilities.[21] The introduction of housing allowances and rent restrictions swelled the demand for housing beyond the existing supply, and in the 1950s and 1960s the shortage of housing in the larger cities was substantial. Long waiting lists frustrated the homeseeker; young couples were compelled either to wait several years for an apartment or to turn to a kind of black market.[22]

These difficulties now lie in the past. By the mid-1970s a couple needing housing in Stockholm could move within hours. In recent years Sweden's rate of housing construction has been the world's highest (13.6 dwellings completed per 1000 persons in 1970).[23] The standard of construction is impressively high. There are no slums. The rapid pace of home building has outstripped demand. Only 3 percent of the population now lives in conditions of extreme overcrowding, defined as more than two to a room, excluding the kitchen. Indeed the very definition of "overcrowding" has been revised to reflect the general improvement in housing standards. Housing policy, once a major critical target, is in fact a brilliant achievement.

The most striking testimonial to the success of the Swedish welfare state is the extent to which traditional class barriers have been razed. Everyday phenomena reveal the presence of substantial social equality. The most obvious evidence of this equality is the fact that Swedish neighborhoods reflect only modest variations in wealth; the normal patterns of social intercourse have an egalitarian character. Ernst Michanek, a former director of social services, writes:

> People from all different classes of society go to the post office to cash children's allowances or national pensions. Different kinds of people live in the same rented multi-family dwellings or in houses of their own in the same district. . . . For a long time it has been considered natural for all of us to enter the same public hospitals and to receive treatment from the best specialists available in these hospitals.[24]

The French economist, Jean Parent, has captured still another aspect of this social equality in his striking phrase, "equality before the risk of death." He means that the factors that make for a high life expectancy—good health care, secure employment, decent housing, and the like—are distributed relatively equally throughout the society; they do not exist solely for the benefit of the more privileged.[25]

Michanek has described the pains that have been taken to avoid invidious distinctions and humiliating procedures in the provision of benefits:

> It was vital, in our opinion, to do away once and for all with the idea—widespread in the days of the old poor relief—that social assistance was something shameful, something of a personal disgrace to the recipient. So we tried to tie the special benefits [for low-income recipients] to certain *objective criteria* in the same way as under the social insurance system: a certain age, certain dwelling standards, a certain number of children or a certain income gave the *right* to a certain benefit. We tried to restrict to a minimum any discretion in the assessment of the individual's need for help and also to lessen the room for arbitrariness on the part of the public authorities concerned. We tried to do away with stinginess in the aid measures, to provide what might be termed as "help toward self-help," and to restrict to a minimum the necessary control. We tried to get rid of the discrimination against needy persons that had created an animosity towards society among her less fortunate children, and which had made both public and private welfare activities despised by many of those who depended thereon. Words like "help" and "subsistence aid" were replaced by words such as "benefit" or "allowance."[26]

Although the stigma attached to the acceptance of public assistance has not been entirely removed, the administration of the system has contributed enormously not only to an objective equality of condition, but to a spirit of equality and mutual respect.

Sweden is not a classless society, but the welfare state has succeeded in effecting a substantial redistribution and equalization of advantages. In the cautious language of an official report on the distribution of purchasing power, "the system of public taxation and transfer payments . . . has a progressive character, and this point holds both for the taxation portion of the system and the transfers portion, although it does not hold for each individual tax or transfer."[27] The accompanying table illustrates that the tax system is in fact considerably more progressive than the transfer payments.

As the table makes clear, transfers do comprise an important part of an average worker's income. The family allowance for a single child is equivalent to approximately five percent of a working-class family's disposable income. These monetary calculations, however, probably understate the actual redistribution of resources, for they neglect the impact of public services such as health care and community planning.

The distinctive tools and successes of Swedish social welfare policy indicate that Sweden is moving beyond the social security state and toward the social welfare state. The pursuit of an active labor market policy, the LO's emphasis on wage solidarity, the profusion of social services extended as citizen rights, and the growing concern with the issues of the work environment and the control of investment distinguish the Swedish version of the welfare state from the British model. The Swedish Social Democrats share with their British Labour comrades a devotion to security, equality, solidarity, liberty, and democracy, but they insist as well upon the need for economic efficiency. Unlike Britain, Sweden has been able to expand social welfare programs, rather than allowing inflation and economic stagnation to erode them. By extending the benefits of these programs to the entire population, rather than just the neediest sectors, Sweden has generated an overwhelming public consensus on the merits of the welfare state. By its example, the emerging Swedish social welfare state tends to confirm the claim, regularly advanced by Swedish Social Democratic theorists, that equality and efficiency are complementary rather than mutually exclusive.

The evidence cited here clearly demonstrates that the welfare state "works." Sweden's achievements in social policy confute both those conservatives who argue that redistributive measures must fail and those radicals who claim that capitalist societies contain structural features that make "genuine" social reform impossible. Sweden's welfare state has not collapsed as a result of internal contradictions or economic inefficiency; rather it has succeeded in revising the operation of a market economy so as to

Disposable Income and Social Class

	Total Income by Crowns	− Taxes =	Income after Taxes	of which Pensions	Transfers (Social-bidrag)
Social Group I	31,500	12,300	19,300	1400	1100
Social Group II	16,900	4,700	12,200	900	1000
Social Group III	12,100	2,800	9,300	1100	1000

Source: Den svenska köpkraftensfördelning 1967 (Stockholm: SOU 1971: 39), p. 52.

produce higher and more evenly distributed levels of welfare. Its critics cannot justifiably claim either that its economy functions inefficiently or that its institutions resemble those of an unregulated capitalism.

Conservative and Radical Criticisms

Conservative critics, unable to argue plausibly that the Swedish economy has been ruined by governmental interference, concentrate their fire on the working of specific sectors of the economy, such as housing and health care, and ominously forecast a future collapse resulting from a loss of economic "initiative." Foreign critics particularly favor these arguments, which they believe demonstrate the impracticality of welfare statist institutions; domestic conservatives, persuaded through experience that the welfare state is a workable and even a desirable form of social organization, employ these criticisms only to discredit specific Social Democratic policies, not the entire apparatus of the welfare state. Hospitals are crowded and doctors in short supply, but these shortages arise because every member of society, not merely the fortunate, can effectively demand these goods and services. On a comparative basis, Swedish hospital facilities fare well:

> There are more hospital beds per capita in Sweden (16.2 per 1000 inhabitants) than are available in the United States (9+ per 1000 inhabitants). The real problem stems from an acute shortage of doctors: one for every 940 Swedes as contrasted with one for every 690 Americans.[28]

The relative scarcity of doctors is partially offset by a more even distribution of doctors within the country. Furthermore, when one looks to the results of the health care system, it is clear that the Swedish system is certainly one of the world's best. By absolute standards, the Swedish housing situation did show and health care does still show obvious deficiencies, but when compared to other advanced industrial societies, the Swedish accomplishment in these areas undermines the conservative case in these areas, rather than strengthening it.

For years it has been a staple of conservative doctrine that governmental efforts to redistribute income and to provide security for workers must ruin the system of incentives and personal initiative upon which (in their view) a properly functioning economy must rest. The case has a moral as well as an economic dimension; elaborate denunciations of sloth and of parasitic dependence upon a noble and productive minority flow from conservative lips and pens. This rhetoric, applied to the Swedish case, finds little support in the facts. Sweden has maintained more rapid rates of economic growth than most of the advanced industrial societies that lack such developed welfare institutions. In steadily increasing numbers Swedes pursue advanced educational programs. To finance a country cottage or some equally tangible sign of superior affluence, more and more Swedish families are taking on additional employment. These developments hardly point to impending indolence and inertia. If anything, the conservative criticism is just the opposite of the facts; the advent of greater social equality has brought an even more intense scramble to demonstrate one's superiority over his neighbors, as Tocqueville forecast it would more than a century ago. The conservative image of economic man, driven to labor by the fear of starvation and poverty, simply cannot do justice to the Swedish experience.

Allusions to moral depravity are a second standard objection offered by conservative critics. In their ranks vivid disquisitions on the "sin-sex-suicide syndrome" (as Joseph Board has aptly termed it) flourish. According to these writers, life in a welfare state encourages sexual promiscuity, suicide, and alcoholism. Not everyone may regard sexual abstinence as one of the hallmarks of a good society, or believe suicide invariably immoral, or consider alcoholism a sign of moral depravity, but in any case there is little evidence to support the view that the welfare state contributes to them.

Evidence with regard to extramarital sexual relations is obviously unlikely ever to be rigorous and complete. One indicator, rough because it can make no allowances for improvements in the technology of birth control, is the percentage of children born out of wedlock. There is no noticeable correlation of such births with the development of the welfare state. In Sweden the rate of "illegitimate" births peaked in the first third of this century, declined rather steadily until the mid-1950s, and has since begun rising again. The suicide rate similarly does not correlate with the development of the welfare state. From 1901–1910, well before the establishment of the welfare state, there were 15.1 suicides per 100,000 inhabitants. By 1961 the rate had increased to 16.9.[29] The most thorough and scholarly study of this issue argues that "Sweden's late but fast-developing industrial capitalism" is a better explanation for this slight rise than the relatively recent social welfare measures."[30]

The claim that the welfare state engenders alcoholism is equally unfounded. Alcoholism is a serious problem in Sweden but again one that predates the development of modern welfare policy.[31] The state actively combats the problem through educational efforts and stiff penalties for drunken driving. It is worth noting that in 1962 Sweden ranked eighth in international comparisons of alcohol consumption—after France, Italy, Switzerland, West Germany, the United States, Great Britain, and Denmark. In short, the case against the welfare state as a singularly iniquitous promoter of moral turpitude rests on conservative prejudices rather than on the facts. Sweden does have serious social problems, but those most commonly discussed have their origins not in the welfare state, but in deep-seated national characteristics and the strains of modern industrial life.

The central conservative argument, however, is not that the welfare state disrupts the economy or even that it fosters moral degeneracy, but that it restricts freedom. Within Sweden and beyond its borders the refrain of the welfare state's detractors has been that governmental intervention has curbed personal freedoms.[32] The validity of such criticisms is not easily determined, for there is no single, readily quantifiable entity known as freedom, but a multitude of distinctive freedoms—the freedom to speak contentious thoughts in public; the freedom to assemble for redress of grievances; to worship or not as one pleases; to determine one's own preferences in food, clothing, and personal associations; and so on, in a virtually endless list. Moreover, these individual liberties may come into conflict with one another and their relative value is not commonly agreed upon. For conservatives the freedom to dispose of "one's own" income or property is a critical liberty; those of a more progressive disposition are quite prepared to limit this "right" if restrictions enhance other people's opportunity to live their lives free from various physical or material hardships. Because personal preferences in this area do differ, facts alone may not resolve the controversy, but they can contribute to a more intelligent weighing of the argument.

Two considerable figures in the debate over the liberal or illiberal character of Swedish society have erred by attempting to give a more definitive answer on this issue than is possible. Albert Rosenthal in *The Social Programs of Sweden* has argued that the large number of Swedes who continue to vote for Social Democratic policies is evidence that they feel sufficiently free and thus must enjoy substantial liberties. Roland Huntford in *The New Totalitarians* claims, on the contrary, that the continued success of the Social Democrats only indicates the insidious skill with which they undermine traditional liberal freedoms and attitudes. Neither position survives critical investigation, particularly since the 1976 election in which the Social Democrats fell from power. Rosenthal's criterion for a free society (not his only criterion, incidentally) is logically inadequate; as Orwell's *1984* demonstrates, feeling free is not the same thing as being free. The logic of Huntford's case is not seriously deficient, but his evidence is; when evidence appears at all, it is often tendentiously selected or inaccurately reported.[33]

The bulk of foreign observers have found the traditional civil liberties carefully preserved in Sweden. The range of political debate extends over a wider spectrum of opinion than in the United States. The general assurance of minimum standards has expanded opportunities for social mobility and personal development among those in the lower reaches of the social hierarchy. Concomitant with these increased possibilities for the less advantaged sectors of the population have come real restraints on the spending of private incomes and on the operation of private businesses. Precisely how one draws the balance with regard to these gains and losses in liberty (and other values) is largely a matter of personal preference. One thing is clear, however; a condemnation of the Swedish welfare state on the grounds that it abrogates traditional civil liberties or eliminates political debate is grossly inaccurate.

The radical criticisms of Swedish society find less support in Western public opinion, but they have a decidedly superior basis in fact. The achievements of social welfare policy compel Swedish radicals to speak in temperate tones, but the major themes of radical criticism continue to be sounded: Sweden, the argument runs, remains an inegalitarian and undemocratic society. This contention, and corresponding calls to action, arise from groups within the Liberal and Social Democratic parties and from what there is of the New Left and of Communism in Sweden.

The persistence of substantial inequalities in the ownership of property, in educational opportunity, and in the exercise of authority in the factory need little documentation. Although considerable redistribution of incomes has occurred, the distribution of property remains highly skewed. At one extreme approximately 55 percent of the adult population lacks any substantial property; at the other extreme stands the near-legendary Wallenberg family, with an enormous fortune that allows them to control, either through majority or strong minority holdings, firms employing about 13 percent of all Swedes employed in the private sector. Through their control of Stockholm's Enskilda Banken and their powerful influence in eight of Sweden's ten largest corporations, the Wallenbergs have carved out a position of power unique in advanced Western industrial societies; even within business circles their immense resources create uneasiness and fear. A number of similar, though smaller, financial concentrations, centered on banks and holding companies, occupy the "commanding heights" of the private sector.[34] In a well-documented and generally respected study the former Communist party leader, C. H. Hermansson, pointed to fifteen families as the great powers in the economy. The French observer, Jean Parent, describes the large financial networks as *"hypergroupes"* comparable to the great economic dynasties of Japan in both power and dynamism.[35] That the ownership and control of Swedish industry remain highly concentrated is a fact conceded by all sides.

Inequalities in the ownership of property are the most glaring, but not the only offense against the norm of equality. In the late 1960s, in the midst of unprecedented affluence, over a third of the total working force earned less than $2000 a year. Nearly 300,000 Swedes had an annual income below $600—distinctly below a subsistence level in the country's high-priced economy.[36] Recognition of these unpalatable facts gave rise to a demand for a new and thorough study of the living standards of low-income recipients. An appropriate commission was established and its reports disclosed significant variations in living standards, with the poorest classes of the population suffering cumulative disabilities and disadvantages. Persons in Social Group III (blue-collar workers) not only had less income and property than those in Social Groups I and II; they also had poorer health, nutrition, housing, educational opportunity, and political resources. On only two of the tens of indicators did Social Group III fare better than the other groups; they consumed less tobacco and less alcohol.

Only 3 percent of Social Group I lived in overcrowded conditions (and many of these were students); more than a quarter of those in Social Group III were poorly housed, with attendant loss of privacy, sleep, and health.[37] In 1967, among the population of university age, a mere 8 percent of Social Group III attended colleges or universities, as opposed to 23 percent in Social Group II and 63 percent in Social Group I.[38] Whereas 21 percent of Social Group I had never contributed to public political debate, 40 percent of Social Group III, nearly twice as great a percentage, remained completely aloof from the formation of public policy. Even more significantly, 86 percent of persons in Social Group I felt capable of protesting against an abuse of public or private authority that affected them adversely; only 32 percent of persons in Social Group III felt that they could initiate procedures to redress a personal grievance.[39] This modest sample of data assembled by the "Low Income Commission" confirms that the standard of welfare in Sweden, measured both in monetary terms and in more direct indicators of living standards, varies sharply and systematically according to social class.

Sweden falls short of being a participatory democracy in which all citizens both can and do engage in public debate and defend their own interests. Moreover, despite a general balance of power among the large organizations in Swedish society, substantial inequalities of power persist *within* these organizations.

> The present scene, one might say, consists of enormous blocs of concentrated power which have largely achieved a state of equilibrium. On the one hand, augmented power is vested in the state and the Government, but on the other, the large organizations are better equipped not only to influence the central authority, but even to thwart it. . . . [But] if large power

blocs can thus be said to counter-balance one another, a distinct tendency towards far-reaching concentration of power *within* these blocs would appear to be in the making.[40]

In the interplay among the large organizations, the Social Democratic party and the national labor federation, the Landesorganisationen, have clearly exerted more influence than other organizations, particularly when they work in concert. Nonetheless, to argue that the Social Democrats and the LO instituted a kind of totalitarian labor regime, as Roland Huntford has suggested, is nonsense. In the words of a sober French observer, "the Social Democrats have not established a dictatorship or anything that could be called an official party regime; they take care to name some notable opposition figures to responsible posts. Public discussion (la propagande) is open to all. . . ."[41]

Centralization has also proceeded apace in the political sphere. In the interests of administrative efficiency the number of local government units is being reduced from 905 in 1968 to 282 by the end of the 1970s. This "modernization" of local government will necessarily lessen opportunities for direct participation in the process of local government. At the national level a growing number of observers have discerned a different sort of centralization, the growth of an "Establishment," a new elite enjoying high positions, income, and status deriving from their authority in the power blocs they represent. In his controversial *Maktspelet i Sverige,* an analysis of the distribution of power in Swedish society, the television journalist Åke Ortmark isolated 250 people as the wielders of decisive power in Swedish society.

> The 250 powerholders in this book—242 men and 8 women— all belong to Sweden's privileged class. It is above all this class who enjoy and make use of the universities, luxury restaurants, theatres, and tennis halls. It is for this class that the best doctors and most skillful jurists are reserved. It is for them that writers write, painters paint, and composers compose. It is for them that housing, bank loans, and abortions are arranged. In this class one finds people of intellectual capacity and breeding, articulate and self-confident. It is this group that has the pleasant and interesting work assignments, the high wages, good reputations, power, and glory.[42]

Ortmark only slightly overstates the material prequisites of Establishment figures, but he considerably exaggerates their actual power. He fails to mention that this group operates within the confines of a parliamentary system in which politicians obtain the right to rule through competition for votes in popular elections. The Establishment enjoys wide discretionary power, but only within the limits of what a democratic majority will tolerate.

Ortmark characterizes Sweden as an "idyllic class society."[43] The welfare state, he observes, has succeeded in providing enormous benefits for the laboring population. Compared to the 1930s, the working family's income, housing, diet, health, education, employment and recreational opportunities, and living environment have improved immensely. The barriers between white- and blue-collar classes have been effaced to a very substantial extent. The movement toward a classless society must still cope, however, with the existence of an "Establishment" and of an underclass which has not fully shared in the general abundance. Critical decisions for the completion of a social welfare state remain to be taken.

Sweden's accomplishments make it natural that other nations should strive to imitate it; however, the extent to which Sweden can serve as a model for American reformers is problematic. Radicals argue that Swedish affluence is parasitic upon Western imperialism, but this claim is questionable. Norway and Denmark can spend sparingly upon defense because of their reliance upon NATO, but Sweden expends six to seven percent of its gross national product for military purposes, one of the world's heaviest defense spending burdens. The Swedish economy does depend heavily upon exports (roughly 30 to 40 percent of GNP), but these export products are not based upon the exploitation of cheap foreign raw materials, but upon Swedish iron ore, forests, water power, and technology. Furthermore, Sweden's economy is sufficiently productive that Sweden may be the only country to meet the United Nations' goal of providing one percent of GNP in aid to developing countries. These considerations suggest that Sweden's successes in social policy result from its own efforts, not from dependence upon the Western powers.

Less easily dismissed is the contention that Sweden's domestic structure has certain unique traits that make its relevance to

American conditions limited. Sweden is a comparatively small country of eight million people; America, a continental nation nearing 250 million inhabitants. Sweden's pressure groups are small in number and operate within a disciplined system of national bargaining and consultation; America's have proliferated and press their interests with minimal restraint. The Swedish Social Democrats held power for forty years; American parties seldom have an effective working majority and then only for short periods. Clearly, the United States would face distinctive administrative and political challenges in constructing a welfare state as successful as the Swedish model.

7

The United States: Origins, Structure, and Performance of the Positive State

This chapter reviews the origins, structure, and performance of American welfare provision. We attempt to account for why government welfare programs are so confused and hard to comprehend, why they cost so much in relation to the benefits they provide, and why the system of government intervention as a whole tends to favor those who are already relatively well-off. A key to understanding these features is found in the historical record. We witness the same curious pattern: The United States began by sharing with other industrial countries (and particularly with Britain) the problems giving rise to calls for reform; this reform has occurred at similar times and at the outset in similar ways as in most industrial countries. But for a series of reasons the United States has ended up with less than other countries achieved, or than the reformers wanted, or than their opponents feared.

The Unique Development of American Welfare Provisions

Until the last years of the nineteenth century, American welfare policy rested on a merger of Elizabethan and New Poor Law reforms.[1] From the former, the administrative structure of poor relief was retained: legal settlement, local responsibility. To this structure were grafted the principles that inspired Chadwick and the contemporary English practitioners of political economy: the reluctance to countenance "outdoor relief" (assistance given outside the local, public institution); the belief that indigence was the mark of personal sloth and fecklessness—sins that tempted most men and which must be repressed sternly; and the firm conviction that state intervention was not to be countenanced both because it almost always ended up by making the problem worse (a line of thought developed in Chapter Three) and because it always involved the restriction of individual freedom. In this connection, the establishment of social insurance in Germany, while furthering similar developments in Sweden in particular, probably retarded American reform by associating insurance with authoritarianism.

The Progressive Era

However much attuned to the American spirit it may have been, this form of poor relief was undermined by the same forces as those in Britain: the collection of statistical evidence showing the social not personal bases of poverty; the associated failure of "scientific charity" (most notably the Charity Organization Society); the advent of reformers and politicians hopeful of bridging the gap between the two nations; and, above all, rapid industrialization that necessitated labor mobility, underlined the collective nature of unemployment, and inspired notions of the utility (for business) of a government-business partnership. These strands combined to initiate the reforms of the "Progressive Era," reforms that were primarily attitudinal, with the old verities of individual responsibility strongly challenged for the first time. The poor, it was now maintained, were not personally culpable, and they could also be assisted through purposeful public policy. Moreover (and here the ascension of England, the land of Gladstonian probity, to the ranks of the social insurers was a key event), foreign models were now employed to demonstrate the backwardness of American policy.[2]

When it came to practice, however, the fruits of reform were modest indeed. A dependent mother's pension was passed (by 1911) in a majority of states; a few states passed an Employer Liability bill for industrial accidents (only to be declared unconstitutional); the pension movement was less than overwhelmingly successful with only four states paying pensions as late as 1930. And, despite much hope and despite its introduction in twenty states by 1917, no health insurance bill was ever passed anywhere. The reasons for this meager legislative response were varied. Certainly constitutional arrangements were important. Teddy Roosevelt might want reform, but persuading Congress was not sufficient; as was often lamented, it seemed to take a reform movement in every state to effect the desired result. The possibility for delay was particularly damaging because the impetus for reform proceeded in waves. To miss the crest was more than a temporary setback, as can be seen in the failure of health insurance which America was probably closer to implementing in 1917 (just at the entrance into World War I) than at any time since. Finally, there were always the courts, periodically prepared to strike down ordinances; until at least 1937, the question of constitutionality was a major obstacle to social reform.

Constitutional considerations aside, advocates of social reform, in comparison to their counterparts in Europe, had to deal with a far more complex social structure that provided, in an ad hoc manner, major nongovernmental forms of relief from individual destitution. In the first place, there already existed *surrogate forms of social insurance,* primarily the huge Civil War pensions falling due in precisely this period, and the series of immigrant mutual aid societies paying sickness, accident, and death benefits. There were literally hundreds of these societies, many with capital in the millions of dollars.[3] The immigrants further diversified the contemporary American working class, which, even taken as a whole, was not the most numerous social class in most American states. As a consequence, it is not surprising to find the virtual absence of widespread organized pressure for social reform. Even organized labor clung to Samuel Gompers' vision of "more" (money) and was neutral or antagonistic toward most reform proposals, especially pensions.

But the major reason for the slackening of the reformist impulse was the construction of the first of many attempts to forestall the development of collective forms of welfare provision. This early effort we shall call businessism. Based on the "principles of scientific management" (the title of a book by Frederick Taylor, a main inspiration for the movement), businessism held that all production and distribution problems could be solved by the application of proper reasoning and technique. This peculiarly American movement (based on the Taylor Society and backed by Herbert Hoover, John D. Rockefeller, Jr., Gerald Swope, President of General Electric, Marion Falson, treasurer of Eastman-Kodak, Henry Ford, and Louis Brandeis among others) argued directly against the European experience. Social insurance, government welfare programs, were a negative intrusion, a disruption of sound business practice; the business of the American people, in Calvin Coolidge's literally apt phrase, is business. And this phrase was not to be interpreted narrowly; business management could, and should, *solve* the ills that called forth state action in Europe. As Rockefeller wrote in "Representation in Industry":

> Shall we cling to the conception of industry as an institution, primarily of private interest, which enables certain individuals to accumulate wealth, too often irrespective of the well-being, the health and the happiness of those engaged in its production?
>
> Or shall we adopt the modern viewpoint and *regard industry as being a form of social service,* quite as much as a revenue-producing process? . . .
>
> The soundest industrial policy is that which has constantly in mind the welfare of employees as well as the making of profits, and which, when human considerations demand it, *subordinates profits to welfare.* . . .[4]

In short, the enlightened self-interest of business could take the place of incipient government welfare provisions abroad.[5]

The New Deal

Whatever one's reactions to businessism as an ideology, it did have the attractive feature of establishing specific criteria on which it was to be judged. In return for public noninterference in business affairs and an absence of profit regulation, business enterprise would keep prices low, raise real wages, and provide ever increasing security for its work force. It seemed to be approaching these goals during the 1920s (in marked contrast to Britain and Germany—both countries, it was noted, with social insurance systems). Then came the Great Depression which, as we recounted in Chapter One, painfully illustrated the flaws not only of unregulated markets but of self-supervised capitalism American style as well. The collapse of production, the mounting unemployment, the inability of farmers to sell their produce at anything approaching cost, the apparently ceaseless fall of industrial prices—all attested to the termination of businessism as a viable organizational principle.

Reactions to the cataclysmic events varied. Some, like Hoover, retreated to the philosophy of the Poor Law: "I am opposed to any direct or indirect government dole. The breakdown and increased unemployment in Europe is due in part to such practices. Our people are providing against distress from unemployment in true American fashion. . . ."[6] Others responded in more creative (or rational) ways. Swope and many other industrialists (including the U.S. Chamber of Commerce) called for government planning, unemployment assistance, and an end to enforcement of the Sherman (antitrust) laws. When Hoover responded that "this stuff was sheer fascism," he was informed by one prominent industrialist that in view of his intransigence "the business world would support Roosevelt with money and influence."[7] The leadership of organized labor (in 1932, forty-two years after a similar shift in British Trade Union opinion) likewise swallowed its dislike of appearing "a ward of the government" and embraced social insurance legislation.[8] The stage was set for reformative political action.

The New Deal reforms laid the groundwork for the "positive state."[9] First, prototypes of government-business cooperation for the production of economic wealth were established. To be sure, cooperation during the 1930s was far from placid because of the loss of status felt by many businessmen, the personal hostility of many businessmen toward Roosevelt (and vice versa), the internal split between large corporations and smaller businesses, and the rise of organized labor. Still, the extent to which these difficulties were largely superficial is seen in the speed with which they dissipated after 1940 when the country mobilized for war. It seems hardly necessary to observe that the association between government and business since the war has been continued and strengthened.

Second, a pattern of government sponsorship and regulation of labor-management bargaining was instituted. Again, the relationship at the outset was stormy. Strikes, violence, and lock-outs were frequent; rhetoric was passionate. The transformation of organized labor from at most a minor appendage of industrial production to an independent force constantly pushing for higher wages and benefits represented another reduction in power and status many businessmen found hard to accept. But again, the cooperation of management and labor imposed by World War II dampened the earlier tensions when it was discovered empirically that high profits and high wages need not be incompatible and were indeed mutually sustaining.

Finally, a movement began to relieve by collective action the more extreme forms of destitution. It is this aspect of New Deal policy that is most often stressed and most often debated. That it was a key consideration for Roosevelt and most of his commentators is apparent both in the works of current and contemporary historians and in the utterances of Roosevelt himself:

> I assert that modern society, acting through government, owes the definite obligation to prevent the starvation or the dire want of any of its fellow men and women who try to maintain themselves but cannot.... To these unfortunate citizens aid must be extended by Government, not as a matter of charity, but as a matter of *social duty*.[10]

Legislation embodying these ideas was restricted primarily to the Social Security Act of 1935. Its main features were: (1) unemployment compensation—states were financially encouraged to set up programs meeting federal standards (by 1938 all had done so); (2) aid for dependent children, as well as state grants for maternal health services; (3) old age assistance consisting of two parts—aid to states for pensions and compulsory old age insurance for qualifying groups paid for by a tax levied on employers and employees. It is this last provision that is commonly identified with "social security."

As it stood, the bill was gauged incomplete even by its strongest supporters, being conceived in haste and passed overwhelmingly under the impetus of the Townsend Movement and similar schemes for income redistribution.[11] A good summary of the next steps deemed logical and necessary to take was given by Paul Douglas in his 1936 book, *Social Security in the United States*. These steps may be collected into three categories:

1. Administrative Rationalizations: Uniformity of state programs. Minimum standards for state personnel. Effective national sanctions.
2. Coverage of Existing Programs: Extended to all citizens. Made adequate to meet minimum needs.
3. Structural Changes: Institution of national health insurance. Payment of benefits to compensate for loss of earnings. Lifting a portion of cost of the program from workers and consumers by tapping general revenue acquired by progressive taxation. Elevation of the wage level.

A comparison of this list with actual progress reveals what was to become a familiar American pattern. The welfare bureaucracies established under the act proceeded to address the problems with vigor and efficiency. Administrative rationalizations and the compliance of state officials were rapidly achieved, and there was a constant push for higher benefits and extended coverage. What quickly petered out was the political commitment, and all reforms requiring further legislative action (health insurance, changes in financing) were postponed with increasing verve. This truncated record calls for an explanation, and again we find factors similar to those bringing the "Progressive Era" to a rapid halt.

First, we have the delaying capability of federal institutions. Even though Roosevelt had been elected overwhelmingly in 1936 on a platform of reform not retrenchment, to be effected reform had to pass the scrutiny of the courts, the Congress, and the states. Only the first, sufficiently chastened by the court-packing attempt, proved more amenable than in 1932. Second, the organizational base for further advance was narrow, resting on the typical triad of Presidential leadership, the persuasion of "reformers" and the associated activities of welfare bureaucracies, and the presence of ad hoc protest movements. Because there was no coherent, organized political pressure for welfare reform, progress toward a social security state rested heavily on the sufferance of particular interest groups (representing insurance companies, doctors, low-wage employers) and on the continual exercise of Presidential pressure. When the Depression waned sufficiently to permit groups to defend their interests more vocally, and when Roosevelt grew tired of the process (ran out of ideas, failed to reorient the Democratic Party, turned his attention to Europe, or whatever explanation), reform ended.

World War II confirmed the solution of the positive state to the troubles of American capitalism and at the same time stifled any latent tendencies toward redistributive reform.[12] Wages soared, unemployment vanished, production multiplied. In only five years (1940–1944) gross income doubled, consumer spending went from $75 billion to $99 billion, coal output rose 71 percent, natural gas 91 percent. America, alone among the belligerent countries, was in a position to produce both "guns" and "butter." Roosevelt saw the occasion to transcend the New Deal, and given the "cult of personality" that permeated all aspects of welfare reform, efforts of men like Henry Wallace to breathe new life into the New Deal were rendered totally ineffective.[13] As Roosevelt explained in his "Dr. Win the War" Press Conference, the ills of the depression had been remedied, and further initiatives were to be postponed until "the time comes."[14]

Besides confirming Roosevelt's decision to postpone further reform until "the time comes," the war brought to the fore two other issues that were to dominate the political agenda for the next two decades—the status of blacks and the attitude toward communism. These issues impeded further welfare reform not only by monopolizing attention, but also by fracturing the New Deal coalition that depended, especially in Congress, on the good will of Southern whites; by 1944 they constituted 54 percent of the Democratic strength in the House and 50 percent in the Senate, as well as continuing to control the most important committees. The nonhomogeneity of America and the immaturity of its political culture was apparent in the agonizing debate over whether a large number of citizens were to be allowed basic human rights.

Finally, and more positively, the war inaugurated yet another alternative to a government sponsored and guaranteed security system, this time a series of union negotiated "fringe benefit" packages covering health costs, supplementary unemployment benefits, pensions, and paid holidays—and most of the packages paid for exclusively by the employer![15] The extent of these benefits will be described below. Here we shall note that this form of economic security, to the extent it is successful, reduces drastically the political appeal of the welfare state. The welfare state, it will be recalled, was established primarily to bring the benefits of economic security (property) to the working class. If the working class could negotiate this security on its own through collective bargaining, what was the purpose of governmental welfare programs? This question is not just "historically" significant; it is a major argument in the current attack on welfare programs, and it continues to drive a wedge between groups that one would expect to be the "natural" pro-welfare state constituency.

The War on Poverty and its Aftermath

The United States, unlike its postwar industrial neighbors, settled into a period of satisfied normalcy. Politically, this state of mind was embodied by Eisenhower. On the one hand, Eisenhower made explicit the adherence of the Republican Party leadership to the programs and the *outlook* of the New Deal. Eisenhower expressed his "philosophy" in the following terms, almost indistinguishable from Roosevelt's earlier quoted conviction that government "owes the definite obligation to prevent the starvation or the dire want of any of its fellow men and women":

> When I refer to the Middle Way, I merely mean the middle way as it represents a practical working basis between extremes, both of whose doctrines I flatly reject. It seems to me that no great intelligence is required to discern the practical necessity of establishing some kind of security for individuals in a specialized and highly industrialized age . . . it [is] impossible for any durable government to ignore hordes of people who through no fault of their own suddenly find themselves poverty stricken.[16]

At the same time, Eisenhower made it plain that he felt this goal had already been mainly achieved, and that what was now required was a reduction in spending and a cutback in the "overcentralization" of government.

That Eisenhower held these views is not particularly remarkable, and neither was the far-from-unanimous decision of the Republican leadership to align the party with them for the sake of electoral advantage. What is surprising is the alacrity with which the *Democratic leadership* responded to these sentiments. That both parties attempted to recruit Eisenhower for the presidency in 1948 is well-known, but its implications have not been stressed enough. And even after Eisenhower in 1951 let it be known that he really was a Republican, having apparently voted that way in the 1950 Congressional election, Democrats continued to campaign on the not overly ambitious grounds that they, not their Republican opponents, better expressed Eisenhower's outlook and program. Eisenhower himself recorded some sympathy with this position.[17]

When this happy consensus was broken in the early 1960s, it was from a diverse assortment of pressures. Eisenhower, with his old-fashioned ideas about balanced budgets and the free market, had never, it was charged, grasped the possibilities for economic growth inherent in the use of government-business partnership by the positive state;[18] it was time to "get the country moving again." All the more reason to do so, because of the discovery that poverty, far from being "completely routed," was indeed endemic in central cities and rural outbacks and showed no sign of self destructing. The persistence of poverty had been an unwelcome finding, as we have seen, in more developed welfare states as well; in the United States it was compounded by the inadequacy of social security benefits and by the system of union-management negotiations that excluded the less organized (and more marginal) workers. In addition, it was noted that many of these poor people were black. Blacks were getting restless and demanding rights that Eisenhower, for one, thought premature. Finally, reformers noted the growth in the number of one-parent families, a specific welfare problem which, as in Britain, social insurance was not equipped to handle. This problem, which the Eisenhower administration typically sought to ignore, seemed to demand for its solution fresh conceptual thinking. And what better way to mobilize the unproductive elements in the economy, to end the scandal of the "other America," to dampen discontent, and to bring a new spirit to public assistance than to launch what President Johnson called in 1964 a "national war on poverty."

The legislative products of this "war" can be aggregated in

three major categories (the wealth of literature on the subject permits us to be brief): First, important policy initiatives were undertaken. The most important was Medicare-Medicaid, under which we might include the qualitative jump in social security payments. Second, a plethora of ad hoc programs was set up addressing particular needs and groups (food stamps, aid to schools in educationally deprived areas, the establishment of mental health clinics, etc.). There are now over 1,100 separate federally administered welfare programs, over five times the number existing in 1963.[19] Third, an effort (mainly through Community Action Agencies and programs like VISTA) was made to increase the political participation of the recipients and to involve the "poor" directly in the administration and formulation of their own welfare programs.

The outcome of the "war" is much more difficult to assess, but a handle can be found if it is viewed within the post-New Deal pattern. Here we see the same political checks and the same loss of interest on the part of the President. For Johnson, victory in Vietnam soon took precedence over victory in Detroit or eastern Tennessee. While the drive to achieve victory abroad did bring about full employment and a rapidly expanding economy that reduced the numbers of the "poor" by 1970, the dissembling of its impact on the federal budget also helped spawn the inflationary-recessionary cycle of the early 1970s, driving up the numbers again, reversing the trend toward higher per capita real income, and ending the slow increase in black income relative to white. And when Johnson retired, his more exposed programs dealing with a potential shift in political power were rapidly overwhelmed. Even attempts to "deradicalize" the initiative (to exclude "troublemakers," to work more closely with city hall) were only marginally successful and did not in the end forestall the dismemberment of O.E.O. Finally, subsequent legislative action practically ceased, and thus ten years after Medicare and forty years after the publication of *Social Security in the United States,* America still lacks a system of national health insurance.

Again, however—and this is what makes the record fundamentally ambiguous—coincident with the political failure of the war, with the inability to meet the professed goals of the reforms, many of the programs themselves have been rationalized and continually expanded. More people are being helped than ever before;

federal minimums are being established (particularly in the Supplemental Security Income program, initiated nationwide in January 1974, for the aged, blind, and disabled); food stamps assistance is being extended to groups previously excluded (primarily the "working poor"). In short, as in the expansion of social security coverage after the New Deal, much of the welfare effort proceeded apace despite the Vietnam War, despite Nixon's preference for work over welfare, and despite the unsympathetic outlook of Gerald Ford. One of the major items we will consider in the remainder of this chapter is whether America has adopted the institutional structure of the social security state by administrative stealth.

The Structure of American Welfare Provision

As we argued in Chapter One, the pattern of welfare provision must be placed within the larger context within which the modern capitalist state operates. Accordingly, before turning our attention to "welfare" per se, we shall review briefly the two major pillars of the contemporary positive state: government-business cooperation, and minimalist full employment policy.

Government-corporate collaboration

Long past are the days when the United States was held up, by Shonfield and others, as a model of how not to operate a modern economy; long past are the days when slower growth was thought an inevitable "cost of freedom." In the last fifteen years we have seen government-corporate collaboration in the production of economic wealth vastly strengthened and solidified.[20] In viewing this relationship we must not reach the conclusion—often broached by students of European politics—that it is weaker than in some other countries because of the relative absence of formal *planning procedures*. Proponents of this view usually overlook that planning can be merely a defensive measure, aimed at shoring up an inadequate capital market (as in France) or at protecting weak enterprises (as in Italy). The United States has a highly adequate capital market and weak enterprises have been treated individually. Planning may also subsume goals such as full employment and income redistribution (as in Sweden), goals tangential to the production of economic wealth and goals to which the United

States does not subscribe. Finally, the large size of American companies (often called multinational which is indicative of their power if not their political base) permits them to do their own planning and arrange their own cooperative enterprises.

Government provides other services—opening up foreign markets, financing basic research, guaranteeing profits, bailing out large bankruptcies, maintaining a steady flow of arms sales abroad. For defense procurement at home alone, the Defense Department awarded contracts in 1975 amounting to forty billion dollars, with the top nine companies receiving $12.5 billion.[21] That corporate leaders value these services is indicated by their general inclination to advocate a return to "free enterprise" for all industries *except* their own.[22] That they were seen, at least in some circles, to have forfeited thereby a portion of their autonomy and integrity is indicated by their solicitation in 1972 for illegal contributions to the Nixon reelection campaign. No company, as far as is known, thought fit to call these proposed levies to the attention of the authorities. Some, displaying great courage and independence, apparently were able to reduce the amount of their tribute.

Minimalist Full Employment Policy

Although the United States recognized the ideal of full employment as early as the Employment Bill of 1946, a glance at the unemployment figures since the war shows that the commitment has been selectively applied. In line with the stress on economic "efficiency," full employment has been deemed essential for those whose skills are vital for corporate production and for other members of the middle class (e.g., aerospace engineers). There is much less concern for the two groups rendered particularly "expendable" by economic development—unskilled youth in major urban centers competing for too few manual jobs; and most residents of economically peripheral areas competing for too few jobs of any sort. Race is an important feature of the first category. In May 1975 the unemployment rate of young blacks was *officially* put at 40 percent. Other estimates are higher, and it is not surprising to find whole areas in the "inner city" in which the notion of a socially sanctioned job for a young person is as foreign as the notion of a trip to Paris or of a street cleared of garbage. As for the second category, the United States provides a case study of the tendency of the modern economy to centralize activities in a few growth areas, leaving the periphery to languish.[23] To summarize, in the employment policy of the United States, we arrive at the somewhat paradoxical but by no means unexplainable finding that those most exposed to the vagaries of unregulated capitalism are those who are helped the least. We shall find this pattern recurring, and it has important implications for the debate over the achievement or nonachievement of a social security state in America.

Provision of Welfare Services

Government welfare programs, according to Hugh Heclo, "appear confused and tangled to the man in the street because they *are* confused and tangled, not because devious middlemen have subverted clear and over-arching purpose."[24] We have suggested above some of the reasons for this confusion—the chasm between the political rhetoric and administrative reality of welfare reform, the presence of nongovernmental welfare provisions, the subordinate and tangential place of "welfare" in the vision and operation of the positive state. These reasons are not, however, of much assistance in imparting coherence to what provisions do exist. For this task we divide "welfare services" into three categories: benefits provided by the state, by private or quasi-private initiatives, and by the individual as best as he or she can.

1. *State Services.* From any perspective, the role of the state in the provision of social welfare is massive, fully adequate to assure a national minimum were that the goal of public policy. Spending for social welfare purposes for FY 1974 totaled $242.4 billion, a 13 percent increase from the preceding year, somewhat *less* than the 1966–1973 average growth. Expenditures now total 18 percent of Gross National Product, up from 5 percent in 1950. Another unabated trend has been the increasing proportion of government spending devoted to social welfare activities, now over 55 percent. And within this mix the federal government has increased its share from approximately 43 percent in 1950 to 47 percent in 1960, to 52 percent in 1970, to 57 percent in 1974.[25] The expenditures for the major federal and state and local programs in 1974 are given below:

Social Welfare Expenditures Under
Public Programs, FY 1974
(in millions)

	Federal	State & Local
Social Insurance...	82,508.0	15,994.0
OASDI (exc. Medicare)	54,951.5	—
OASDI (inc. Medicare)	66,273.4	—
Public Employees Retirement	10,549.4	5,939.0
Unemployment Insurance	1,705.3	4,954.7
Other	3,979.9	5,100.3
Public Aid...	21,237.3	12,390.8
Public Assistance	13,664.6	11,747.6
Other	7,572.7	643.2
Health and Medical Programs	8,005.0	6,049.4
Hospital and Medical Care	3,742.0	3,989.4
Construction and Research	2,793.0	894.0
Other	1,470.0	1,166.0
Veterans Programs...	13,877.7	45.0
Education...	8,045.6	64,717.3
Elementary and Secondary	4,128.4	50,867.3
Higher	2,725.6	10,900.0
Vocational & Adult	975.6	2,950.0
Housing	2,131.7	450.0
Public	1,233.0	N.A.
Other	898.0	N.A.
Other Social Welfare	3,774.2	3,160.0
Total	139,579.9	102,806.4

Source: Skolnik and Dales, "Social Welfare Expenditures, Fiscal Year 1974," Social Security Bulletin, 38, 1 (January 1975).

This massive effort can be divided roughly into those programs which provide benefits *in cash,* those which provide benefits *in kind,* and those which target benefits to *particular groups* (not necessarily with the aim of reducing poverty). The major cash transfer program is Old Age, Survivors, and Disability Insurance (OASDI), commonly known as Social Security.[26] OASDI now pays benefits to over 30 million Americans or about 90 percent of the nation's elderly. The system is financed by a payroll tax paid half by the covered employee and half by his employer, and by a tax paid by self-employed people on their earnings. Approximately 90 percent of the nation's employed labor force pay contributions; as of January 1, 1975, employees paid a total tax of 5.85 percent on earnings up to $14,100. (The actual OASDI tax is 4.95 percent; the remaining .9 percent goes to Medicare.) Tax-free benefits (1974) for a disabled worker or a worker retiring at age 65 range from $93.80 to $304.90 for an individual, the precise amount varying upon his previous income and years of participation in the system; in July 1974 the average monthly benefit for retired workers was $186.71. The administrative costs of the system ran about 1.6 percent of total total payments, equivalent to the British.[27]

OASDI benefits significantly alleviate poverty. In 1972 three-fourths of all aged non-married OASDI recipients had incomes below the poverty level before receiving benefits; after benefits, only 36 percent still fell below the threshold. Of aged married couples, 53 percent of OASDI beneficiaries fell below the poverty line before benefits, but only 10 percent did so after benefits. Nevertheless OASDI was not designed primarily as a redistributive measure for alleviating poverty but as a means to provide *earnings-related* income security for workers. Its minimum benefit assures roughly 50 percent of the poverty-level income for a single adult.[28] Blacks, who on the average have less secure and less well-paid employment, have fared particularly badly. To begin with, only 80 percent of blacks over the age of 65 (compared with 92 percent of whites) are receiving OASDI benefits at all; one can, or more likely one cannot, imagine the position of those other 20 percent. And the ratio of average monthly benefits black-white is only .80, basically unchanged since 1960.[29] The inability of OASDI to underwrite a national minimum is clear.

A second social insurance program, similarly designed to protect against loss of income, is the federal-state unemployment compensation system. It, too, is financed by a payroll tax, but one that falls only upon the employer. The tax varies from .3 to 3.7 percent of the taxable wages, depending upon the state administering the program. As these figures suggest, unemployment insurance is not a national program directed by an agency like the Social Security Administration, but a federal program administered by the Labor Department through various state programs. Benefits vary from state to state in relation to the size of the payroll tax, and are calculated in accordance with the size of the recipient's previous income. Forty-two states extend basic benefits for a period of 26 weeks. Recent legislation has established extended unemployment compensation for 13 to 26 additional weeks and a special unemployment assistance program to compensate victims of the latest recession. The unemployment insurance system "caters quite well to people in covered employment with a regular job history," for they are eligible for modestly respectable payments, but the system's general coverage is inadequate. Although approximately 85 percent of wage and salaried employees are covered by some form of unemployment insurance, the system does not cover the unemployed who have never succeeded in obtaining regular employment or those who work at jobs (e.g., in agriculture or domestic service) not covered by unemployment compensation. Thus, as with most insurance programs—public or private—it is precisely the neediest whom the system fails to aid.[30]

A third component of the current welfare system, the previously mentioned Supplemental Security Income for the aged, blind, and disabled (SSI), unlike the programs already discussed, is a means-tested, not an insurance, program. SSI pays benefits from general revenues to aged, blind, or disabled individuals and spouses on the basis of need; the recipient's income and resources may not exceed specified limits; in 1975 the cut-off was $1,500 for an individual and $2,250 for a couple (with a number of excludable items). Inaugurated in 1974, SSI replaces the previous state-administered, federally reimbursed programs with a national program providing a uniform minimum cash benefit with incentives for state supplementation; it is a testimony to the inadequacy of the earlier structure that this reform almost doubled the number of persons receiving assistance—from 3.2 to 6.2 million.[31]

The fourth program, Aid to Families with Dependent Children, (AFDC) is the most controversial; when analysts speak of a "welfare crises," their complaints focus on AFDC. AFDC formed part of the original Social Security Act of 1935, but significantly it has come to be known as "welfare" with all the negative connotations that word carries in the United States rather than "social security," a term with favorable overtones. As of September 1975 over three and a half million families (eleven million individuals) were receiving assistance. Benefits averaged $71.30 per recipient a month and ranged from $14.40 in Mississippi to $120.49 in Massachusetts.[32] AFDC payments are designed for families in which there is a dependent child who has been deprived of parental support or care by reason of death, continued absence, or incapacity. States *may* pay benefits in cases where the child lacks support because the father is unemployed (AFDC-UF), but only twenty-four states have elected to provide this coverage, and where it is provided the eligibility conditions are very narrowly drawn. It is hardly possible to overstress that this central element of the current welfare system is not a program of general assistance to the needy. AFDC does not aid single persons, adult couples, the working poor, or, in twenty-six states, the children of the unemployed.

The administration of AFDC is an organization theorist's nightmare. The School and Rehabilitation Service of the Department of Health, Education, and Welfare provides grants to the states. Slightly over half of the states then administer the program directly; the remainder delegate administrative authority to the local level. The consequences of this organizational laissez-faire is remarkable variation among states and consequent inequity to intended beneficiaries. The dependent child's prospects of decent support vary sharply according to where he or she is reared—a cruel lottery that results from the lack of a well-defined social policy.

These four programs and a variety of other minor ones disburse aid in cash. The needy who derive little or no benefit from these programs must rely on the vagaries of state and local general assistance, private charity, and national programs that provide benefits in kind. The levels of general assistance vary sharply from locality to locality, but in general reproduce the AFDC pattern of high outlays in the more progressive states and low expenditures in backward states. The mitigating effects of private charity are hard to calculate, for there are undoubtedly numerous cases where the prying eye of social science does not see what the generous do in secret. But, in any case—as observers as early as Hobbes have noted—the workings of private charity are essentially random and offer no guarantee that misery will be alleviated. Therefore, it becomes appropriate to proceed next to a consideration of those elements of the current federal system that provide benefits *in kind*.

Although the United States still lacks a national health program, it has had since 1965 health insurance programs for the aged, disabled, and indigent. Medicare provides hospital (not general medical) insurance for persons eligible for social security who are either disabled or aged. The program is financed through a payroll tax collected with social security taxes. It is administered by the Social Security Administration with the assistance of various intermediaries—such as Blue Cross and private insurance companies—which determine the amount of payments due and process claims. Participation in the program entitles the beneficiary to in-patient hospital services up to 90 days (less a deductible that the patient must pay), to post-hospital care for 100 days (again less a coinsurance sum for each day after 20 days), and to certain post-hospital home health care services. The second major health program, Medicaid, is a means-tested rather than an insurance program. Medicaid allows each state, at its option, to provide medical assistance to AFDC and SSI recipients and to the "medically indigent." Only twenty-five states extend coverage to the latter group, defined roughly as those persons whose income minus medical expenses is less than 133 percent of the standard of need the state sets for financial assistance under AFDC or SSI.

A second major category of benefits provided in kind is housing. The Department of Housing and Urban Development (HUD) operates a variety of programs to provide decent, safe, and low-cost housing to the poor. Its record in attaining this objective, however, is at best undistinguished. Actual construction of public housing has lagged far behind demand; less than 10 percent of households eligible for housing assistance receive it.[33]

The uneven geographic dispersion of public housing projects means that, once again, needy persons' prospects of assistance depend upon their place of residence. This basic inadequacy, combined with the high costs, scandal, and administrative troubles of current programs, has induced HUD to experiment with housing allowances that would enlarge the consumer's ability to obtain housing of his own choice.[34] The new approach would effectively shift the focus of housing policy from supply to demand; rather than subsidizing producers and owners of housing, the resources of marginal consumers would (in theory) be supplemented.

Food stamps, the third variety of aid provided essentially in kind, constitute the most dramatic recent expansion of welfare policy. In 1968 the food stamp program served fewer than two million people; in 1975 it aided fifteen million in a typical month (and about twenty-one million in the course of the year), at a cost of over $3.8 billion.[35] Food stamps are available to all recipients of public assistance or general assistance and to other households falling below certain income standards. They vary in price with the size of the recipient's income. The Federal Government is committed to paying the full cost of bonus coupons and half of all administrative costs. The appropriations are open-ended; that is, the government must fund the program to meet the demand that is forthcoming. Both the scope and open-ended nature of the program are under increasing legislative attack. With estimated eligibility put at 40 to 50 million people, this move again seems a reform in the wrong direction.[36]

In addition to these major undertakings to provide benefits in cash and in kind, the government funds a host of specific programs. Many of these were launched under the aegis of the "war on poverty"; some (e.g., "impacted areas" money) bear at best a tangential relationship to relieving poverty; others, like mental clinics, have apparently become reoriented to the needs of the middle class. Together they form an important drain on federal resources (witness the large sums devoted to "other" expenditures in Table I). And while some programs may add the financial or service piece necessary to upgrade the recipient to a recognized minimum level, their multiplicity and diversity add to the "social pork barrel" aura of welfare programs[37] and to the difficulties of coherent assessment.

2. *Nonpublic Provisions.* A cursory examination of the current public programs indicates that while their scope and benefit levels have increased significantly, the many disparities and exceptions they contain, separately or in concert, foreclose the opportunity to establish a benefit floor at a national minimum level. How this finding is to be interpreted depends, of course, on a determination of what additional benefits, if any, an individual is able to receive. Thus we are led to the amorphous category of nonpublic provisions encompassing group health plans, extra unemployment benefits secured through collective bargaining, annuities partially funded by employer and employee—none of which are the product either of public programs or of individual financing. It is the noncollective form of welfare provision, always present in the American experience but coming to fruition after World War II, that is often held to be the unique contribution of the American system, vitiating the need for more comprehensive and expensive governmental intervention.

The scope of these plans is indeed extensive. In 1973, 70 percent of the civilian labor force had both group hospital and surgical insurance, a third had major medical insurance. Among wage and salary workers in private industry 47 percent had temporary disability plans (16 percent long-term disability), and 44 percent were enrolled in retirement programs. Benefits paid in 1973 amounted to $36 billion, including $18 billion for health and over $11 billion for retirement. Contributions to the plans totaled almost $50 billion paid by an employer-employee ratio of more than six to one.[38]

Moreover, these plans have been coming under increasing governmental scrutiny and control in order to insure standardization and the actual payment of benefits. This movement is strongest in the field of retirement pensions, with the landmark provision set forth in the "Retirement Income Security for Employees Act" (the Williams-Javits Bill) passed overwhelmingly by Congress in 1974. The bill has three major aims: to establish minimum vesting rights to which all plans must adhere; to provide back-up governmental insurance should the plan fail; and to establish some controls to ensure adequate financing.[39] The bill would not only preclude a repetition of cases of workers losing all benefits if the company folded (as happened at Studebaker in 1963 when 4,500 employees lost 85 percent of their vested benefits), but also permit workers changing companies to retain some pension rights. These reforms were hailed by Senator Javits as "truly monumental," "the greatest development in the life of the American worker since social security."[40]

But the inadequacies of nonpublic provisions are inescapable. In the first place, the majority of American workers (56 percent) are entirely unaffected by the "monumental" development. More serious for the future, the trend toward enrolling a greater percentage of workers has slowed markedly since 1960 to about .4 percent a year, suggesting that the pool of possible enrollees could be almost exhausted. Finally, nothing has been done to control how much is actually paid; the amount fluctuates wildly, with well-paid employees in industries with strong unions doing far better than others. Thus we see a repetition of the pattern described earlier with social security benefits: those relatively well off tend to get more; those less well off tend to get less. This time, however, the less well off tend to get nothing at all. A 1975 study prepared for the Senate Finance Committee indicates that 40 percent of full-time wage and salary workers making less than $5,000 (20 percent of the employed population) had no group health insurance; *eight* percent of those earning more than $25,000 were in a similar position.[41] Of course, the poor continue to help fund the plans by paying more for the goods and services they buy.

There are also indications that the effective operation of these plans is predicated on prosperous and stable economic conditions; either inflation or unemployment greatly lessens their attraction even for those who are covered. Mainly because of the rapid rise in the cost of living, for example, the average pension has actually decreased in real terms since 1967.[42] The 1974–1975 recession brought greater hardships. It is estimated that up to 80 percent of workers laid off in 1974 lost all health coverage, and since nongroup family health plans run from 20 to 33 percent of average unemployment benefits, it is unlikely that many had made individual provisions.[43] The percentage of these losing benefits might have been less, but then only from the noncomforting discovery that "the 'last hired, first fired' phenomenon may result in unemployment. . . , but not necessarily *loss* of group health insurance coverage, since the affected workers were never covered."[44]

174

Indeed, the general crisis in funding health delivery has become so severe that the government has had to be brought in, often sub rosa, to shore up the structure. Americans now spend well over $120 billion a year for medical care, equivalent to about 8.5 percent of G.N.P., a percentage, as we have seen, close to that in Sweden, more than in Britain. What is rarely appreciated is the size of the public commitment. As the following table indicates, the percentage of nonpublic funding since World War II leapt forward, and the percentage of payments by individuals directly measurable fell steadily. Since the mid 1960s, however, insurance benefits have not increased their share significantly, and the short-fall has been made up by the government, primarily by Medicare-Medicaid.[45]

In light of this altered situation, one might expect government to use its leverage to institute changes. But not at all. Despite many proposals for major reform,[46] actual government policies in the past ten years have had the specific consequences of first aiding Blue Cross (accurately described by Sylvia Law as the "financing arm of American hospitals") by providing guaranteed money in the form of Medicare payments,[47] constructing hospitals and generally providing free infrastructure to the health profession, financing medical research and education, and relieving hospital charity in a random way from much of the burden of treatment for the poor. Needless to say, the total autonomy of the medical profession to set the terms and content of its work has never been challenged.[48]

Percentage Distribution of Personal Health Care Expenditures (in %)

	Private: Direct Payments	Nonpublic: Insurance	Other	Public
1929	88.5	—	2.6	8.9
1935	82.6	—	2.7	14.8
1950	68.3	8.5	3.0	20.2
1960	55.3	20.7	2.3	21.7
1965	52.5	24.7	2.0	20.8
1970	40.4	24.0	1.5	34.2
1974	35.4	25.6	1.4	37.6

Source: Nancy Worthington, "National Health Expenditures 1929–74," *Social Security Bulletin,* 38, 2 (February 1975).

To sum up, the contribution of nonpublic provision to the welfare and security of Americans is indeed vital. The benefits are needed by millions of workers to maintain a standard of living approaching that achieved when they were in good health and full employment (and they confirm thereby the previously discussed split in the "natural" pro-welfare state constituency). But these benefits can in no way be seen as a substitute for the obvious inadequacies of public welfare state programs. They are most inadequate precisely where the public programs fail. Cost difficulties, particularly in health care, necessitate ever-increasing governmental intervention and support. The result is that a large burden of welfare maintenance is left in individual hands.

3. *Individual Provisions.* The spotty nature of the welfare system means that almost everyone must seek some sort of extra protection. The extent to which one must rely on his or her own resources is neither uniform nor random. Rather, in the same familiar and depressing pattern, those who by any objective measurement would seem least able to do so are compelled to do more. The casualties of the industrial order described in Chapter One remain precisely that. How many people fall into this category is not known, a fact that in itself is an indictment of the American welfare "system"; for whereas the concern in Britain and Sweden is to get all the eligibles on the rolls, in the United States the main effort is focused on purging the "unworthy." A consideration of the case of retired citizens does, however, shed light on the nature of the problem.

Public assistance for the elderly has always been among the most popular welfare measures. By definition no one can accuse the elderly of malingering; and traditionally in the United States, as elsewhere, there has been the presumption that those who put in a lifetime of toil "deserve" to live out their remaining years in dignity and without fear. This positive attitude toward helping the elderly indeed inspired the catch-all structure of the 1935 Social Security Act—it was felt essential to combine the other benefits with those for retirement lest Congress vote old age pensions only.[49] A determination of whether retired people actually do have a decent standard of living, therefore, seems a fair—indeed, generous—touchstone for the effectiveness of public policy. In making this assessment, it is first necessary to determine the extent to which people can compensate for the loss of earnings by using their own accumulated assets. The Retirement History Study, a continuing longitudinal research project conducted by the Social Security Administration, is revealing for the first time the amount and the changes in asset holdings of respondents. The findings are summarized in the accompanying table.[50]

This table highlights both the large minority (36 percent of married men) who retire with a rather comfortable "nest egg" (over $25,000) and the large minority (36 percent of the total and over 50 percent of single people) who retire with no or negligible (under $5,000) assets upon which to draw. These figures show that despite the "affluence" of the United States, industrialization and its associated social changes continue to deprive large segments of the population from securing their own future through the acquisition of property. Moreover, if we exclude home ownership from consideration of net assets, the picture worsens, with the percentage of those with no or negligible assets rising to 59 for the total sample, 69 for unmarried men, and 70 for unmarried women. The picture is made even more bleak when it emerges that those without owned houses have less than homeowners in the way of other financial assets. Seventy-eight percent of the married men, for example, were homeowners whereas only 40 percent of unmarried men were. But of the unmarried men with assets of over $25,000 two-thirds owned their home.

Here, then, is prima facie evidence of the need for collective assistance. And, as can be seen from the first table in this chapter, public outlays have been substantial, with payments under OASDI

Amount of Net Worth Upon Retirement: Percentage Distribution by Sex and Marital Status, 1969

.mount of et Worth	Total (n=5112)	Married Men (n=3025)	Single Men (n=594)	Single Women (n=1493)
tive or none	19	11	36	27
than $5,000	17	12	24	24
)o to $15,000	22	23	16	22
)oo to $25,000	14	16	7	11
$25,000	28	36	18	16

: SSA, "Retirement History Study."

alone totaling over $13 billion in 1970 (the date of the above
study). Nevertheless, the amount disbursed has been by itsel
inadequate, averaging around $160 a month in December 197
for retired workers. This produced an average income of $1,92
for retirees, 59 percent of whom held no significant assets apar
from their house, and 36 percent of whom held no significan
assets of any kind. It might be thought that here is the place fo
private-union-government pensions to bring yearly income up to
the "poverty line," and of course it is. But once again these
nonpublic provisions are neither extensive enough nor do the
concentrate benefits where they are most needed. Over 40 per
cent of all respondents listed social security as the only expected
source of post-retirement income.[51] The percentage anticipatin
income from other pensions is given in the accompanying table.[5

Other Pension Sources (in %)

	Total	Married Men	Single Men	Single Wo
Railroad	2.6	2.5	4.6	1.9
Veterans	2.2	1.8	5.2	2.6
Government	7.2	7.3	6.8	7.2
Private	25.9	29.2	24.0	13.9

Source: SSA, "Retirement History Study."

The pattern becomes clearer when pensions are broken dow
by yield.[53]

Annual Income Expected from
Private Employer or Union Pensions (in %)

	Total	Married Men	Single Men	Single Wo
Less than $500	12.2	10.9	14.1	20.5
$500–$2,000	48.5	46.7	45.9	65.8
$2,000–$5.000	30.7	32.5	34.5	12.9
More than $5,000	8.6	9.9	5.5	.8

Source: SSA, "Retirement History Study."

A final source of income might be sharing among family mem
bers. But again, in line with the disintegration of the extended
family, this is not a widely anticipated option. Only 3.5 percent o

respondents expected help from relatives (the percentage did rise to 9.2 for single women).[54] In sum (except for help from families), the various sources of income tend to cluster. Those with significant assets upon retirement tend to own their own home, and to receive pensions that are relatively large.

An Assessment of the Positive State

This survey of American welfare provisions demonstrates both their anarchical character and their traditional neglect of the most disadvantaged. Clearly, these initiatives do not cohere into anything that could remotely qualify as a system; still less do they represent a policy commitment to a minimum standard. On the other hand, the vast array of overlapping programs might offer *individuals* the opportunity to combine public, private, and individual provisions to secure an acceptable standard of living (i.e., one above the poverty line). Has the United States then absentmindedly groped its way toward the social security state, erecting suitable programs that require only modest adjustments?

The argument in favor of this proposition rests on four interrelated points. First, the welfare gains over the past few years have too often been obscured by the well-publicized failure of Great Society programs to meet their professed goals and by the constant rhetoric regarding a "welfare crisis." Second, these welfare provisions taken as a whole do more for recipients than would most proffered alternatives. In particular, Nixon's "good deed," the Family Assistance Plan, would have provided less aid to the working poor than do food stamps.[55] Third, current weaknesses in welfare provision can be overcome within the context of existing programs and politics. "The need now is to fill in gaps that remain and take steps—some quite important ones—to improve and rationalize existing programs, rather than replace them with a comprehensive new system."[56] Finally, there exists an internal dynamic force that can fill these gaps through incremental adjustments. This idea we have found to have had a certain force particularly in the broadening and upgrading of the provisions of the original Social Security Act: Once a program is established it tends to develop its own momentum in the direction of expanded coverage. This being the case, legislative enactments need only spur this process along, correcting ad hoc what now can be described as technical not political problems (e.g., that minimum benefit levels are established for SSI but not for AFDC).

This argument, however enticing, is inadequate. First, like most contemporary American discussions of welfare reform, it overlooks the fact that a social security state (or a national minimum) rests on more than high benefit levels. Equally vital are two other props—a full employment policy to prevent recourse to compensatory benefits and a system of national health insurance to secure minimal levels of health care. The United States has neither in a fully developed form. To achieve either one requires a political commitment to major structural changes that incremental reform by its very nature cannot address.

Second, this argument fails to recognize that a viable national minimum rests on a social commitment that each individual is *entitled* to this minimum. He or she must possess a valid claim to it simply by being a citizen. The courts have recognized that citizens may possess claims to certain welfare provisions—that certain benefits are not simply public largesse to be terminated at will, but "statutory entitlements for persons qualified to receive them."[57] These rights pertain only to specific programs, however, and not to a generalized minimum standard of living.

The degree to which even our "liberal" social commentary has to go in the direction of a national minimum is indicated by Gilbert Steiner's comment in 1974 that "admitting more of the needy poor to the relief rolls, no matter how reluctantly, rather than keeping them off, no matter how ingeniously, is the quintessence of [American] welfare reform."[58] This development, while perhaps laudable, is no guarantee of entitlement. It does not lead to a political concern with adequate benefit levels; neither does it encourage an effort to find out who exactly is below the minimum and how he or she might be brought up to it. Steiner's term "needy poor" encapsulates the attitude of the positive state. In a social security state the word "needy" is redundant. All poor are needy by definition. Americans have yet to make an attitudinal break with the outlook of the new poor law: the feeling that it is basically inappropriate for the "poor" to get, let alone *demand,* welfare services at all. Thus there arises the telling difference that in Britain and Sweden there is great concern over "take-up rates" (i.e., whether all eligible people actually participate in programs), but in the United States the concern is to "purge the rolls" whether the purge affects the eligible or not.[59] For the poor, individual provision (which often means in practice individual abnegation) remains the public norm if not typically public policy. Public policy by stealth cannot effect a guaranteed minimum.

The third flaw in the apology for the current welfare system is its failure to recognize that the complexity of current arrangements effectively curtails provision of benefits. The whole issue of entitlement and benefit levels is so complex that few recipients possess the basic information on how much they ought to get.[60] Many welfare workers also lack the mastery of the available programs that would enable them to maximize recipients' benefits. Incremental reform may well complicate this problem still further. To serve its neediest clients effectively, a welfare system must be simple, and incremental reform cannot achieve this fundamental objective.

The fourth and decisive indictment of current welfare provisions is that despite public expenditures in the neighborhood of $150 billion, large numbers of Americans slip through the porous social safety nets and live lives of rugged poverty. The best data available to demonstrate this point have been collected by the University of Michigan Survey Research Center. These data allow one "to evaluate the adequacy of the transfer system in alleviating poverty" in 1971.[61] (The survey defined transfers as benefits from both social insurance and public assistance, including state general assistance; they excluded subsidized housing and medicare payments.) The data show that 15,059,000 American families (21 percent of the total) had incomes below the poverty level before the receipt of transfer benefits. Of these 15 million families, 20 percent, concentrated among male-headed families, received no transfer income whatever. Even after transfers, 57 percent, or more than eight million families, remained poor. The subsequent development of SSI and the expansion of food stamps have helped reduce the number of post-transfer poor, but the worsening of general economic conditions has tended to offset these gains. The welfare system does achieve some notable successes—without public transfer programs over half of aged and disabled families would have been poor—but the effectiveness of the transfer system in alleviating poverty is spotty at best, and our attentive readers can doubtless no longer restrain themselves from raising the query of the irate American taxpayer: Why, with all this spending, does poverty persist?

Regrettably, the statistics available do not allow a conclusive answer to this question, and consequently the explanation proffered retains an element of speculation. First, one must point to the large sums involved in federal income security programs that by policy choice are not targeted directly on the poor. By far the largest component of these outlays is Social Security, but of Social Security recipients only about a fifth are poor; the poor account for roughly the same percentage of medicare recipients.[62]

Secondly, there is little doubt that the current plethora of programs results in administrative duplication, waste, and inefficiency. The quality control system instituted by HEW to reduce errors in the AFDC program found in mid-1973 an error rate of 10.2 percent on eligibility, 22.8 percent on overpayments, and 8.1 percent on underpayments. The study concludes that:

> There is no doubt at all ... that the administrative cost component increases dramatically with both the degree of administrative discretion and the proliferation of separate programs. The administrative costs of the Institute for Research on Poverty's recently completed urban and rural negative income tax experiments are substantially less per family than those in the AFDC program. For a program that covered all families and unrelated individuals below 150 percent of the poverty level, such differences in administration would lead to differences in cost of about $3 billion.[63]

Efforts to enforce work requirements in welfare programs add further administrative costs. Scandal, perpetuated by unscrupulous housing operatives and devising academics persuaded that "there's money in poverty," further depletes the resources that actually reach the poor.

Finally, however, the essential reason why poverty persists despite sizable government programs is that the operation of American welfare institutions is not designed to relieve it; there is no concerted effort to provide security for the large number of economic casualties of the industrial order. At this point we might discuss the thought that economic growth will solve the problem without further public initiatives. First, the poor are unlikely to reap much benefit from growth:

> An increasing percentage of poor families are headed by someone who works only part of the year—or more often, who does not work at all because of ill health, old age, or home responsibilities, not from inability to find a job.[64]

Economic growth cannot provide immediate benefits to those who are at best only marginal members of the labor force. Secondly, economic growth not only moves persons up the income hierarchy, it drops them as well, leaving the aged, the unskilled, and the technologically outdated as its refuse. Thirdly, as we have seen, there is no indication that high aggregate levels of growth permit the universal acquisition of significant amounts of individual property. Finally, there is no evidence to indicate that economic growth eliminates poverty as inequality rather than poverty as income deficiency.[65] The number of persons suffering absolute deprivation has decreased as the American economy has grown, but the relative position of the poor has not improved. The poorest fifth of the population received 5.1 percent of total national income in 1947, 5.4 percent in 1974.[66]

The consideration that poverty is inequality and not just income deficiency introduces a broader-ranging indictment of American welfare institutions. Thus far, the analysis has proceeded on the postulate that informs most American analysis—the social security state assumption that the purpose of social welfare policy is to secure a minimum standard of living for all citizens. American welfare policy fails this test, but by substituting the assumption of the social welfare state—that the aim of policy is to produce a more egalitarian society—a more fundamental critique emerges. The exponent of the social welfare state cannot restrict his glance to the efficacy of the welfare system in protecting persons against poverty. He looks to the quality of life enjoyed by all members of the society. The egalitarian values upon which this sort of investigation are grounded may not be congenial to all, but at the very least this enterprise exposes the value preferences that permeate prevailing analyses. From this point of view, the total effect of social policy—the combination of government, quasi-private, and individual welfare arrangements—is radically deficient, not merely because it perpetuates poverty, but because it fails even to trifle with the structural inequalities and class privileges of the society. We pursue this argument in the next chapter.

8

Toward an American Social Welfare State

Our comparative analysis of social welfare policy in Britain, Sweden, and the United States suggests that interventionist regimes differ significantly. They vary in the policy instruments they employ and in the aims they pursue. Furthermore, these differences matter; they affect the security of individual citizens, the quality of living conditions, and the moral tone of the society. They give substance to the claim that the social security state, the social welfare state, and the positive state represent the three available sets of policy choices for interventionist regimes desiring to promote the well-being of their citizens.

Great Britain's social welfare policy still bears the stamp of Beveridge's principles. Its emphasis upon the provision of a secure national minimum, but not general equality, for its citizens casts it in the social-security state mold. Its neglect of economic efficiency has led to erosion of benefits and placed the entire system on shaky foundations, a sobering reminder of the way the attractive gains of the social security state can be imperiled by economic stagnation.

Sweden shows signs of moving beyond the social security state toward the social welfare state. The labor movement, the hitherto dominant force in Swedish politics, has shifted the social balance of power and succeeded in devising economic and social policies that have greatly benefited Swedish workers. While vast inequality of personal wealth remains, Sweden has not only protected its citizens against stark impoverishment, but created a rough general equality of living conditions.

The American positive state services the corporate sector more effectively than it does small business, workers in small businesses, and the needy. Private welfare provisions benefit those employed in the corporate sector, state programs benefit state employees, but the plethora of uncoordinated programs designed to aid welfare recipients fails to provide a satisfactory national minimum. Class differences in life styles remain blatant and political power continues to rest with the leaders of the corporate sector and their representatives.

The point of this comparative survey is not to equate Britain with the social security state and Sweden with the social welfare state—in some ways the British National Health Service corresponds more closely to the social-welfare state model than the Swedish program—and then to recommend that the United States imitate these countries. Rather, it is to give empirical grounding to the claim that the different models of policy choice represent critical alternatives for citizens and societies. We now want to argue that the social-welfare state model is the most attractive goal for American social welfare policy, one that is unrecognized and unduly neglected in current welfare reform proposals. After considering these proposals and their underlying values in the light of social-welfare statist aims, we present a program of reforms, assess the prospects of implementing it, and answer popular objections to it.

Current Reform Proposals

Two sets of reform proposals currently under debate could, if implemented, create an American social security state. The first, based on the conservative normative premises discussed in Chapter Three, would institute a negative income tax. The negative income tax guarantees every household a minimum income that is determined by the size of the family. The higher a household's earnings, the lower its public transfer payment becomes. At a certain level of income—the break-even level—the household becomes a net payer of taxes rather than a recipient of transfers. The primary aim of negative income tax proposals is to eliminate poverty at minimum cost without eliminating work incentives. As Christopher Green has written, "Negative income taxation, as it has been presented by Friedman and Lampman, represents a means to attack poverty with a minimum of income redistribution."[1]

Plans circulated within HEW and the Executive branch in 1974 would have established an Income Supplement Program (ISP) that would provide a basic income of $3,600 for a family of four. ISP would be universal in coverage and would extend cash payments only; it would replace three current programs, Aid to Families with Dependent Children, Supplemental Security Income, and food stamps. States could (and it is assumed, about 25 states would) supplement the basic benefit. The plan has a marginal tax rate of 50 percent, deemed sufficiently low to provide a strong work incentive. Despite skepticism about the value of work tests, the program includes one, if only for political reasons. By approximately halving current administrative costs, ISP's projected net cost over current programs is reckoned at about $4–$5 billion.[2]

The Income Supplement Program is the culmination of governmental discussion of income maintenance proposals that originated at least as early as 1968, when President Johnson appointed a Commission on Income Maintenance Programs. With the exception of the level of the minimum income guarantee and the work test provision, devised to appease the wrath of conservative legislators, ISP is a model of social-security state legislation. It bears all the attractive features of negative income tax plans: It is universal rather than categorical or restrictive in its coverage. It does not tax the earnings of the poor at confiscatory rates. It alleviates or removes the stigma attached to being on relief. It eliminates incentives for family instability. It allows the recipient to choose how to spend his or her income. It simplifies administration. It reduces the opportunities for social workers or other public agents to intrude upon the recipient's rights.

Nonetheless, there are disadvantages. The consolidation of existing programs may result in lower current benefits and reduced future increases for recipients; ex-HEW secretary Wein-

186

Income Supplement Program (ISP)

	Benefits at various earnings levels				Total income at various earnings level				Break-even level of earnings total income (benefit = 0)
	$0	$2000	$4000	$6000	$0	$2000	$4000	$6000	
Single individual	$1200	200	*	*	1200	2200	*	*	$2400
Childless couple	2400	1400	400	*	2400	3400	4400	*	4800
Single parent, one child	2400	1400	400	*	2400	3400	4400	*	4800
Single parent, three children	3600	2600	1600	600	3600	4600	5600	6600	7200
Two parents, two children	3600	2600	1600	600	3600	4600	5600	6600	7200
SSI individual	2300	1300	300	*	2300	3300	4300	*	4600
SSI couple	3300	2300	1300	300	3300	4300	5300	6300	6600
Disabled parent, three children	4050	3050	2050	1050	4050	5050	6050	7050	8100

Source: HEW department. Cited by John Inglehart, "Welfare Report: HEW Wants Welfare Programs Replaced by Negative Income Tax," *National Journal Reports*, 6, 42 (October 19, 1974), p. 1563.

berger supported ISP, among other reasons, because he believed it would minimize the costs of public welfare.[3] The provision of income in cash affords no assurance that recipients will employ it upon such necessities as food and shelter. ISP will bring its own administrative complexities, such as how to define income, households, and accounting periods, and how to reach recipients. Finally, from a social welfare state point of view, the income supplement program would mark only the beginning of the substantial redistribution of income, wealth, and power that American society requires. It neglects and perhaps undermines the objectives of full employment and economic efficiency by attacking the problems of poverty through income transfers alone without giving attention to general economic policy. It makes no provision for comprehensive national health care.

The second major reform proposal, "incremental reform," accepts many of the arguments against negative income tax proposals and contends further that negative income tax plans are politically less feasible than incremental improvements. The incrementalist case stresses, as we described in Chapter Seven, the recent revisions of the welfare system that have extended coverage and increased benefits: increases in Social Security payments, the inception of the Supplemental Security Income system, emergency unemployment compensation, Medicare and Medicaid, revenue sharing, the liberalization of Aid to Families with Dependent Children, and in particular the expansion of food stamps. It maintains that while the welfare system still requires important adjustments, it can be brought toward the social-security state level by strengthening and rationalizing existing programs.

The defects in the incrementalist program are simply the arguments for the negative income tax in another guise: The incrementalist's strategy would perpetuate administrative overlap; it would not allow the recipient a wide choice in spending his or her income; it would maintain current programs that stigmatize recipients. It would also need to be supplemented by a maximalist full employment policy and a national health care program, if the United States were to become a social welfare state. Of the two strategies, the relative simplicity of the negative income tax makes it superior to incremental reform, but either, properly implemented, could bring immense improvement in the condition of the disadvantaged.

Education plays virtually no role in either program. This fact is at once the greatest difference and the most significant advance on the antipoverty legislation of the 1960s. As a dominant strategy for eliminating poverty, education is out of place. As Miller and Roby correctly argue:

> By itself, the educational strategy for poverty reduction suffers from four major limitations: the strategy neglects many poor people [those not of school age, particularly the elderly and the very young]; its goals are difficult to achieve, requiring a radical redistribution of resources and first-rate staffs; the strategy is only partially effective for those youths who do obtain education because discrimination and other factors intervene between education and income; its heavy emphasis damages individuals and society by constricting channels of occupational mobility and by restricting the pluralism of social values.[4]

And, Miller and Roby might have added, most of the benefits of spending on education flow in any case to middle-class professionals and their children. The recognition of these points has meant an appropriately reduced role for education in antipoverty strategies.

The Underlying Values of Social Welfare Policy

The presumptions of the contemporary discussion of welfare reform virtually coincide with the goals of the social security state. The proposals and their justifications assume that the problem of social policy is how to eliminate poverty by ensuring the least advantaged a minimum standard of civilized life. Continued social inequality above the minimum standard is assumed, as the lengthy and detailed inquiries into preservation of work incentives, opportunity for upward mobility, and justice among various strata of the working and nonworking poor abundantly demonstrate. Similarly, the necessity for increasing the political power of the disadvantaged goes unaddressed, save for a few unrepentant antipoverty warriors still attracted by community action programs.[5]

The welfare reformers do not camouflage their ideological foundations, for they assume that their values are not controversial. The Congressional Joint Economic Committee's *Studies in Public Welfare* argue explicitly for the values of adequacy, incentives, and equity.[6] The committee's studies place primary emphasis upon the provision of sufficient benefits, the preservation of work incentives without encouragement of procreation or family separation, and the attainment of equity among different categories of aid recipients and the poor. The vision of a social policy dedicated to a classless society never appears.

Still more revealing about the climate of discussion is the HEW study, *Toward an Effective Income Support System: Problems, Prospects and Choices.*[7] This paper, prepared for an administration task force on welfare reform, is a product of the rethinking that followed the demise of the Nixon Family Assistance Plan. In the measured language with which it insinuates the case for a negative income tax, it gives the most detailed view available of the administrative position on welfare reform. What is particularly striking for the present discussion is the list of "Goals of an Income-Tested Welfare System" set down in the document.

The authors preface these goals with the remark that:

> Perceptions of exactly what problem areas constitute the "welfare mess" and how welfare reform should proceed depend largely on the goals established for an income-tested transfer system. Although there is likely to be disagreement about relative priorities and the means of accomplishment, *hopefully there can be fairly general agreement about the desirability of several general principles.* [Our emphasis.][8]

The general principles are listed as: *adequacy* (of income); *target-efficiency* (benefits concentrated upon the neediest); *administrative efficiency; horizontal equity* (people in similar circumstances or need receive similar treatment); *vertical equity* (people who earn more receive more total income than those earning less); *work incentives; family stability incentives; personal independence or self-sufficiency;* and *coherency and control* (the system is understandable in its operation and effect, and subject to policy and fiscal control). The HEW study concludes that "these goals should serve as the basis for evaluating the structuring or restructuring of a welfare system."[9]

It need hardly be said that these principles reflect the traditional liberal values of American society. With their stress on "target-efficiency," the work ethic, and formal justice they remain securely locked within the mold of the social security state. The assumption of consensus on values implies that technocratic solutions rather than political debates are in order. Nonetheless, could these principles (in particular, adequacy) be realized in practice, the result would be a far more effective and attractive system.

The continuation of the HEW paper vitiates any notion that its stipulated goals provide an adequate guide for policy formulation: "It must be emphasized . . . that these goals are not fully consistent with each other."[10] For example, to enhance work incentives, one must ensure that as welfare recipients earn higher wages, they are not rapidly stripped of their welfare benefits. But lowering the rate at which their benefits are reduced entails providing more benefits to persons in relatively higher income classes; it thus contradicts the goals of target efficiency or concentrating resources upon the poorest. If instead one attempts to preserve work incentives by lowering benefits at the bottom of the income scale, then the principle of adequacy is imperiled. "Trade-offs such as these," the authors conclude, "are unfortunate but unavoidable."[11]

Given these trade-offs, the "general agreement" about "general principles" is not very helpful, for the "relative priorities" of these goals is precisely the point at issue. Until one specifies which of these goals take preference, the ostensible consensus on principles can provide no direction. The conscious advocate of the social security state is certainly prepared to establish such priorities: For him adequacy must be the overriding criterion. Work incentives accordingly must give way somewhat, a sensible decision since the available evidence indicates that the obsession with the willingness to work of the poor is misplaced.[12]

The proponent of the social welfare state finds the goals of the social security state attractive, but eventually inadequate. Like Richard Titmuss, he believes that the whole welfare problem must be reformulated and that

... our frame of reference in the past has been too narrow. Thought, research, and action have focused too heavily on the poor; poverty engineering has thus been abstracted from society. Social policy has been seen as an *ad hoc* appendage to economic growth. The provision of benefits, not the formulation of rights [sic].

If we are in the future to include the poor in our societies we shall have to widen the frames of reference. We shall need to shift the emphasis from poverty to inequality, from *ad hoc* programs to integrated social rights, from economic growth to social growth.[13]

This appeal, couched in the tradition of R. H. Tawney, demonstrates how the values of the social welfare state require a conception of the tasks and purposes of social policy that is broader and more ambitious than prevailing conceptions of welfare reform.

Reform Proposals

The objectives of the social welfare state, it bears repeating, differ fundamentally from those of the social security state. Not merely adequate living standards for all, but a general equality of condition ought to prevail. Freedom not merely to develop one's own potential, but to participate in the formation of policy and the defense of one's rights is essential. Security provided through an efficient and relatively waste-free economy, and a greater degree of solidarity and fraternity represent aspirations more demanding than those of the social security state. These goals— equality, freedom, democracy, security, economic efficiency, and solidarity—constitute the touchstones of an advanced social welfare policy.

They entail proposals more radical than those required to establish a social security state. The aim of these proposals is not to destroy market mechanisms and private property, but to reorient these institutions so that they fulfill the most urgent needs of citizens. They must offer benefits not for the poor alone, but for the great majority of citizens. They require not merely care for the victims of advanced industrial society, but preventive efforts to forestall unemployment, disease, waste, and urban squalor. Accordingly, the agenda for an American social welfare state must include:

1. *Maximalist Full Employment.* Full employment provides the basis for economic growth, individual self-sufficiency, and expenditures on social welfare policy. It is, consequently, the fundamental objective of public policy. The full employment target should be set at 1.5 to 2.0 unemployment as currently defined; acceptance of a 5 or 5.5 percent unemployment rate as "full employment" is intolerable. This new target cannot be met and relatively stable prices maintained simply by regulating aggregate demand; more specific labor market policies are required. Special programs should be established to promote greater employment of minority teenagers, women, and the handicapped. Not only should growth be stimulated, but its direction should be altered by progressive taxation and by government investment in housing and railway construction, thus opening opportunities for less skilled workers.

2. *A National Health Service.* Medical care should be reckoned a right equivalent to education, provided essentially at public expense from general revenues in accordance with need. Ideally medical care should be organized as a public service, possibly with modest user charges. A public insurance program covering basic health care costs would be a second-best but acceptable solution. Greater emphasis ought to fall on preventive medicine, especially during pregnancy and childhood. What cannot be tolerated is a system built on private insurance with invidious distinctions among citizens who can and cannot afford such coverage.

3. *Housing Allowances.* A decent and prosperous society will assure each household suitable housing, for like education and medical care, adequate housing deserves to be a fundamental right of citizenship. Housing allowances might originally be based on need so as to prevent excessive start-up costs.

4. *A Public Pension System.* The goal of security requires that the chaotic private pension system be replaced with a public program guaranteeing income security for all retirees. The immense resources that will accumulate in this system offer an ideal lever by which public representatives can sway corporate investment decisions in the direction of greater economic efficiency and public utility.

5. *A Guaranteed Annual Income.* This program will operate like

a negative income tax, save that it will go to every citizen by right. The economic effect will be precisely the same, but the organizational principle will stress the equality of all members of the community rather than the special needs of the poor. Unlike most current negative income tax proposals it will undergird other social welfare programs rather than replace them; it forms part of a universal program of income security rather than being a residual device for coping with the poor.

6. *Progressive Taxation of Incomes and Capital.* The goals of equality and social solidarity forbid vast discrepancies among citizens' personal resources. The primary purpose of these tax measures is to decrease the extent of these differentials, and thus promote social solidarity and the freedom of the less advantaged. This tax policy is consistent with a lowering of corporate taxation, the incidence of which is normally passed on to the consumer, so long as unearned income from dividends is stiffly taxed.

7. *Community Planning and Land-Use Regulation.* The enormous social costs of private development and unregulated urban and industrial expansion must be reduced. The development of safe and attractive living and working environments and the preservation of natural amenities presupposes institutions of public control that narrow private interests cannot dominate.

8. *Termination of Capitalist Hegemony in the Cultural Sphere.* Personal and corporate wealth cannot be allowed sovereignty in determining the goods and services people use or the entertainments that they enjoy. The particular consequences of this principle are detailed and far-reaching, but at a minimum they imply greater public scrutiny and direction of large investment decisions and the elimination of commercial advertising on radio and television.

9. *Expanded Opportunities for Public Participation in Politics.* The extensive apparatus of American democracy affords vast opportunities for participation to those who have the resources of money and of time required. Through the creation of greater equality of resources, the social welfare state will improve the background conditions of politics and enhance access to public decision-making, but new arenas of political participation must open as well. The worker should have greater authority over his conditions of employment, the reci-

pient of public assistance greater discretion over the character of assistance he receives, and all citizens greater access to legal services. (To object that this program politicizes new spheres of life is unavailing; these spheres are already politicized, but without being democratized.)

This list of reform measures conforms to the description of social-welfare statist means in Chapter Two. It includes initiatives to improve the functioning of the market economy (1), to compensate for the inequities of the market (2–6), and to enhance public direction of community life (7–9). The agenda is not meant to be comprehensive or final, but only to highlight the major public initiatives required in the near future. Such undertakings as pursuit of solidaristic wage policy must result from private efforts and hence do not properly constitute part of this agenda.

The ideological bearing of these proposals resembles the position of advanced European Social Democrats, like the Swedish party commission chaired by Alva Myrdal which produced *Towards Equality*.[14] They differ from either traditional communism or capitalism, both of which focus on the formal ownership of the means of production. The social welfare statist considers formal ownership of secondary importance. "What is of prime importance is the distribution in society of the economic and political functions which are hidden beneath formal ownership."[15] This fact renders traditional ideological debate about the relative merits of private and public ownership both outdated and irrelevant.

In the American political arena social-welfare statist proposals fall well to the left of Republican and Democratic positions. Neither of the established parties has proved capable of clearly formulating issues or of provoking intelligent public debate about the real problems of the 1970s and 1980s, as the 1976 Presidential campaign demonstrated once again. The Republicans, despite their practical adjustment to the realities of government's role in a modern economy, still mouth the platitudes of the twenties. The Democrats, bent on electoral success, pursue a rampant incremental expansion of public spending with no coherent conception of its object or purpose. In reaction, some "new" Democrats have suggested public retrenchment and reject the policy of turning to government to solve public problems.[16] The social-welfare statist's proposals offer a coherent democratic and egalitarian alternative, free from both the lack of vision of the traditional parties and the defeatism of the "new" Democrats.

The eventual consideration and implementation of these proposals might effect a radical restructuring of the American party system. Both parties currently flounder in disorder. Intriguing consequences might result from the transformation of the two parties into a conservative party dedicated to the principles of the social security state and a social democratic party pushing for creation of the social welfare state. Farfetched as this proposal may seem at first, it amounts to little more than a modest evolutionary change from the current situation; and is, in fact, a sensible political strategy for both parties. The Republicans need voters, and *pace* conservative theoreticians like Phillips and Rusher, they will not find them by beating the anti-welfare statist drum, but rather by telling the party's country club establishment that it will have to accommodate itself to a new era. The Democrats require a bond to cement their upper middle-class and working-class supporters; the principles of the social welfare state, deftly handled, would provide this link.

Implementation

Proposals do not enact themselves; there must be a coalition of political forces that will endorse and execute them. There must be a political strategy that will define potential supporters of the proposals and rally their assistance. At times the portents appear dismal: The word "welfare" grates on millions of American ears, and conservative publicists flood the media with attacks on the modest social programs now in existence. Even the most incurable optimist would have to admit that resistance to an American welfare state is strong. Nonetheless, there are some encouraging signs.

First, the American welfare system as it now stands is far from ideal—expensive to operate, haphazard in its benefits, hard to comprehend, and inequitable in its results. The economy's recent bout with "stagflation" has exposed these problems anew. High levels of unemployment demonstrate the disadvantages for organized labor of nonpublic welfare provisions; health policies lapse and supplemental unemployment funds run dry. The "middle class" suffers from a double difficulty—the cost of essential nonpublic services (particularly health) escalates far faster than real wages, while the increasingly expensive policies produced by the welfare state machine no longer seem directly beneficial.[17]

Second, certain elements of the program, long deemed utopian and impractical, if not downright wicked, are now close to general acceptance. National health insurance has built such a substantial following that the question no longer is whether, but when and in what form it will appear. HUD has experimented with housing allowances and found them to possess advantages over current housing policy. The negative income tax has strong bureaucratic support and in the form of Nixon's Family Assistance Plan came close to passage, failing because some liberals voted against it. Pension reform, slowed by recent legislation, should regain momentum as the gaps in current coverage appear. All of these programs clearly have a place on the national agenda, for they have both bureaucratic and interest group support and are verging on general public acceptance, if only some relatively painless means of extracting the necessary revenues can be found. A re-expanding economy may not only generate these higher tax revenues, but even require them as a check on inflation.

A broad section of the population is prepared to entertain reformist measures. Public opinion polls show that the general public maintains an unstudied ambiguity toward social welfare programs. Polls in the mid-sixties showed:

> wide acceptance of proposals for national health insurance, federal government responsibility to do away with poverty, and increased spending in urban renewal, along with majority sentiment that relief rolls are loaded with chiselers, that any able-bodied person who really wants to work can earn a living, and that we should rely more on individual initiative and less on welfare.[18]

There is little reason to think that these views have changed, and the fact that the social welfare state can appeal to both sets of views (by stressing full employment as well as solidarity with the needy) suggests that the political situation is far more fluid than most commentators will allow.

Certain social-welfare statist proposals—notably full employment and the measures to democratize community life—attack fundamental capitalist privileges. They threaten to make the labor market a sellers' market and to redistribute political and social power. Accordingly, they generate far greater controversy and opposition. Their adoption will be more difficult. The remoteness of full employment under the Ford administration was painfully evident. Land-use planning is much discussed, but it is hotly contested wherever it threatens to undermine established business practices. Industrial democracy and restrictions upon commercial advertising on television and radio seem distinctly foreign notions.

Clearly these measures, absolutely essential if the positive state operating for business interests is to be transformed into a social welfare state serving the interests of non-propertied classes, require more than bureaucratic initiatives, interest group support, and public toleration. They will not pass without strong, enthusiastic, and even somewhat tumultuous support from the general public. Only in novels and social fantasies do privileged classes voluntarily renounce their birthright. In defense of the proposition that a strong popular consensus for these measures can be constructed, one might have resort to the accidents and abrupt swings of American political life, but there is a firmer basis for this claim.

A reservoir of potential supporters of the more radical social-welfare statist measures exists. The American labor movement, for all its flaws, remains committed to an improved existence for its members, at least in part through public legislation to redress the inequities produced by a capitalist economy. The civil rights movement contains similar currents. Meanwhile the opposing forces may be weakening. Vested interests have recently had to absorb some substantial blows. Top executives are forced to admit illegalities in open court. Watergate has left a stench of corruption around the Republican party. Environmental and energy problems continue to befuddle a nation accustomed to individualist rhetoric rather than solidaristic policy. Support for staunchly conservative policies has eroded; how much is unclear, but the possibility of major reorientation cannot be discounted.

The direction of this reorientation is admittedly less certain, as the support for Wallace and Reagan indicates. Here the social welfare statist places his faith in the fundamental decency of the population and the superior attractions of his position. As Barrington Moore has written,

> The practical failure of a set of institutions to live up to what is expected of them provides an atmosphere receptive to demands for a more or less extensive overhaul of the status quo. At this juncture the future course of events depends heavily upon the models of a better world that become available to various strategic groups in the population.[19]

The American people have long subscribed to the ideals of equality, liberty, democracy, and economic efficiency. The increasing vagaries of advanced industrialism have persuaded Americans that security is a valuable goal. It is the conception of solidarity that gives them pause, but the social welfare statist can appeal to the moral superiority of this ideal and to the increasing impotence of individualistic striving in a highly organized society. His task of persuasion is eased by the fact that only these values and proposals can give Americans what they most desire: good secure jobs, readily available health care, protection against the hazards of modern industrial life, attractive communities, and a sense of participation in the common life. With time the principles of the social welfare state will no longer seem utopian, but rather the only practical remedy to insufferable conditions.

Popular Objections

Simply presenting the case for the social welfare state, its program, and its potential supporters will not suffice to persuade many Americans of its merits. Certain notions are so deeply rooted in the popular consciousness that they must be faced directly and refuted. The fears aroused by these notions have long delayed essential reforms; thus one needs to show that the social welfare state does not promote inflation, sloth, environmental damage, inefficiency, or tyranny.

Are the social-welfare statist programs inflationary? In the short term the answer is quite probably yes, for certain spheres of the economy. Effective national health, housing, and pension programs would certainly raise demand in each area, simply because essential needs have long been neglected. For a time the new demands may outstrip available resources, creating inflationary pressures, though careful planning may permit rapid expansion of the supply of medical personnel, housing materials, and the like. Furthermore, it may be possible to eliminate the present duplication and waste of the private sector and to achieve economies of scale.

In the economy as a whole, however, the greater efficiency of the social welfare state should dampen inflationary pressures. Full employment should eliminate the current waste of human potential and reduce (though not eliminate) expenditures to cope with the social pathology that results from unemployment. The redistribution of income and wealth should increase work incentives for the rich, and partially purge the private sector of its propensity to waste and the production of trivia. Increased worker participation in industrial management should improve morale and possibly even productivity. In short, there is no reason to believe that the rise of the social welfare state would precipitate ruinous inflation.

Would the social welfare state impair economic efficiency by dampening work incentives and constricting the flow of savings and investment? In a recent and stimulating short study Arthur Okun, former chairman of the President's Council of Economic Advisors and himself a modest egalitarian, contends that the trade-off

> ... between equality and efficiency... is our biggest socioeconomic trade-off, and it plagues us in dozens of dimensions of social policy. We can't have our cake of market efficiency and share it equally.[20]

Yet Okun's own evidence strongly undermines this claim. As he correctly observes, current researchers have discovered virtually no significant effects of the present tax system upon the work effort of the affluent. The New Jersey work incentive experiment and related experiments indicate that public transfer payments have scarcely any effect upon primary earners' efforts, though they do reduce slightly the work effort of secondary earners (i.e., workers other than the head of the family).[21] The decline of work is a red herring, assiduously dragged out by conservative spokesmen, as is the notion that the progressive taxation of the social welfare state would depress the nation's rate of investment. In

1929, when federal taxes were low and barely progressive, the United States saved and invested 16 percent of its gross national product; in 1973, despite business lamentation about "soaking the rich," the nation saved and invested the same 16 percent of GNP.[22] What might be damaged is the incentive to innovate, should the social welfare state fail to provide enterprising smaller firms some counterweight against the large corporate sector, but this danger exists already in the positive state.

Would the social-welfare state's agenda be detrimental to the environment? Not to the human or social environment—its entire thrust is to recast these structures in more satisfying and humane forms. Nor is it likely that this agenda would seriously damage the natural environment. It does presume a high standard of material welfare, but at the same time it establishes limitations upon activities with high social costs. It encourages efficient production. And it inculcates a different view of human satisfaction; the human being is no longer regarded as an essentially acquisitive creature seeking to gratify his urge to consume. Instead persons are looked upon as creative rather than consuming beings, as creatures destined to order their environment, not ravage it.

Is the social-welfare state program bureaucratic? Certainly— there is no way to provide public services without large-scale organization. Large-scale organization, however, does not necessarily produce excessive inefficiency, regulation, or domination. The internal structure of the organization makes an enormous difference as the relative performance of the Social Security Administration and the Penn Central Railroad, or of Swedish and American welfare services at the local level demonstrates. Furthermore, as a constant antidote to bureaucratic rigidity the social welfare state enhances the opportunities for public criticism of, supervision over, and participation in, bureaucratic institutions.

Does the social welfare state lead down the "road to serfdom," by gradually curtailing individual rights and expanding governmental power?[23] Hardly—its ideology is based on liberty, equality, and democracy. It limits its incursions on traditional rights to property rights, particularly as they are vested in corporations. It leaves civil liberties inviolate, and indeed advocates a more consistent application of these principles than the United States has normally followed. To check potential abuses of public power it encourages citizen participation in interest groups such as labor unions, business groups, farm organizations, and public interest lobbies. To prevent an inadvertent and unintended descent into governmental domination the traditional mechanisms of electoral and judicial controls are supplemented with administrative remedies (like those provided taxpayers by the IRS), public review boards, and ombudsmen.

The development of the social welfare state will not produce a utopia. Certain attractive practices of liberal society will suffer. Supporting one's parents and relatives through an impersonal social insurance system is never likely to have the same human quality as direct familial support. Private philanthropy will necessarily contract as high progressive taxation takes effect; the opportunities for wealthy eccentrics will shrink. Small independent family businesses will probably continue to decline. None of these activities is an unmixed blessing, but at their best they typify an attractive bourgeois ideal of responsibility and service. It would take a modern Tocqueville to do justice to the relative gains and losses accompanying the arrival of the social welfare state, but the present argument will have served its purpose if it has persuaded readers of the strong relative advantages of the social welfare state and the weakness of popular objections to it.

The most serious objection to an American social welfare state has little popular backing. Indeed, it has scarcely been raised, though it is eminently worthy of debate: The United States may be too politically fragmented to produce the consensus required for effective administration of a social welfare state. Federalism confounds efforts to erect a satisfactory national income maintenance system and affords interest groups innumerable points of entry to bias policy in favor of their private interests.[24] The diffuseness of the private sphere creates obstacles of its own. With only about a fifth of the labor force unionized, there is no national wage-bargaining structure nor unified workers' movement. The economic and social policies of the social welfare state require the ability to plan coherently and administer impartially over lengthy periods, but the fragmentation and continental scope of American politics make the necessary consensus difficult to obtain and harder to maintain.[25]

To produce this consensus, with or without constitutional revision, will be the greatest challenge facing advocates of the welfare state. When consensus has been created, the United States has had minimal difficulty in establishing new structures to overcome the administrative hazards of the federal structure, as the adoption of Social Security (OASDI), the development of the interstate highway system, and civil rights legislation testify. The adoption of reforms is less a question of administrative feasibility than it is of power. The private structure to complement public initiatives may be slow to develop. The unions show few signs of readiness for a coordinated wages policy, and in any case they cannot claim to represent more than a minority of the labor force. As the assurance of full employment and individual economic security spreads, however, unions may be more prepared to suppress private interests in favor of coherent and solidaristic wage policies. In this way reforms may stimulate the desire for structural change and still more radical reforms.

Summary

The policy choices for advanced Western societies in general and the United States in particular are not "totalitarianism" and "democracy" or "capitalism" and "communism." These formulations only obscure policy-making and retard efforts to establish the proper forms and objectives of government intervention in economic markets and property relations. The real issue is whether public policy will approximate the model of the corporate-oriented positive state, the social security state with its national minimum, or the radically democratic and egalitarian social welfare state. By comparing the origins, structure, and performance of welfare policy in Britain, Sweden, and the United States, we have shown wide variations in regimes all often (though in the latter case, improperly) termed welfare states and thus indicated the empirical and political relevance of the three models of policy choice.

We have contended that the establishment of a social security state would greatly advance American social welfare policy, but that the creation of a social welfare state is an even worthier objective. The case for the social welfare state rests not only on the attractive record of Sweden, the closest approximation to it now in existence, but upon a distinct set of values and policy instruments. Equality, liberty, democracy, security, solidarity, and economic efficiency constitute the major goals of policy. Budgetary planning, active labor market policy, and solidaristic wage policy improve the functioning of private enterprise economies. Public services, social insurance, transfer payments, and progressive taxation redress the distributional inequities produced by an unregulated market system. Finally, various modes of participation enhance citizens' opportunities to oversee this apparatus and to give public guidance to community life. Neither the conservative claim that these institutions and policies diminish personal freedom nor the radical objection that these changes are superficial bears conviction. On this foundation we argue for our program of social democratic reforms and rest the case for an American social welfare state.

BIBLIOGRAPHY

This bibliography presents basic material for readers wishing to pursue the study of the theory and operation of the welfare state. It makes no pretense of being exhaustive.

I. Political Theory and the Welfare State

Arblaster, Anthony. "Liberal Values and Socialist Values," *The Socialist Register 1972*, eds. Ralph Miliband and John Savile. London: Merlin, 1972, pp. 83–104.

Baran, Paul. *The Political Economy of Growth.* New York: Monthly Review Press, 1957.

Berle, Adolf, and Gardiner Means. *The Modern Corporation and Private Property.* New York: Macmillan, 1937.

Bernstein, Eduard. *Evolutionary Socialism.* New York: Schocken, 1961.

Bodin, Jean. *Six Books of a Commonweale.* Cambridge, Mass: Harvard University Press, 1959.

Buber, Martin. *Paths in Utopia.* Boston: Beacon Press, 1960.

Buchanan, James. *The Limits of Liberty.* Chicago: University of Chicago Press, 1975.

Burke, Edmund. *Reflections on the Revolution in France.* Indianapolis: Liberal Arts Press, 1955.

Cohn-Bendit, Daniel and Gabriel. *Obsolete Communism.* New York: McGraw-Hill, 1968.

Cole, G. D. H. *Guild Socialism Restated.* London: Leonard Parsons, 1920.
———. *Self Government in Industry.* London: G. Bell and Sons, 1917.

Dahl, Robert, and Charles Lindblom. *Politics, Economics and Welfare.* New York: Harper, 1953.

Dietze, Gottfried. *In Defense of Property.* Baltimore: Johns Hopkins University Press, 1963.

Efron, Edith. "Conservatism: A Libertarian Challenge," *The Alternative* (October 1975).

Forsyth, Murray. "Property and Property Distribution Policy," London: P.E.P. Broadsheet No. 528, July 1971.

Friedman, Milton. *Capitalism and Freedom*. Chicago: University of Chicago Press, 1962.

Furniss, Edgar S. *The Position of the Laborer in a System of Nationalism*. Boston: Houghton Mifflin Company, 1918.

Furubotyn, Eirik, and Svetozar Pejovich. "Property Rights and Economic Theory: A Survey of Recent Literature," *Journal of Economic Literature* (December 1972).

Galbraith, John Kenneth. *The Affluent Society*. Boston: Houghton Mifflin, 1969.

————. *The New Industrial State*. Boston: Houghton Mifflin, 1971.

Gintis, Herbert. *Neo-Classical Welfare Economics and Individual Development* Cambridge, Mass.: M.I.T. Press, 1971.

Gorz, André. *Socialism and Revolution*. Garden City, N.Y.: Anchor Books, 1973.

Gramm, Warren. "Industrial Capitalism and the Breakdown of the Liberal Rule of Law," *Journal of Economic Issues*, 7, 4 (December 1973).

Greenberg, Edward. "Capitalism and the Welfare State: A Radical Critique." (Paper prepared for delivery at the Annual Meeting of the American Political Science Association, San Francisco, September 2–5, 1975).

Harbour, William. "The Foundations of Conservative Thought." Ph.D. dissertation, Indiana University, 1976.

Harrington, Michael. *Socialism*. New York: Bantam Books, 1972.

Harris, Ralph, ed. *Freedom or Free-for-all: Essays in Welfare, Trade and Choice*. London: Institute of Economic Affairs, 1965.

Hayek, Friedrich. *The Constitution of Liberty*. Chicago: University of Chicago Press, 1960.

————. *The Road to Serfdom*. Chicago: University of Chicago Press, 1944.

Heckscher, Eli. *Mercantilism*. London: George Allen & Unwin Ltd., 1955.

Hobhouse, L. T. *Liberalism*. New York: Oxford University Press, 1964.

Jewkes, John. *The New Ordeal by Planning*. London: Macmillan, 1968.

Keynes, John Maynard. *Essays in Persuasion*. London: Macmillan, 1972.

————. *The General Theory of Employment, Interest, and Money*. London: Macmillan, 1973.

Lenin, V. I. *What Is to be Done?* Oxford: Oxford University Press, 1963.

Lothstein, Arthur, ed. *All We Are Saying*. New York: Capricorn Books, 1971.

Luxemburg, Rosa. *Reform or Revolution*. New York: Pathfinder, 1970.

MacCallum, Gerald. "Negative and Positive Freedom," *Philosophical Review*, 76, 3 (1967).

Macmillan, Harold. *The Middle Way: A Study of the Problem of Economic and*

Social Progress in a Free and Democratic Society. London: Macmillan, 1938.

Maitland, Friedric William. "A Historical Sketch of Liberty and Equality," in *Collected Papers.* Cambridge, England: The University Press, 1911, Vol. I.

Mannheim, Karl. "Conservative Thought," in Kurt Wolfe, *From Karl Mannheim.* New York: Oxford University Press, 1971.

————. *Freedom, Power and Democratic Planning.* New York: Oxford University Press, 1950.

Marcuse, Herbert. *Eros and Civilization.* New York: Vintage, 1962.

————. *One-Dimensional Man.* Boston: Beacon Press, 1962.

————. "Repressive Tolerance," in Robert Paul Wolff, Barrington Moore, Jr., and Herbert Marcuse, *A Critique of Pure Tolerance.* Boston: Beacon Press, 1965.

Marx, Karl, and Friedrich Engels. *Basic Writings on Politics and Philosophy,* ed. Lewis Feuer. Garden City, N.Y.: Anchor, 1959.

Meade, J. E. *Efficiency, Equality, and the Ownership of Property.* Cambridge, Mass.: Harvard University Press, 1964.

Miliband, Ralph. *The State in Capitalist Society.* London: Weidenfeld & Nicolson, 1969.

Moore, Barrington. *Reflections on the Causes of Human Misery.* Boston: Beacon Press, 1972.

Moynihan, Daniel. "The United States in Opposition." *Commentary,* 59 (March 1975).

Myrdal, Alva. *Nation and Family.* Cambridge, Mass.: M.I.T. Press, 1968.

Myrdal, Gunnar. *Beyond the Welfare State.* New Haven: Yale University Press, 1960.

Nozick, Robert, *Anarchy, State and Utopia.* New York: Basic Books, 1974.

Oakeshott, Michael. *Rationalism in Politics and Other Essays.* New York: Basic Books, 1962.

Oates, Wallace. "An Economist's Perspective on Fiscal Federalism" (Paper presented at the ISPE Conference, January, 1976).

O'Connor, James. *The Fiscal Crisis of the State.* New York: St. Martin's Press, 1973.

Offe, Claus. "Advanced Capitalism and the Welfare State," *Politics and Society,* 3 (Summer 1972).

————. *Wohlfahrtsstaat und Massenloyalität.* Köln: Kiepenhauer & Witsch, 1975.

Ostrom, Vincent. *The Political Theory of a Compound Republic.* Blacksburg, Va.: Virginia Polytechnic Institute and State University, 1971.

Pateman, Carole. *Participation and Democratic Theory.* Cambridge, England: University Press, 1970.

Polanyi, Karl. *The Great Transformation.* New York: Rinehart, 1944.

Rawls, John. *Theory of Justice.* Cambridge, Mass.: Harvard University Press, 1971.
Schottland, C. I., ed. *The Welfare State.* New York: Harper & Row, 1967.
Shonfield, Andrew. *Modern Capitalism.* London: Oxford University Press, 1966.
Spencer, Herbert. *Data on Ethics.* London: Williams and Norgate, 1907.
Stretton, Hugh. *Capitalism, Socialism and the Environment.* Cambridge, England: University Press, 1976.
Sumner, William Graham. *The Challenge of Facts and Other Essays.* New Haven: Yale University Press, 1914.
Tawney, R. H. *The Acquisitive Society.* New York: Harcourt, Brace, 1920.
──── . *Equality.* London: Unwin Books, 1964.
Titmuss, Richard. *Commitment to Welfare.* London: Allen & Unwin, 1968.
──── . *Essays on 'The Welfare State'.* London: Unwin, 1963.
──── . *The Gift Relationship: From Human Blood to Social Policy.* New York: Pantheon, 1971.
Thurow, Lester. "Toward a Definition of Economic Justice," *Public Interest,* No. 31 (Spring 1973).
Towards Equality. Stockholm: Prisma, 1970.
Voegelin, Eric. *Science, Politics, and Gnosticism.* Chicago: E. Regnery, 1968.
De Vroey, Michel. *Propriété et Pouvoir dans les Grandes Entreprises.* Brussels: C.R.I.S.P., 1973.
Walzer, Michael. "Politics in the Welfare State," *Dissent* (January 1968).
Webb, Sidney and Beatrice. *The Break-Up of the Poor Law: The Minority Report of the Poor Law Commission.* London: Longmans, Green 1909.
Weber, Max. *The Methodology of the Social Sciences.* New York: Free Press, 1949.
Wigforss, Ernst, *Från Klasskamp till Samverkan.* (Stockholm, 1941).
──── . *Frihet et Gemenskap.* Stockholm: Tidens Förlag, 1962.
──── . *Socialism i Vår Tid.* Stockholm: Tidens Förlag, 1952.
──── . *Ur Mina Minnen.* Stockholm: Tiden, 1964.
──── . *Vision och Verklighet.* Stockholm: Prisma, 1967.
Wolin, Sheldon. *Politics and Vision.* Boston: Little, Brown, 1960.
Young, Michael. *The Rise of the Meritocracy.* Baltimore: Penguin, 1967.

II. The Welfare State in Practice

A. THE UNITED KINGDOM

Abel-Smith, Brian, and Peter Townsend. *The Poor and the Poorest.* London: G. Bell & Sons, 1965.

Atkinson, Anthony Barnes. *The Economics of Inequality*. Oxford: Clarendon, 1975.

———. *Poverty in Britain and the Reform of Social Security*. Cambridge, England: University Press, 1969.

Beveridge, William. *Full Employment in a Free Society*. London: Allen & Unwin, 1944.

———. *Power and Influence*. London: Hodder and Stoughton, 1953.

———. *Social Insurance and Allied Services*. New York: Macmillan, 1942.

———. *Unemployment: A Problem for Industry*. London: Longmans, Green, 1909.

Booth, Charles. *Life and Labour of the People in London*. London: Macmillan, 1902, Vol. II.

Brown, John. "Ideas Concerning Social Policy and Their Influence on Legislation in Britain 1902–1911." Ph.D. thesis, University of London, 1964.

Bruce, Maurice. *The Coming of the Welfare State*. London: B. T. Botsford, 1965.

Chester, T. E. *The British National Health Service*. Paris: O.E.C.D., 1975.

Eckstein, Harry. *The English Health Service*. Cambridge, Mass.: Harvard University Press, 1959.

Edsall, Nicholas. *The Anti-Poor Law Movement 1834–44*. Manchester, England: University Press, 1959.

Forder, A. *Penelope Hall's Social Services of England and Wales*. London: Routledge, 1971.

Fraser, Derek. *The Evolution of the British Welfare State*. London: Macmillan, 1973.

Furniss, Norman. "The Welfare Debate in Britain: Implications for the United States," *Public Administration Review*, 51 (May–June 1975).

Gilbert, Bentley. "Winston Churchill versus the Webbs: The Origins of British Unemployment Insurance," *American Historical Review*, 71, 3 (April 1966).

Harris, Jose. *Unemployment and Politics: A Study of English Social Policy 1886–1914*. Oxford: Clarendon Press, 1972.

Hoggart, Richard. *The Uses of Literacy: Aspects of Working Class Life*. London: Chatto and Windus, 1957.

Mackenzie, Norman, ed. *Conviction*. London: MacGibbon & Kee, 1958.

Marsh, David. *The Future of the Welfare State*. Baltimore: Penguin, 1964.

Nicholls, George. *A History of the English Poor Law*. London: John Murray, 1834.

Polanyi, George and Priscilla. *Failing the Nation: The Record of the Nationalized Industries*. London: Fraser Ansbacher, 1974.

Royal Commission on the Poor Laws and Relief of Distress. (1909). *Minutes of Evidence*.

Rowntree, B. Seebohm. *Poverty, A Study in Town Life*. London: Macmillan, 1902.

Slater, H. C. "Controlling the Cost of the British National Health Service," *International Social Security Review*, 25, 1 (1972).

Titmuss, Richard. *Income Distribution and Social Change*. Toronto: University of Toronto Press, 1962.

Townsend, Peter. *The Social Minority*. London: Allen Lane, 1973.

Walley, Sir John. *Social Security: Another British Failure?* London: C. Knight & Co., 1972.

Williams, Gertrude. *The Coming of the Welfare State*. London: Allen & Unwin, 1967.

Willnott, Phyllis, ed. *Public Social Services*. London: Bedford Square Press, 1973.

B. SWEDEN

Adler-Karlsson, Gunnar. *Reclaiming the Canadian Economy*. Toronto: Anansi, 1970. Originally published as *Functional Socialism: A Swedish Theory for Democratic Socialization*. Stockholm: Prisma, 1969.

Board, Joseph. *The Government and Politics of Sweden*. Boston: Houghton Mifflin, 1970.

Childs, Marquis. *Sweden: The Middle Way*. New Haven, Conn.: Yale University Press, 1961.

Cole, Margaret, and Charles Smith, eds. *Democratic Sweden*. London, 1936.

Hadenius, Stig, Björn Molin, and Hans Wieslander, *Sverige efter 1900: En modern politisk historia*. Stockholm: Aldus/Bonniers, 1972.

Hancock, M. Donald. *Sweden: The Politics of Post-Industrial Change*. Hinsdale, Ill.: Dryden, 1972.

Hendin, Herbert. *Suicide and Scandinavia*. New York: Grune and Stratton, 1964.

Hermansson, C. H. *Monopol och storfinans—de 15 familjerna*. Stockholm: Rabén & Sjögren, 1965.

Historisk statistik för Sverige. Del 1. Befolkning 1720–1967. Stockholm: Statistiske Centralbyrån, 1969.

Höjer, Karl. *Den Svenska Socialpolitiken*. Stockholm: Norstedt, 1969.

Holmberg, Per. "Svensk Socialpolitik—Nulage och Tendenser," in Bo Södersten, ed., *Svensk Ekonomi*. Stockholm: Raben & Sjögren, 1970.

Huntford, Roland. *The New Totalitarians*. New York: Stein and Day, 1972.

Inghe, Gunnar and Maj-Britt, *Den ofärdige välfärden*. Stockholm: Tiden, Folksam, 1970.

Israel, Joachim. "The Welfare State—A Manifestation of Late Capitalism," *Acta Sociologica*, 17, 4 (1974).

Jämlikhet, the Alva Myrdal Report to the Swedish Social Democratic Party, Stockholm: Prisma, 1969.

Jenkins, David. *Sweden and the Price of Progress.* New York: Coward-McCann, 1968.

Johansson, Lena. *Den vuxna befolkningens bostadsförhållanden 1968.* (Stockholm, 1971).

Johansson, Sten. *Politiska resurser: Om den vuxna befolkningens deltagande i de politiska beslutsprocesserna.* Stockholm, 1971.

Korpi, Walter. *Fattigdom i välfärden.* Stockholm: Tiden, 1971.

Landesorganisationen i Sverige. *Economic Expansion and Structural Change,* trans. T. L. Johnston. London: Allen & Unwin, 1963.

Lewin, Leif. *Planhushållnings Debatten.* Stockholm: Almqvist & Wiksell, 1967.

Meidner, Rudolf. *Co-ordination and Solidarity, An Approach to Wages Policy* Stockholm: Prisma, 1974.

Michanek, Ernst. *For and Against the Welfare State: Swedish Experiences.* Lecture given in Berlin, October, 1963. Stockholm: The Swedish Institute, 1964.

Myrdal, Alva. *Nation and Family.* Cambridge, Mass.: M.I.T. Press, 1968.

Myrdal, Gunnar, "Socialpolitikens Dilemma," *Spektrum,* 2, 3 and 4 (1932).

Nasenius, Jan, and Kristin Ritter, *Delad Välfärd.* Stockholm: Scandinavian University Books, 1974.

Ortmark, Åke. *Maktspelet i Sverige.* Malmö: Wahlström & Widstrand, 1967.

Parent, Jean. *Le Modèle Suédois.* Paris: Calmann-Levy, 1970.

Robinson, Derek. *Solidaristic Wage Policy in Sweden.* Paris: O.E.C.D., 1974.

Rosenthal, Albert. *The Social Programs of Sweden: A Search for Security in a Free Society.* Minneapolis: University of Minnesota Press, 1967.

Rustow, Dankwart. *Politics of Compromise.* Princeton, N.J.: Princeton University Press, 1955.

Snavely, William. "Macroeconomic Institutional Innovation: Some Observations from the Swedish Experience," *Journal of Economic Issues,* 6 (December, 1972).

Socialdepartmentet *Socialvården: Mål och medel.* Stockholm: Statens offentliga utredningar, No. 39, 1974.

Den Svenska Köpkraftensfördelning 1967. Stockholm: SOU 1971: 39.

Therborn, Göran, ed. *En ny vänster.* Stockholm: Rabén & Sjögren 1966.

Tilton, Timothy. "The Social Origins of Liberal Democracy: The Swedish Case," *American Political Science Review,* 68 (June 1974).

Tomasson, Richard. *Sweden: Prototype of Modern Society.* New York: Random House, 1970.

Verney, Douglas. "The Foundations of Modern Sweden: The Swift Rise and Fall of Swedish Liberalism," *Political Studies,* XX, 1 (March 1972).

C. THE UNITED STATES

Altmeyer, Arthur. *The Formative Years of Social Security.* Madison: University of Wisconsin Press, 1966.

Angus, Anne. "The Gains and Losses of the Poverty Programme," *New Society* (April 3, 1975).

Banfield, Edward C. *The Unheavenly City.* Boston: Little, Brown, 1968.

Barth, Michael, George Carcagno, and John Palmer. *Toward an Effective Income Support System.* Madison, Wis.: Institute for Research on Poverty, 1974.

Berle, Adolf, and Gardner Means. *The Modern Corporation and Private Property.* New York: Macmillan, 1932.

Bernstein, Barton. "The New Deal: The Conservative Achievements of Liberal Reform," in Bernstein, ed., *Towards a New Past.* New York: Random House, 1968.

Burke, Vincent and Vee. *Nixon's Good Deed: Welfare Reform.* New York: Columbia University Press, 1974.

Douglas, Paul. *Social Security in the United States.* New York: Whittlesey House, 1936.

Freeman, Roger. *The Growth of American Government: A Morphology of the Welfare State.* Stanford, California: Hoover Institution Press, Stanford University. 1975.

Galbraith, John K. "The Conservative Majority Fallacy," *New York* (December 22, 1975).

Glazer, Nathan. "The Limits of Social Policy," *Commentary,* 52, 3 (September 1971).

Goodwin, Leonard. *Do the Poor Want to Work?* Washington, D.C.: Brookings 1972.

Greenberg, Edward. *Serving the Few: Corporate Capitalism and the Basis of Government Policy.* New York: John Wiley, 1974.

Harrington, Michael. *The Other America.* Baltimore: Penguin, 1963.

Heclo, Hugh. "The Welfare State: The Costs of American Self-Sufficiency," in Richard Rose ed., *Lessons from America: An Exploration.* London: Macmillan, 1974.

Hennessey, Timothy, and Richard Feen. "Social Science as Social Philosophy: Edward C. Banfield and the 'New Realism' in Urban Politics," *American Behavioral Scientist* 17 (November–December 1973).

Humphrey, Hubert. *The Political Philosophy of the New Deal.* Baton Rouge, La.: Louisiana State University Press, 1970.

Inglehart, John. "Welfare Report: HEW Wants Welfare Programs Replaced by Negative Income Tax," *National Journal Reports,* 6, 42 (October 19, 1974).

Kirkendall, Richard, ed., *The New Deal: The Historical Debate.* New York: Wylie, 1973.

Kolko, Gabriel. *Wealth and Power in America.* New York: Praeger, 1962.

Kolodrubetz, Walter. "Employee-Benefit Plans, 1973," *Social Security Bulletin,* 38, 5 (May 1975).

Law, Sylvia. *Blue Cross: What Went Wrong?* New Haven, Conn.: Yale University Press, 1974.

Levine, Robert. *The Poor Ye Need Not Have with You.* Cambridge, Mass.: M.I.T. Press, 1970.

Marris, Peter, and Martin Rein. *Dilemmas of Social Reform.* Chicago: Aldine, 1973.

Miller, Arthur. "The Legal Foundations of the Corporate State," *Journal of Economic Issues,* 6, 1 (March 1970).

Miller, S. M., and Pamela Roby. *The Future of Inequality.* New York: Basic Books, 1970.

Moynihan, Daniel. *Maximum Feasible Misunderstanding.* New York: Free Press, 1969.

Myers, Robert. *Social Security.* Bryn Mawr, Pa.: McCahan Foundation, 1975.

Nathan, Richard P. "Food Stamps and Welfare Reform." (Address given at Fredericksburg, Va., February 4, 1975.)

——— . "Tax Aid to the Poor—Reconsidered," *The Wall Street Journal* (April 24, 1974).

Nelson, Daniel. *Unemployment Insurance: The American Experience, 1915–1935.* Madison: University of Wisconsin Press, 1969.

Okun, Arthur. *Equality and Efficiency: The Big Trade-off.* Washington, D.C.: Brookings, 1975.

Pechman, Joseph, and Michael Timpane. *Work Incentives and Income Guarantees: The New Jersey Negative Income Tax Experiment.* Washington, D.C.: Brookings, 1975.

Piven, Frances Fox, and Richard Cloward. *Regulating the Poor.* New York: Pantheon Books, 1971.

Polenberg, Richard. *War and Society: The United States 1941–1945.* Philadelphia: Lippincott, 1972.

Schweitzer, Arthur. "American Competitive Capitalism," *Schweizerische Zeitschrift für Volkswirtschaft und Statistik,* 92, 1 (1956).

Skolnik, Alfred. "Workmen's Compensation Under Scrutiny," *Social Security Bulletin,* 37, 10 (October 1974).

Social Security Administration, Office of Research and Statistics, "Retirement History Study" (Ongoing Studies published periodically in the *Social Security Bulletin*).

Steiner, Gilbert. "Reform Follows Reality: The Growth of Welfare," *The Public Interest* (Winter 1974).

——— . *The State of Welfare.* Washington: Brookings, 1971.

Stockman, David. "The Social Pork Barrel," *The Public Interest* (Spring 1975).

Swope, Gerald. "The Responsibilities of Modern Industry," *Industrial Management: The Engineering Magazine* 62, 6 (December 1926).

Thompson, Gayle. "Blacks and Social Security Benefits; Trends, 1960–73," *Social Security Bulletin*, 38, 4 (April 1975).

U.S. Congress, Joint Economic Committee. *Studies in Public Welfare* Papers 1–20 (Washington, D.C., 1972–1974).

Witte, Edwin. *The Development of the Social Security Act*. Madison: University of Wisconsin Press, 1962.

———, ed. *Social Security Perspectives*. (Madison University of Wisconsin Press, 1962.

Worthington, Nancy. "National Health Expenditures 1929–74," *Social Security Bulletin*, 38, 2 (February 1975).

D. COMPARATIVE

Anderson, Odin. *Health Care: Can There be Equity?* New York: Wiley, 1972.

Briggs, Asa. "The Welfare State in Historical Perspective," *Archives Européenes de Sociologie* (1961).

Collier, David, and Richard Messick. "Prerequisites versus Diffusion: Testing Alternative Patterns of Social Security Adoption," *American Political Science Review*, 59, 4 (December 1975).

Dorwat, Reinhold. *The Prussian Welfare State Before 1740*. Cambridge, Mass.: Harvard University Press, 1971.

Green, Christopher. *Negative Taxes and the Poverty Problem*. Washington, D.C.: Brookings, 1966.

Heclo, Hugh. "Frontiers of Social Policy in Europe and America," *Policy Sciences*, 6 (1975).

———. *Modern Social Politics in Britain and Sweden*. New Haven, Conn.: Yale University Press, 1974.

Heidenheimer, Arnold, Hugh Heclo, and Carolyn Adams. *Comparative Public Policy: The Politics of Social Choice in Europe and America*. New York: St. Martin's, 1975.

King, Anthony. "Ideas, Institutions and the Policies of Governments: A Comparative Analysis," *British Journal of Political Science* V, 3, 4.

Lindberg, Leon, et al. *Stress and Contradiction in Modern Capitalism*. Lexington, Mass.: Lexington Books, 1975.

Marshall, T. H., "The Welfare State," *Archives Européenes de Sociologie* (1961).

Mukherjee, Santosh. "Making Labour Markets Work," *Political and Economic Planning* (Broadsheet 532: January 1972).

Pachter, Henry, "Three Economic Models," in Irving Howe, ed., *Essential Works of Socialism*. New York: Holt, Rinehart and Winston, 1970.

Parkin, Frank. *Class Inequality and Political Order*. New York: Praeger, 1972.

Rein, Martin, and Hugh Heclo. "Welfare & A Comparison," *New Society*, 27, 59 (January 1974).

Rennison, G. A. *We Live Among Strangers: A Sociology of the Welfare State.* Melbourne: University of Australia Press, 1970.

Scase, Richard. "Images of Inequality in Sweden and Britain," *Human Relations*, 28, 3 (April 1975).

Shonfield, Andrew. *Modern Capitalism.* London: Oxford University Press, 1965.

Sleeman, J. F. *The Welfare State: Its Aims, Benefits and Costs.* London: Allen & Unwin, 1973.

Thoenes, Piet. *The Elite in the Welfare State.* London: Faber, 1966.

Titmuss, Richard. "Choice and the 'welfare state'" (Fabian Tract 370: February 1967).

————. *Social Policy.* London: Allen and Unwin, 1974.

Touraine, Alain. *The Post Industrial Society.* New York: Random House, 1971.

Waltman, Jerold. "Comparing Public Policies." Ph.D. dissertation, Indiana University, 1975.

Wilensky, Harold. *The Welfare State and Equality.* Berkeley: University of California Press, 1975.

Notes

Introduction

1. Max Weber, "Objectivity in Social Science and Social Policy," *The Methodology of the Social Sciences* (New York: Free Press, 1949), pp. 56–57. Italics in original.

2. John Plamenatz, "The Uses of Political Theory," in A. Quinton, ed., *Political Philosophy* (New York: Oxford University Press, 1967), p. 25. Italics in original.

3. Lawrence Frank has cogently argued the need for a new political theory in America. "The New Deal, which enlarged governmental services and financial support, was followed by the New Frontier, and now by the Great Society programs. Although these slogans have evoked support for often reluctantly adopted measures, they have not been productive of a new political theory rationalizing these departures from our accepted beliefs about the limited powers and responsibilities of government." "The Need for a New Political Theory," in Daniel Bell, ed., *Toward the Year 2000* (Boston: Beacon Press, 1970), p. 179.

Chapter 1

1. A. F. K. Organski, *Stages of Political Development* (New York: Knopf, 1967), p. 176.

2. Cf. David Collier and Richard Messick, "Prerequisites versus Diffusion: Testing Alternative Patterns of Social Security Adoption," *American Political Science Review*, 59,4 (December 1975), 1299–1315.

3. Reinhold Dorwat, *The Prussian Welfare State Before 1740* (Cambridge, Mass.: Harvard University Press, 1971), pp. 19–21.

4. Jean Bodin, *Six Books of a Commonweale* (Cambridge, Mass.: Harvard University Press, 1959), p. 9. No definitive version of the *Republic* (Six Books) was made. The work was first written in French and then rewritten with omissions and additions in Latin. The 1606 Knolles translation (edited by Kenneth D. McRae) used here is a composite of the two. We have modernized the spelling and some word ordering.

5. Ibid.

6. Bodin, p. 675. Our italics.

7. Bodin, p. 11.

8. See, for example, the account in Eli Heckscher, *Mercantilism* (London: George Allen & Unwin, 1955), Vol. II, pp. 13–49, 238–261.

9. This issue is considered in detail by Edgar S. Furniss, *The Position of the Laborer in a System of Nationalism* (Boston: Houghton-Mifflin, 1918), pp. 157–197.

10. Daniel Defoe, *Giving Alms no Charity, and Employing the Poor a Grievance to the Nation* (London, 1704), p. 27.

11. Bodin, p. 84. For a brief discussion of the universalization of the French term "sovereignty," see Alexander Passerin d'Entrèves, *The Notion of the State* (Oxford: Oxford University Press, 1967), pp. 99–103.

12. *Entick* v. *Carrington.* State Trials, XIX, 1029 (1765). Nelson Lasson, *The History and Development of the Fourth Amendment to the United States Constitution* (Baltimore: Johns Hopkins University Press, 1937), pp. 13–50, remains an excellent source on the early development of this concept. See also Richard Harris, "The Liberties of Every Man," *The New Yorker* (November 3, 1975).

13. The development in liberal thought of the distinction between government and society and the identification of the latter with economics is presented by Sheldon Wolin, *Politics and Vision* (Boston: Little Brown, 1960), pp. 286–351. The quotation is from page 291.

14. Karl Polanyi, *The Great Transformation* (New York: Rinehart, 1944), p. 57.

15. The two most prominent semi-exceptions were France and the United States. France didn't really experience a consumer boom; the United States, for example, remained well below the 1926–1928 level. See David Landes, *The Unbound Prometheus* (London: Cambridge University Press, 1969).

16. Landes, p. 391.

17. Data taken from the United Nations Economic Commission for Europe: Publication No. 1954 II E.3, *Growth and Stagnation in the European Economy* (Ingvar Sverrilson, author), tables A.22, A.28, A.31.

18. *Statistical Abstract of the United States, 1939.* In Britain the plight of some localities such as Ebbw Vale where the iron-steel plant closed in 1929 gained particular notoriety. The division of countries into different "nations" depending on their reliance on heavy industry is given powerful expression by J. B. Priestly, *English Journey* (New York: Harper and Brothers, 1934).

19. *Growth and Stagnation of the European Economy,* table 3; *Statistical Abstract of the United States, 1950.*

20. Cross-national data on consumption patterns are sketchy. The

record for the United States, however, seems clear. See S. H. Hymans, "The Cyclical Behavior of Consumers Spending, 1921–61," *Southern Economic Journal*, 32, 1 (July 1965), 23–33. This uniqueness of the Great Depression has been used to propose a greater identity between "classical" and "Keynesian" economics than is popularly supposed. Keynes in his *General Theory*, it is advanced, was describing only a *particular* case. It was, of course, the case that mattered. For an excellent discussion of this question see Axel Leijonhufvud, *Keynes and the Classics* (London: Institute of Economic Affairs, 1971), Occasional Paper No. 30.

21.   "American Competitive Capitalism," *Schweizerische Zeitschrift für Volkswirtschaft und Statistik*, 92, 1 (1956), 35–36. Our italics.

22.   See the discussion by Gottfried Dietze, *In Defense of Property* (Baltimore: Johns Hopkins University Press, 1963), pp. 109–111.

23.   Charles Dickens, Charles Napier, Léon Faucher, and Alexis de Tocqueville. Quoted in Steven Marcus, *Engels, Manchester, and the Working Class* (New York: Random House, 1974), pp. 28–66.

24.   Charles Booth, *Life and Labour of the People in London* (London: Macmillan, 1902), Vol. II.

25.   This was the conclusion of B. Seebohm Rowntree's classic study of York: *Poverty, A Study in Town Life* (London: Macmillan, 1901). Rowntree's research also laid to rest the belief that London was peculiarly afflicted as the catchment area for the dregs of society, and that poverty would be significantly less in the provinces.

26.   Whether, as Adolf Berle and Gardiner Means contended in their classic study, *The Modern Corporation and Private Property* (New York: Macmillan, 1937), control has become vested in management or whether, as Michel de Vroey argues persuasively in *Propriété et Pouvoir dans les Grandes Entreprises* (Brussels: R.I.S.P., 1973), large property owners remain in charge is as yet not relevant to our discussion.

27.   Wallace Peterson, "The Corporate State, Economic Performance, and Social Policy," *Journal of Economic Issues*, 8,2 (June 1974), 487.

28.   Indeed, the general consensus is that it cannot. For an overview see Eirik Furubotyn and Svetozar Pejovich, "Property Rights and Economic Theory: A Survey of Recent Literature," *Journal of Economic Literature* (December 1972), 1137–1162. The difficulty of justifying taxation on pollution generated by the exercise of property is used by the "property rights school" to argue against such levies. The difficulty can also be overcome by attenuating the property rights themselves.

29.   This position follows from the tenets of "political economy" which rest on the assumption of discrete units each intent on maximizing its self interest. Wallace Oates states that "the outcome is efficient resource allocation in the public sector." "An Economist's Perspective on Fiscal Federalism" (Paper presented at the ISPE conference, January 1976), 10.

30. See the discussion of Hillel's saying in Kurt Wolff, ed., *From Karl Mannheim* (New York: Oxford University Press, 1971), CVIII–CXII. This issue was central in all of Mannheim's writings after his departure from Germany. For an extended review see "Thought at the level of Planning," and "Freedom at the Level of Planning," in *Man and Society in an Age of Reconstruction* (London: Routledge, 1940), pp. 147–236, 269–281.

31. It might be useful to note explicitly that while the models correspond roughly to the institutional structure in the United States, Britain, and Sweden respectively, none is congruent with all the features of any state. It is especially important to avoid the identification of our normative preference, the social welfare state, with the political culture of Sweden which is unique and separable.

32. This term has been widely used to describe the legal position of corporations in America. For an excellent review see Arthur Miller, "The Legal Foundations of the Corporate State," *Journal of Economic Issues*, 6,1 (March 1972), 60–73. The term has recently been applied specifically to welfare issues by Edward Greenberg, *Serving the Few: Corporate Capitalism and the Basis of Government Policy* (New York: John Wiley, 1974), esp. pp. 3–32. Greenberg would tend to see its applicability to all modern capitalist states. We review this argument in Chapter Four.

33. Warren Gramm, "Industrial Capitalism and the Breakdown of the Liberal Rule of Law," *Journal of Economic Issues*, 7,4 (December 1973), 579. The legal implications of this relationship are detailed at some length by Kenneth Davis, *Discretionary Justice* (Baton Rouge: Louisiana State University Press, 1969).

34. That the pattern of distribution produced by government-business cooperation is somehow optimally efficient is a notion that permeates the ideas even of "liberal" American economists. For an example see Arthur Okun, *Equality and Efficiency: The Big Trade-off* (Washington, D.C.: Brookings, 1975).

35. Richard Titmuss, *Social Policy* (New York: Pantheon, 1974), p. 48.

36. William Beveridge, *Social Insurance and Allied Services* (New York: Macmillan, 1942), p. 13.

37. Ibid., pp. 6–7.

38. Ernst Wigforss, "Förstamajtal 1962," *Frihet och Gemenskap* (Stockholm: Tidens Förlag, 1962), pp. 149–150.

39. An excellent (and somewhat envious) account is provided by Santosh Mukherjee, "Making Labour Markets Work," *Political and Economic Planning* (Broadsheet 532: January 1972). We discuss this policy further in Chapter Six.

40. The program was first elaborated fully in the 1951 Report, "Trade Unions and Full Employment." A useful summary is given by Derek Robinson, *Solidaristic Wage Policy in Sweden* (Paris: O.E.C.D., 1974).

41. Harold Wilensky, *The Welfare State and Equality* (Berkeley: University of California Press, 1975), pp. 116–119, makes what might appear a similar contrast between what he calls the welfare state (our social security state) and the welfare society. In his description of the latter, however, he avoids discussing notions of equality or participation and concentrates on "universal issues of citizen survival"—mainly crime and pollution. In this sense he can suggest that the welfare state might inhibit a welfare society; the latter remains an elite activity. The social welfare state as we describe it entails a shift in *political power*. Safeguards against pollution are far from the most important of its activities.

42. So essential is this shift that Andrew Martin declares that for a social welfare state to be successful a working class party must be in continuous political control. See his interesting article, "Is Democratic Control of Capitalist Economies Possible?" in Leon Lindberg, et al., eds., *Stress and Contradiction in Modern Capitalism* (Lexington, Mass.: Lexington Books, 1975), pp. 13–56.

43. See Wilensky, *The Welfare State and Equality*, pp. 15–19.

Chapter 2

1. Sidney Hook, "'Welfare State'—A Debate that Isn't" in C. I. Schottland, ed., *The Welfare State* (New York: Harper & Row, 1967), p. 165.

2. Maurice Bruce, *The Coming of the Welfare State* (London: B. T. Botsford, 1965), pp. 16, 17, 259.

3. Gunnar Adler-Karlsson, *Reclaiming the Canadian Economy* (Toronto: Anansi, 1970), pp. 3, 2. Originally published as *Functional Socialism: A Swedish Theory for Democratic Socialization* (Stockholm: Prisma, 1969).

4. Piet Thoenes, *The Elite in the Welfare State* (London: Faber, 1966), p. 133.

5. Ibid. Barrington Moore has argued that these "negative" aims are actually the most compelling, *Reflections on the Causes of Human Misery* (Boston: Beacon, 1972).

6. Gunnar Myrdal, "Socialpolitikens Dilemma, I" *Spektrum*, 2, 3 (1932), p. 6.

7. George Wright, "The High Cost of Rawls' Inegalitarianism," *Western Political Quarterly*, 30,1 (March 1977).

8. Ernst Wigforss, *Socialism i vår tid* (Stockholm: Tidens Förlag, 1952), p. 24.

9. As Michael Young has shown in *The Rise of the Meritocracy* (Baltimore: Penguin, 1967). See Chapter Four for a more detailed discussion of this point.

10. *Towards Equality* (Stockholm: Prisma, 1970), p. 15.

11. Arthur Okun, *Equality and Efficiency: The Big Trade-off* (Washington, D.C.: Brookings, 1975).

12. Ibid., p. 79.

13. *Towards Equality*, p. 16. This discussion of the ends and means of the social welfare state is substantially indebted to this volume.

14. Gerald MacCallum, "Negative and Positive Freedom," *Philosophical Review*, 76, 3 (1967), 314.

15. R. H. Tawney, *Equality* (London: Unwin Books, 1964), p. 164.

16. L. T. Hobhouse, *Liberalism* (New York: Oxford University Press, 1964), p. 17.

17. Eduard Bernstein, *Evolutionary Socialism* (New York: Schocken, 1961), pp. 149–159.

18. Ernst Wigforss, *Från Klasskamp till Samverkan* (Stockholm, 1941), p. 25. A valuable discussion of liberal and socialist views of freedom, to which we are indebted, is Anthony Arblaster, "Liberal Values and Socialist Values," in Ralph Miliband and John Savile, eds., *The Socialist Register, 1972* (London: Merlin, 1972), pp. 83–104.

19. See R. H. Titmuss, *The Gift Relationship* (New York: Pantheon, 1971).

20. Hobhouse, *Liberalism*, p. 67.

21. "The need for security is the strongest impulse behind the development of the modern welfare society. It manifests itself on both the material and on the spiritual or psychic plane, in the need for security as a basis for physical existence as well as in the need for a secure anchorage in society and in relations with other people. Freedom has little meaning for those who do not possess security. Bourgeois, and in particular liberal, ideologies have often tried to see a conflict between security and freedom, and still more between security and efficiency. The utilitarian psychology of the eighteenth century, which provided the basis for this ideology, interprets human beings as fundamentally calculating and selfish; and on this view the only spurs to increased effort are intense competition, insecurity, and the prospect of material gain. This psychology is at the root of the doctrine of free competition and its superiority, and of the whole view of society on which modern capitalism has been founded.

"However, the modern social sciences see in security a very important factor in the development both of the individual and of society. Human beings are regarded primarily as social creatures, whose complicated and often irrational character and behavior develop through close interaction with their surroundings, and who have a great need of secure relations with this environment in order to live harmoniously. Security is [thus] a prerequisite of liberty and efficiency." Landesorganisationen i Sverige, *Economic Expansion and Structural Change*, trans. T. L. Johnston (London: Allen & Unwin, 1963), pp. 30–31.

22. Myrdal, "Socialpolitikens Dilemma."

23. Daniel Moynihan, "The United States in Opposition," *Commentary*, 59 (March 1975), 19–26.

24. The Swedish Social Democrats see these aims as complementary, contending that "socialism should be seen as a freedom movement, in which freedom from the pressure of external circumstances, class divisions and insecurity is considered a *prerequisite* for new human relationships marked more by cooperation and community and less by self-assertion, competition and conflict among various groups in society." *Towards Equality*, p. 15.

25. Lester Thurow, "Toward a Definition of Economic Justice," *Public Interest*, No. 31 (Spring, 1973), 57.

26. Thus a Swedish trade union study concludes: "Free competition and planning are often contrasted with one another as pure systems of economic policy. We have not based our program on either, but have instead begun quite empirically from the mixed economy characteristic of the present structure of our economy. . . .

"In an economy of the present type we cannot expect competition to become so wide in scope that it alone could determine the course of development. Even if, against all the odds, this were to prove possible we would not regard it as a fortunate solution. Many major needs cannot be satisfied through the typical profit economy; much intervention and redistribution are necessary. At the same time, competition can *to some extent, within the framework* of certain government controls and intervention and, in particular, through free trade, be *one* of the measures at work in an economic policy directed to bringing about structural adjustment.

"A completely planned economy which satisfied our requirement of free choice by consumers would encounter many grave problems. It would be susceptible to political pressures and the stresses that can arise when great expectations and practicable results cannot be reconciled. At the same time, the size of the public sector and the need for various forms of social intervention in the economy mean that a large measure of official direction is inevitable. This should be as well planned and coordinated as possible." Landesorganisationen, *Economic Expansion and Structural Change*, pp. 167–168

27. Adler-Karlsson, *Reclaiming the Canadian Economy*, p. 16.

28. J. M. Keynes, *Essays in Persuasion* (New York: Harcourt, Brace, 1932), p. 321. Our emphasis.

29. David Jenkins, *Sweden and the Price of Progress* (New York: Coward-McCann, 1968), p. 86.

30. Harold Wilensky, *The Welfare State and Equality* (Berkeley: University of California Press, 1975), p. 37.

Chapter 3

1. John Rawls, *Theory of Justice* (Cambridge, Mass.: Harvard University Press, 1971), pp. 12–15: Robert Nozick, *Anarchy, State, and Utopia* (New York: Basic Books, 1974), pp. 150–182. In a state properly ordered on a market basis, Nozick does not feel that the proviso would have much, if any, actual relevance.

2. This point is made with his typical vigor in a private communication by Charles Hyneman.

3. Edith Efron, "Conservatism: A Libertarian Challenge," *The Alternative* (October 1975), 10, 11.

4. *Reflections on the Revolution in France* (Indianapolis: Liberal Arts Press, 1955), p. 110.

5. In an important and relatively neglected essay, Karl Mannheim has shown that soon after Burke this "organic society" disappeared. "Conservative Thought," collected in Kurt Wolff, *From Karl Mannheim* (New York: Oxford University Press, 1971), pp. 132–222.

6. *Reflections*, p. 109.

7. For a development of a theory of the state from the perspective of the "Property Rights School" see James Buchanan, *The Limits of Liberty* (Chicago: University of Chicago Press, 1975).

8. As Peter Witonski states, "The point I have tried to make in my writings . . . is that there is no conservative *gestaltprinzip*. I could not call myself a conservative in, say, Spain or France, or any other country where the conservative tradition is predicated upon authoritarian nostrums. But, as an American I gladly embrace the term, because I understand the American orthodoxy as being a liberal orthodoxy, and, like most of my fellows, I wish to conserve it." Letter in *The Alternative* (December 1975), 37. For those who object to the designation "conservative," Friedrich Hayek has suggested "Old Whigism": "Why I am not a Conservative," in *The Constitution of Liberty* (Chicago: University of Chicago Press, 1960), pp. 395–411. The term "neo-conservative" has also enjoyed a recent vogue.

9. The quotation is from Jean-Baptiste Say, *A Treatise on Political Economy* (New York: "Reprints of Economic Classics, 1964), p. 200. First published in 1820, Say's work is probably the first economic "text" and as such was widely disseminated.

10. Adam Smith, *The Wealth of Nations* (Oxford: Clarendon Press, 1880), Vol. II, Book 4, Chapter 5. Quotation, p. 97.

11. Edward Stanley Robertson, "The Impracticality of Socialism," in Thomas Mackay, ed., *A Plea for Liberty* (New York: D. Appleton, 1891), pp. 56–67.

12. *The Economist* May 28, 1921. The document quoted from is the "Committee Appointed to Collect Information on Russia" (Cmd. 1240).

13. Frederic William Maitland, "A Historical Sketch of Liberty and Equality," in *Collected Papers* (Cambridge, England: The University Press, 1911), Vol. 1, pp. 107–109. Our italics.

14. *The Constitution of Liberty*, p. 29. Our italics.

15. This point is well developed in the seminal work of R. H. Coase, "The Problem of Social Cost," *The Journal of Law and Economics*, 3, 1 (October 1960), 1–44.

16. See Maitland, pp. 107–108. This argument is developed at some length by Herbert Spencer in an appropriately titled work, *Data on Ethics* (London: William and Morgate, 1907).

17. Cf. William Graham Sumner, "Reply to a Socialist," in *The Challenge of Facts and Other Essays* (New Haven, Conn.: Yale University Press, 1914). Sumner maintains inter alia that "I am by no means arguing that everything is for the best in the best of worlds . . . I am, on the contrary, one of those who think that there is a great deal to be dissatisfied about" (p. 60).

18. Herbert Spencer, "From Freedom to Bondage," in Mackay, p. 24.

19. John Maynard Keynes, *The General Theory of Employment, Interest, and Money* (London: Macmillan, 1973), pp. 260–269.

20. Ibid., p. 129.

21. For an excellent discussion of physical planning and its employment by the first Labour Government in Britain after the war see Andrew Shonfield, *Modern Capitalism* (London: Oxford University Press, 1966), pp. 88–91. Many commentators have made the error of linking the defects of physical planning with the alleged intrinsic difficulties of *all forms* of economic and social planning. For an example see John Jewkes, *The New Ordeal by Planning* (London: Macmillan, 1968).

22. This policy was outlined most completely by Alva Myrdal, *Nation and Family* (Cambridge, Mass.: M.I.T. Press, 1968; first published in 1941). The most famous legislative enactment is the French Code de la Famille (1939), which provided allowances that increased with the number of children.

23. For a review of the evidence see Charles Kindleberger, *Economic Growth in France and Britain* (Cambridge, Mass.: Harvard University Press, 1964), pp. 72–80.

24. For an optimistic evaluation see J. B. Pieters, "Nature Conservation in the Netherlands," in *Planning and Development in the Netherlands* (1970), pp. 192 ff.

25. For a complete and fascinating account in one city see A. J.

Youngson, *The Making of Classical Edinburgh* (Edinburgh: University Press, 1966).

26.   See E. A. Gaitkind, *International History of City Development* (New York: Free Press, 1971), Vol. VI.

27.   For a discussion of the role of New Towns see Frederic Osborn and Arnold Whittick, *The New Towns: The Answer to Megalopolis* (London: Leonard Hill, 1969).

28.   For a fairly recent example of the latter see David Jacobs, "The Impact of Planning on a City of Suburbs: A long view of Long Island," *New York Times Magazine* (February 17, 1974). Because of the ambiguity surrounding the legitimacy of planning in the United States, much of it, as Jacobs recounts, has to be carried out by stealth. Paradoxically, this results in *less public control* of planners than in most welfare states.

29.   Gottfried Dietze, *In Defense of Property* (Baltimore: Johns Hopkins University Press, 1963), p. 173. If Dietze means his charges to be taken in any but an allegorical sense, we would expect to find that in welfare states employment levels would drop, the number of calls for unneeded public assistance would soar, there would be a great run on medical and psychiatric facilities, and economic progress would, at best, stop. None of these things has occurred. Specific refutations are provided in Chapters Five and Six.

30.   Roger A. Freeman, *The Growth of American Government: A Morphology of the Welfare State* (Stanford, California: Hoover Institution Press, 1975), p. 171. Mr. Freeman is a senior fellow at the Hoover Institution. His book has been cited by a number of "conservative commentators" as a brilliant exposé of the welfare state.

31.   Ernest van den Haag, "Economics is Not Enough—Notes on the Anticapitalist Spirit," *The Public Interest*, 45 (Fall 1976), 116–117.

32.   Edward C. Banfield, *The Unheavenly City* (Boston: Little, Brown, 1968), p. 2. Timothy Hennessey and Richard Feen have written a fine article noting the similarity (if not the identity) of position between Banfield and William Graham Sumner, "Social Science as Social Philosophy: Edward C. Banfield and the 'New Realism' in Urban Politics," *American Behavioral Scientist*, 17 (November–December 1973), 171–204. In defense of Sumner, it must be noted that, writing in the 1890s, he had much more cause for adopting his position.

33.   Perhaps this comment is unfair, but we have been unable to find anywhere in *Anarchy, State, and Utopia* an account of why we have these rights, or indeed what their content is.

34.   Nozick denigrates this notion somewhat hastily by offering this example to support his contention that "holdings to which [p]eople are entitled may not be seized, even to provide equality of opportunity for

others." "*Is* it unfair that a child be raised in a home with a swimming pool, using it daily even though he is no more *deserving* than another child whose home is without one?" (*Anarchy, State, and Utopia,* pp. 235, 238). Maybe not, but *is* it unfair that a child be raised in a home without access to medical care so that he grew up physically and mentally *stunted?* Maybe so. It is this sort of distinction that a prudent presupposition in favor of laissez-faire might be able to make.

35. This procedure is undertaken systematically by E. G. West, *Education and the State: A Study in Political Economy* (London: Institute of Economic Affairs, 1965). West is able to conclude that in most instances compulsory state education (the "collectivist assumption") is neither necessary nor desirable.

36. This discussion represents our own composite. For a critical commentary on this notion see Richard Titmuss, "Choice and the 'welfare state,'" (Fabian Tract 370: February 1967).

37. The accommodation approach is obviously less useful when dealing with a country that is *not* a welfare state. The difficulties will be considered in Chapter Seven.

38. Ralph Harris, "Introduction," to *Freedom or Free-for-all: Essays in Welfare, Trade and Choice* (London: Institute of Economic Affairs, 1965), pp. 15–16.

39. For an interesting attempt to apply this reasoning to a reform of the British National Health Service see D. S. Lees, "Health Through Choice," in *Freedom or Free-for-all: Essays in Welfare, Trade and Choice.*

40. Milton Friedman, *Capitalism and Freedom* (Chicago: University of Chicago Press, 1962), pp. 191–192.

41. This argument is rarely offered in any systematic form. For a major exception see Murray Forsyth, "Property and Property Distribution Policy" (P.E.P. Broadsheet No. 528, July 1971).

Chapter 4

1. Karl Marx, "Critique of the Gotha Program," in Karl Marx and Friedrich Engels, *Basic Writings on Politics and Philosophy,* ed. Lewis Feuer (Garden City, N.Y.: Anchor Books, 1959), p. 120.

2. Alva Myrdal, *Nation and Family* (Cambridge, Mass.: M.I.T. Press, 1968), pp. 151–153.

3. Karl Marx, "Communist Manifesto," in *Basic Writings,* p. 9.

4. Rosa Luxemburg, *Reform or Revolution* (New York: Pathfinder, 1970).

5. Ibid., p. 35.

6. Ibid., p. 19.

7. Ibid., p. 23.

8. V. I. Lenin, *What Is to Be Done?* (Oxford: Oxford University Press, 1963), p. 41. George Lichtheim warns against fully equating the "economists" with the German revisionists: "In particular, there is very little to support the notion—energetically propagated by Lenin himself, and subsequently elevated to the rank of dogma by his followers—that the split corresponded to the revisionist controversy in the West." *Marxism* (New York: Praeger, 1961), p. 329.

9. Richard Titmuss, *Income Distribution and Social Change* (Toronto: University of Toronto Press, 1962), p. 198.

10. Ibid., p. 193.

11. Brian Abel-Smith, "Whose Welfare State?" in Norman Mackenzie, ed., *Conviction* (London: MacGibbon & Kee, 1958), pp. 55–56.

12. Gabriel Kolko, *Wealth and Power in America* (New York: Praeger, 1962), p. 132.

13. Francis Fox Piven and Richard Cloward, *Regulating the Poor* (New York: Pantheon Books, 1971).

14. Michael Harrington, *The Other America* (Baltimore: Penguin, 1963).

15. Åke Ortmark, *Maktspelet i Sverige* (Malmö: Wahlström & Widstrand, 1967), p. 75; Villy Bergstrom, "Inkomstfördelningen under efterkrigstiden," *Välståndsklyftor och standardhöjning* (Stockholm, 1967), pp. 11–33.

16. For some specific results of the Låginkomst Kommission's study, see Chapter Six.

17. Walter Korpi, *Fattigdom i välfärden* (Stockholm: Tiden, 1971); Gunnar and Maj-Britt Inghe, *Den ofärdige välfärden* (Stockholm: Tiden, Folksam, 1970).

18. Per Holmberg, "Svensk Socialpolitik—Nulage och Tendenser," in Bo Södersten, ed., *Svensk ekonomi* (Stockholm: Raben & Sjögren, 1970), p. 276.

19. Michael Harrington, *Socialism* (New York: Bantam Books, 1972), pp. 332–333.

20. Herbert Marcuse, *One-Dimensional Man* (Boston: Beacon Press, 1962), esp. pp. 48 ff.

21. Paul Baran, *The Political Economy of Growth* (New York: Monthly Review Press, 1957).

22. Herbert Marcuse, "Repressive Tolerance," in Robert Paul Wolff, Barrington Moore, Jr., and Herbert Marcuse, *A Critique of Pure Tolerance* (Boston: Beacon Press, 1965).

23. André Gorz, *Socialism and Revolution* (Garden City, N.Y.: Anchor Books, 1973), p. 103.

24. Ralph Miliband, *The State in Capitalist Society* (London: Weidenfeld & Nicolson, 1969).

25. Göran Therborn, ed., *En ny vänster* (Stockholm: Rabén & Sjögren, 1966), p. 212.

26. Gorz, *Socialism and Revolution*, p. 138.

27. For analyses of the social conditions for radical reformism see Timothy Tilton, "The Social Origins of Liberal Democracy: The Swedish Case," *American Political Science Review*, 68, 2 (June 1974), 561–571; Joseph Hamburger, *James Mill and the Art of Revolution* (New Haven, Conn.: Yale University Press, 1963); Albert Hirschman, *Journeys Toward Progress* (Garden City, N.Y.: Anchor Books, 1965), esp. pp. 360 ff.

28. James O'Connor, *The Fiscal Crisis of the State* (New York: St. Martin's Press, 1973), p. 1.

29. Claus Offe is a second important radical author who revises the classical Marxist theory of the state to take note of its legitimizing activities. Offe's work, much of it available only in German, consistently asserts that the welfare state does not and cannot fundamentally alter capitalist society. His evidence for this claim is drawn primarily from American and West German society, not from Scandinavia, and thus avoids the real challenge to his argument. His reasoning suffers from a failure to explain adequately why any legitimizing work is necessary and why it can remain limited. See "Advanced Capitalism and the Welfare State," *Politics and Society*, 3 (Summer 1972), 479–488, and his introduction to Wolf-Dieter Narr and Claus Offe, eds., *Wohlfahrtsstaat und Massenloyalität* (Köln: Kiepenhauer & Witsch, 1975), pp. 9–46.

30. Michael Young, *The Rise of the Meritocracy* (Baltimore: Penguin, 1967), pp. 167–168.

31. Ibid., p. 108.

32. Ibid., p. 46.

33. Frank Parkin, *Class Inequality and Political Order* (New York: Praeger, 1972) pp. 122 ff., 127.

34. For a liberal view, John Rawls, *A Theory of Justice* (Cambridge, Mass.: Harvard University Press, 1971), esp. pp. 100 ff; for a social democratic view, *Towards Equality* (Stockholm: Prisma, 1971), esp. ch. 1.

35. *Towards Equality*, p. 17.

36. Rawls, *A Theory of Justice*, p. 102.

37. Gorz, *Socialism and Revolution*, p. 103.

38. G. D. H. Cole, *Guild Socialism Restated* (London: Leonard Parsons, 1920), pp. 31, 15.

39. For interesting examples of greater participation at work see ibid., and Carole Pateman, *Participation and Democratic Theory* (Cambridge: Cambridge University Press, 1970), esp. chs. 3–6.

40. Murray Bookchin, "Listen, Marxist!" *All We Are Saying* (New York: Capricorn Books, 1971), p. 104.

41. Ibid., p. 105.

42.   Situationist International, "Ten Days That Shook the University," *All We Are Saying*, pp. 89, 90.
43.   Ibid., p. 360. Cf. also Herbert Marcuse, *Eros and Civilization* (New York: Vintage, 1962).
44.   "Socially, bourgeois exploitation and manipulation have brought everyday life to the most excruciating point of vacuity and boredom. In converting society into a factory and market place, the very rationale of life is reduced to production for its own sake—and consumption for its own sake. For all its different historical forms and combinations, capitalism has never transcended the commodity nexus and the banalization of experience to the level of 'business as usual.' Hence everyday life becomes a business, marriage a partnership, children an investment. One budgets time and saves space. . . . This commodity mode of society is beyond reform." Murray Bookchin, "Post-Scarcity Anarchy," *All We Are Saying*, pp. 346–347.
45.   Herbert Gintis, *Neo-Classical Welfare Economics and Individual Development* (Cambridge, Mass., 1971), p. 40.
46.   Ibid., p. 8.
47.   Raymond Williams, "Culture is Ordinary," *Conviction*, p. 80.
48.   Martin Buber, *Paths in Utopia* (Boston: Beacon Press, 1960), p. 80.
49.   Daniel and Gabriel Cohn-Bendit, *Obsolete Communism* (New York: McGraw-Hill, 1968).
50.   Ibid., p. 90. The term "anti-bureaucratic utopia" we owe to our colleague, Alfred Diamant.
51.   Iris Murdoch, "A House of Theory," *Conviction*, p. 230.
52.   Alain Touraine, *The Post-Industrial Society* (New York: Random House, 1971), p. 63.
53.   Adler-Karlsson, *Reclaiming the Canadian Economy*, p. 12.

Chapter 5

1.   This is the theme of Jerold Waltman, "Comparing Public Policies" (Ph.D. Dissertation, Indiana University, 1975).
2.   Scottish procedures, greatly influenced by the strictures of John Knox, were dissimilar. Ecclesiastical authorities, for example, retained responsibility for poor relief until 1834.
3.   This consideration—too often ignored in most discussions of British "welfare state" development which tend to concentrate on public policy outputs to the exclusion of their social, let alone religious, bases—is powerfully argued by R. H. Tawney, *Religion and the Rise of Capitalism* (New York: Harcourt, Brace, 1926).
4.   An extended treatment of mercantilist thought on employment

and proper wage rates is given by Edgar S. Furniss, *The Position of the Laborer in a System of Nationalism* (Boston: Houghton Mifflin, 1920).

5. Ethel Hampson makes the following conclusion from an extensive study of Cambridgeshire: "Even within the confines of a single county contradictory policies repeatedly characterize places but a few miles apart.... Complete local autonomy resulted in the most varied administration—legal, extra-legal, illegal." *The Treatment of Poverty in Cambridgeshire 1597–1834* (Cambridge: University Press, 1934), p. 260.

6. The most famous initiative was the development of the "Speenhamland System" which set the minimum wage for a laborer on the double basis of the price of bread and family size. It was precisely this type of relief that the 1834 reform was intended to terminate.

7. Quoted in Sir John Walley, *Social Security: Another British Failure?* (London: C. Knight, 1972), p. 22. An excellent brief account of the development of the intellectual underpinnings of the New Poor Law can be found in Derek Fraser, *The Evolution of the British Welfare State* (London: Macmillan, 1973), pp. 34–50.

8. *On Political Economy in Connection with the Moral State and Moral Prospects of Society* (Glasgow: William Collins, 1832), pp. 404, 405, 415. In regards to the bounds of private charity the good doctor voiced the happy thought that "when Christianity becomes universal, ... the poor will wish for no more than the rich will be delighted to bestow." "On the Great Law of Reciprocity Between Man" in *Works* (Philadelphia: A Tower, 1833), p. 262.

9. This consideration was in the forefront of the Royal Commission deliberations and in the parliamentary debate surrounding the 1834 act. For a sympathetic description see Sir George Nicholls, *A History of the English Poor Law* (London: John Murray, 1834), Vol. II, pp. 252–304.

10. Quoted in Fraser, p. 38. That previous "ill effects" had been totally unsubstantiated except rhetorically was pointed out at the time. Needless to say, this argument had no impact on the theoretical discussion. See *Cobbett's Weekly Political Register*, 1833–1834, passim, especially 12 July 1834.

11. Nassau Senior's manuscript narrative of the Poor Law Amendment Bill. Quoted in Nicholls, p. 287.

12. A good account of the opposition is provided by Nicholas Edsall, *The Anti-Poor Law Movement 1834–44* (Manchester, England: University Press, 1971).

13. A useful statistical summary is found in the Royal Commission on the Poor Laws and Relief of Distress (1909), *Minutes of Evidence* (Appendix Vol. IA), Cd 4626.

14. Sidney and Beatrice Webb, *The Break-Up of the Poor Law* (The Minority Report of the Poor Law Commission) (London: Longmans, Green, 1909), pp. 3–25.

15. Nicholls, p. 286. Written in 1856.

16. Just one of these institutions, Toynbee Hall (established in the East end of London in 1872 by Samuel Barnett, Vicar of St. Jude's, White Chapel), housed within the space of five years two of the civil servants most responsible for the 1908–1911 reforms—Llewellyn Smith and Joseph Nicholson, plus William Beveridge and R. H. Tawney.

17. This theme permeates Beveridge's account of his experiences at Toynbee Hall in *Power and Influence* (London: Hodder and Stoughton, 1953). Beatrice Webb expressed her sentiments with typical directness in her diary: "Who would want to imprison the intellect in this smelly kitchen of social life were it not for the ever-present 'thirty percent,' with the background of the terrible East End streets? The memory of the low, cunning brutal faces of the loafers and cadgers who hang about the Mint haunts me when I feel inclined to put down the Trade Union reports and take up a bit of good literature." *My Apprenticeship* (London, 1926), p. 413.

18. One can be brief because of the excellent literature on the subject. The works of Beveridge, Booth, Rowntree, and the Webbs are, of course, essential. Their ideas are summarized and magnificently interpreted by Jose Harris, *Unemployment and Politics: A Study of English Social Policy 1886–1914* (Oxford: Clarendon Press, 1972), pp. 102–347. What we consider to be the best account of the more general development of social thought has unfortunately not been published: John Brown, "Ideas Concerning Social Policy and their Influence on Legislation in Britain 1902–1911" (Ph.D. Thesis, University of London, 1964).

19. *Poverty, A Study in Town Life* (London: Macmillan, 1902).

20. Evidence before the Royal Commission on Poor Laws and the Relief of Distress (1909). *Memoranda* (Cd 4983), p. 38. Booth in 1892 recommended state labor colonies to which the underclass of London would be forcibly removed.

21. This was the conclusion, based in part on empirical observations, of William Beveridge, *Unemployment: A Problem for Industry* (London: Longmans, Green, 1909).

22. The most famous of the "scientific charities," the London Charity Organization Society, was found by the 1908 Royal Commission to have administrative costs approximately ⅓ its total budget (evidence of Harry Toynbee, Secretary). The general rise and decline of organized charity is described by Harris, pp. 102–115.

23. As even Lloyd George admitted, "in general, those who called themselves Radicals at the end of the Boer War, had no distinctive outlook on domestic policy." Quoted in Brown, p. 47.

24. Quoted in Brown, p. 300.

25. Beveridge's interpretation of this is given in *Power and Influence*, pp. 39–92. A fine study is provided by Bentley Gilbert, "Winston Chur-

231

chill versus the Webbs: The Origins of British Unemployment Insurance," *American Historical Review*, 71, 3 (April 1966), 844–862. We might note that Hugh Heclo, *Modern Social Politics in Britain and Sweden* (New Haven, Conn.: Yale University Press, 1974), pp. 78–92, gives more weight to the independent role of civil servants, in particular Llewellyn Smith. Here we emphasize the role of politicians as catalysts of reform and as sponsors of sympathetic civil servants (Smith and, above all, Beveridge).

26. See Harris, pp. 211–272.

27. Brown, pp. 61–78.

28. The story is well presented by Hugh Heclo, *Modern Social Politics in Britain and Sweden*, pp. 65–226. See also Fraser, pp. 135–191.

29. For this reason the measure was strenuously opposed by Beveridge who objected to its blanket nature and to the absence of regulation: "The grant of pensions might have gilded the bitter pill of registration" (article in the *Morning Post*, May 8, 1908).

30. Gilbert, p. 856.

31. This divergence from the European pattern, later to be enshrined in the Beveridge Plan, is often cited as the major inherent fault of the British system. A powerful statement to this effect is made by Sir John Walley, *Social Security: Another British Failure?*

32. Thus as late as 1919 the Secretary of the Treasury could state that he could not "admit any inherent natural right in an aged person to receive maintenance at the expense of the community." Quoted in Heclo, p. 199.

33. This was admitted as early as the Final Report of the 1931 Royal Commission on Unemployment Insurance (Cd. 4185).

34. See the Report of the Economic Advisory Council on Empire Migration, May 1932 (Cd. 4075). Malthus made a similar recommendation 144 years earlier.

35. In the "Beveridge Papers" (Vol. LXI). The typed paper was probably written in July 1941.

36. In a letter to Asquith, March 14, 1908. Quoted in Brown, p. 340.

37. The analysis given in *Newsweek* (December 7, 1942).

38. Letter to Frau Dr. Bremme (June 1957). Beveridge Papers (Vol. VIII, 48).

39. Comparative statutes are usefully laid out by Joseph P. Newhouse, "Medical Care Expenditure: A Cross-National Survey" (Rand Corporation Paper P-5608: February 1976). Estimates on administrative costs are provided by H. C. Slater, "Controlling the Cost of the British National Health Service," *International Social Security Review*, 25, 1 (1972), 20.

40. Data (for 1967) from Odin Anderson, *Health Care: Can There Be Equity?* (New York: Wiley, 1972), p. 125.

41.   Basic information and a discussion of difficulties in comparison are both found in Anderson. It might be noted that at the inception of the National Health Service the British figures were worse. Infant mortality rates in 1950 were 31.4 per thousand in Britain and in 1968 they were 18.3; in the U.S. the figures were 29.2 and 21.8. The decline in the rate was thus 41.7 percent in Britain; 25.3 percent in the United States (38.1 percent in Sweden).

42.   Statistics drawn from an excellent comparative study by Political and Economic Planning, *Social Security in Europe* (London, 1975).

43.   For details see Heclo, pp. 253–283.

44.   Its scope and importance can be seen in its length, 122 sections involving the partial or total repeal of 24 previous statutes.

45.   "Education Bill," Sections 8, 1 and 76. *The Statutes Revised* 5 and 6 Geo. VI to 7 and 8 Geo. VI (1941–44), Vol. xxvi.

46.   See Hansard, Vol. 408 (13 February–9 March 1945), 385.

47.   Richard Scase, "Images of Inequality in Sweden and Britain," *Human Relations,* 28, 3 (April 1975), 264. Multiple responses were allowed to the questions.

48.   For an excellent account of the domestic changes during World War II see Angus Calder, *The People's War* (London: Jonathan Cape, 1969).

49.   Such that, for example, someone suffering an industrial accident would, until such time as he could resume work, have to vacate his flat, shun his friends, etc.

50.   In *New Society* (March 13, 1975).

51.   In their famous study, "The Poor and the Poorest" (London: Occasional Papers on Social Administration, No. 17, 1965), Abel-Smith and Townsend estimated that 3.8 percent of the population was below the National Assistance (now Supplementary Benefits) scale in 1960. This percentage can be raised by making the poverty level forty percent above the scale or by discounting the sharing of income among family members, but even when the percentage becomes only fourteen and nine respectively. See A. B. Atkinson, *Poverty in Britain and the Reform of Social Security* (Cambridge, England: University Press, 1969), pp. 29–43.

52.   Further details on the position of the "poverty lobby" are given by Norman Furniss, "The Welfare Debate in Britain: Implications for the United States, *Public Administration Review* (May–June 1975), 300–310.

53.   From 1950 through 1968 the total cost of the health care system increased by 912% per capita in Sweden, 221% in the United States, 159% in Britain (Anderson, p. 215). Again, we do not argue that Britain needed to increase her expenditures at the Swedish rate—given the structure of the Health Service in 1950 she undoubtedly did not. But we do maintain (1) that Britain has not had the luxury even to contemplate such an increase, and (2) that the rise she has managed has been insufficient.

54. The figures are from the "Finer Report," "Report of the Committee on One-Parent Families," July 1974 (Cmnd. 5629). The political implications are spelled out in the *Times* (January 24, 1977).

55. Beginning at least with the evidence taken before the Royal Commission on the Poor Laws there has been a constant stream of comment that the "traditional horror" of the workhouse/means test/supplementary benefits was a result of picturing the procedure "as it was, not as it is" ("Report by Miss Constance Williams" cd. 4690, Appendix Vol. xvii). That these hesitations are still strong is shown in the table given by Atkinson (*Poverty in Britain,* p. 58) on the reasons pensioners given for not applying for assistance:

Major Reasons for Not Applying for Assistance (1965)

Proportion listing (multiple answers allowed)	Married Couples	Single Men	Single Women
Lack of knowledge, misperception	37	34	35
"Managing all right"	20	30	38
Pride, dislike of charity, dislike of going to means test	33	27	23

56. These data have been obtained from interviews at the Ministry of Health and Social Security, June–July 1973.

57. Alex Prain, "The Beveridge Report Answered" (Glasgow, 1943).

58. The *Economist* (February 2, 1946), 162. Assumptions A, B, and C were a full employment policy, a central administration, and a national health scheme.

59. "The Conservative Manifesto 1951," in F. W. S. Craig, ed., *British General Election Manifestos 1918–1966* (Chichester: Political Reference Publications, 1970), p. 144.

60. From his column "Kneeling Nuns, Shame on Us!" (July 9, 1975).

61. Vermont Royster, "Britain: A Model Study," in the *Wall Street Journal* (August 20, 1975), 14. Mr. Royster was editor of the *Journal* from 1958 through 1971 and is now (among other things) a director of Dow Jones and Co. This evocation now seems to be staple intellectual fare. For additional examples see William Cotter, "Social Security, The Frankenstein Monster," *Vital Speeches of the Day,* 42, 2 (November 1, 1975) and Milton Friedman, "The Line We Dare Not Cross," *Encounter* (November 1976).

62. (London: April 1975). Another useful compendia of statistics, "The Common Market and the Common Man," is put out periodically by

the European Communities Press and Information Service. Britain's pension rate relative to earnings is detailed comparatively in "Earnings Replacement Rate of Old-Age Pensions for Workers Retiring at End of 1972" (*Social Security Bulletin,* December 1974). A very concise summary is given in "Welfare in a Cold Climate," *Economist* (September 20, 1975), 46–52.

63. Cf. Daniel Defoe's previously cited tract, *Giving Alms no Charity, and Employing the Poor a Grievance to the Nation* (London, 1704). Defoe contrasts unfavorably the wastefulness and general debauchery of the English working class with the thrift and moral rectitude of the Dutch.

64. Thus there is considerable force in the radical critique that the social security state can be a useful adjunct to capitalism, not an essential variant or challenge. This point is well argued by Edward Greenberg, "Capitalism and the Welfare State: A Radical Critique" (Paper prepared for delivery at the Annual Meeting of the American Political Science Association, San Francisco, September 2–5, 1975). Our argument is that the social welfare state does lead toward different principles, a point the radical critique would tend to deny. Again see Greenberg.

65. Scase, p. 271.

Chapter 6

1. Marquis Childs, *Sweden: The Middle Way* (New Haven, Conn.: Yale University Press, 1936, 1947, 1961).

2. Margaret Cole and Charles Smith, eds., *Democratic Sweden* (London, 1936).

3. Jean Parent, *Le Modèle Suédois* (Paris: Calmann-Levy, 1970); Richard Tomasson, *Sweden: Prototype of Modern Society* (New York: Random House, 1970); Roland Huntford, *The New Totalitarians* (London: Penguin Press, 1971). M. Donald Hancock, *Sweden: The Politics of Post-Industrial Change* (Hinsdale, Ill.: Dryden, 1972) is an excellent, balanced account.

4. Ernst Michanek, *For and Against the Welfare State: Swedish Experiences.* Lecture given in Berlin, October, 1963 (Stockholm: The Swedish Institute, 1964), p. 43.

5. "It was during the Liberal era of 1900–20, and especially 1910–20, that the foundations of the social policy of modern Sweden were laid." Douglas Verney, "The Foundations of Modern Sweden: The Swift Rise and Fall of Swedish Liberalism," *Political Studies,* 20, 1 (March 1972), 46.

6. Karl Höjer, *Den svenska socialpolitiken* (Stockholm, 1969), p. 19.

7. Ibid., p. 23.

8. Stig Hadenius, Björn Molin, Hans Wieslander, *Sverige efter 1900: En modern politisk historia* (Stockholm: Aldus/Bonniers, 1972), p. 180.

9. Ibid., p. 198.

10. Dankwart Rustow, *Politics of Compromise* (Princeton, N.J.: Princeton University Press, 1965).

11. Joseph Board, *The Government and Politics of Sweden* (Boston: Houghton Mifflin, 1970), p. 231.

12. The following analysis is drawn from Sleeman, *The Welfare State,* pp. 141–142.

13. The rationale for these programs is spelled out in Alva Myrdal, *Nation and Family* (Cambridge, Mass.: The M.I.T. Press, 1968). This edition, a reprint of the 1941 original, contains a foreword by Daniel Moynihan which strongly indicates his indebtedness to the Myrdal view for his own family assistance plan.

14. "In Sweden, labour market policy developed rapidly from an *unemployment* policy with unemployment benefits and emergency works to see active *employment* policy.... We try to achieve not only full employment but as *productive*—and this well-paid—employment as possible for all who are able to work." Michanek, *For and Against the Welfare State,* p. 12.

15. *Svenska Dagbladet,* July 28, 1973.

16. *The Swedish Budget 1973/74* (Stockholm: Ministry of Finance, 1973), p. 140.

17. Ernst Wigforss, *Ur mina minnen* (Stockholm: Tiden, 1964), p. 212. Also available in *Vision och verklighet* (Stockholm: Prisma, 1967), p. 19.

18. For a more detailed consideration of solidaristic wage policy see Rudolf Meidner, *Coordination and Solidarity: An Approach to Wages Policy* (Stockholm: Prisma, 1974), and Derek Robinson, *Solidaristic Wage Policy in Sweden* (Paris: Organization for Economic Cooperation and Development, 1974).

19. *Historisk statistik för Sverige. Del 1. Befolkning 1720–1967.* (Stockholm: Statistika Centralbyrån, 1969), pp. 91, 118.

20. Walter Korpi, *Fattigdom i välfärden* (Stockholm: Tiden, 1971), p. 12; Jan Nasenius and Kristin Ritter *Delad Välfärd* (Stockholm: Esselte Studium, 1974), pp. 82–86.

21. *Statistisk Årsbok för Sverige 1937* (Stockholm: Statistiska Centralbyrån, 1937), pp. 232–234.

22. For a distinctly contrary view Huntford, *The New Totalitarians.* Huntford fails to note such peculiarities of the Swedish situation as the unusually high rate of formation of separate households; that is, for equivalent populations, Sweden displays a higher number of separate households and thus has a greater demand for housing. Huntford also fails to adduce international comparisons.

23. *The Swedish Budget,* p. 140.

24. Michanek, *For and Against the Welfare State,* p. 13.

25. Parent, *Le Modèle Suédois,* p. 25.

26. Michanek, *For and Against the Welfare State*, p. 10.

27. *Den svenska köpkraftensfördelning 1967* (Stockholm: SOU 1971: 39), p. 9.

28. Board, *Government and Politics of Sweden*, p. 234.

29. Albert Rosenthal, *The Social Programs of Sweden: A Search for Security in a Free Society* (Minneapolis: University of Minnesota Press, 1967), p. 166.

30. Herbert Hendin, *Suicide and Scandinavia* (New York: Grune and Stratton, 1964), p. 4.

31. Michanek, *For and Against the Welfare State*, pp. 38–41; Rosenthal, *The Social Programs of Sweden*, p. 166.

32. The classic discussion of the Swedish debate over freedom in the welfare state is Leif Lewin, *Planhushållnings debatten* (Stockholm: Almqvist & Wiksell, 1967).

33. To take only one glaring example: Huntford argues that during the 1930s the Swedes "were indoctrinated with the ideas of State direction and intervention in the economy. These became part of the national political canon so that when, in later years, more radical measures were introduced, opposition was absent and the controversy known in the West was avoided in Sweden." The insinuation that Social Democratic propaganda stifled opposition is absolute nonsense, as the vehement debates over the Social Democrats' postwar program and supplemental pension reform and now over the Meidner proposals demonstrate. (This argument was originally written before the 1976 elections; the Social Democrats' defeat in this election makes a mockery of Huntford's allusions to an insidious Social Democratic dictatorship.)

34. Åke Ortmark, *Maktspelet i Sverige* (Malmö: Wahlström and Widstrand, 1967), pp. 167–192.

35. C. H. Hermansson, *Monopol och storfinans—de 15 familjerna* (Stockholm: Rabén & Sjögren, 1965); Parent, *Le Modèle Suédois*, pp. 147 ff.

36. *Statistisk årsbok 1968*, p. 346. Cited in Hancock, *Sweden*, p. 82.

37. Lena Johansson, *Den vuxna befolkningens bostadsförhållanden 1968* (Stockholm: 1971), p. 14.

38. *Jämlikhet*, the Alva Myrdal Report to the Swedish Social Democratic Party (Stockholm: Prisma, 1969), ch. 3.

39. Sten Johansson, *Politiska resurser: Om den vuxna befolkningens deltagande i de politiska beslutsprocesserna* (Stockholm, 1971). Cited in *Kompendium om Låginkomstutredningen* (Stockholm, 1971), p. 110.

40. Kurt Samuelsson, *From Great Power to Welfare State* (London: Allen & Unwin, 1968), pp. 267, 272.

41. Parent, *Le Modèle Suédois*, p. 32.

42. Ortmark, *Maktspelet i Sverige*, pp. 233–234.

43. Ibid., p. 233.

Chapter 7

1. We do not intend to give a full history of the development of American welfare institutions; such an undertaking would require a volume at least the size of this one. Rather, we use the historical record to highlight certain themes of current as well as contemporary relevance. The references given below provide sources for further exploration.

2. This was a constant theme of Theodore Roosevelt and of pressure groups supporting reform. For an excellent account see Hace Tishler, *Self-Reliance and Social Security 1870–1917* (Port Washington, N.Y.: Kennikat Press, 1971), pp. 97–104.

3. For an account (these societies have been relatively underexplored) see Robert Part and Herbert Miller, *Old World Traits Transplanted* (New York: Harper Brothers, 1921), esp. pp. 119–144.

4. *Address before the War Emergency and Reconstruction Conference of the Chamber of Commerce of the United States* (1918), pp. 5–6. The pamphlet names no publisher or publication date. Swope voiced similar sentiments: "From the standpoint of the public, my conception of industry is not primarily for profits but for service." In "The Responsibilities of Modern Industry," *Industrial Management: The Engineering Magazine*, 6 (December 1926), 335–336. It is interesting to note that the fascination with "social engineering" began in America in the business community and spread to government only after the Depression.

5. Good accounts of the movement, its ideas and actions, are given by Herman Feldman, *The Regularization of Employment* (New York: Harper, 1925), and Daniel Nelson, *Unemployment Insurance: The American Experience, 1915–1935* (Madison, Wis.: University of Wisconsin Press, 1969). Henry Ford provides a memorial of an unreconstructed Taylorite in "The American Way to Health and Happiness," in Justus Frederick, ed., *A Philosophy of Production* (New York: The Business Bourse, 1930).

6. Quoted in Frances Piven and Richard Cloward, *Regulating the Poor: The Functions of Public Welfare* (New York: Random House, 1971), p. 53.

7. As recounted in his memoirs. Quoted in Nelson, pp. 144–145.

8. The change is well described in Nelson, pp. 152–161.

9. The debate over the "radical" nature of these reforms is well set out in the following sources: Barton Bernstein, "The New Deal: The Conservative Achievements of Liberal Reform, " in Bernstein, ed., *Towards a New Past* (New York: Random House, 1968), pp. 263–285; Edward Greenberg, *Serving the Few: Corporate Capitalism and the Bias of Government Policy* (New York: Wylie, 1974), pp. 103–127; Richard Kirkendall, ed., *The New Deal: The Historical Debate* (New York: Wylie, 1973). Kirkendall's article, "The New Deal as Watershed," *Journal of American History* (March 1968), 839–852, is also worth reviewing.

10. Quoted in Hubert Humphrey, *The Political Philosophy of the New Deal* (Baton Rouge, La.: Louisiana State University Press, 1970), p. 46. This book (originally a 1940 Master's essay) is not only a good commentary on the motivations of the New Deal leadership, it is also a useful introduction to the political philosophy of Senator Humphrey. Roosevelt (in the semi-private forum of a press conference) even allowed himself to muse that "what we are trying to do is to build up national income with special reference to increasing the share of national income to [the bottom] one-third." *Complete Presidential Press Conferences* (New York: Da Capo Press, 1972), Vol. 9, 437–438 (June 15, 1937).

11. The basic accounts of the development and implementation of the Social Security Act are given by Arthur Altmeyer, *The Formative Years of Social Security* (Madison, Wis.: University of Wisconsin Press, 1966); Paul Douglas, *Social Security in the United States* (New York: Whittlesey House, 1936); Abraham Epstein, *Insecurity: A Challenge to America* (New York: Agathon Press, 1968); and Edwin Witte, *The Development of the Social Security Act* (Madison, Wis.: University of Wisconsin Press, 1962).

12. A good introduction to the nonreforms of the World War II period is given by Richard Polenberg, *War and Society: The United States 1941–1945* (Philadelphia: Lippincott, 1972).

13. The conundrum for Wallace and others is related magnificently by Norman Markowitz, *The Rise and Fall of the People's Century: Henry Wallace and American Liberalism* (New York: Free Press, 1973). It is sad reading, akin in form to the plaint of "old bolsheviks": If only Stalin knew what was being done under his name! Of course, Stalin (and Roosevelt) knew perfectly well

14. Roosevelt outlined his thinking in satisfied tones to May Craig:

> Suppose—in eighteen hundred and sixty-five—after the Civil War, there was a definite program ... of repression of the whole south. Well, they didn't like it at all—the country didn't. And finally, after ten years, they threw it out.
>
> Now, do you think that twenty-five years later, in 1890, that we should have gone back to the same old policy? ... You have a program to meet the needs of the country. ... We are not thinking in terms of the 1939 program. We have done nearly all of that, but that doesn't avoid or make impossible or unneedful another program, when the time comes. When the time comes.
>
> QUESTION: That's the answer?
> THE PRESIDENT: When the time comes.

Franklin Roosevelt, *Complete Presidential Press Conferences*, Vol. 22, 246–254 (December 28, 1943).

15. These packages received strong impetus from the various wage restraints imposed during the war and were seen in fact as indirect wages—thus an additional reason for management to shoulder the entire burden.

16. Dwight D. Eisenhower, *Mandate for Change* (New York: Doubleday, 1963), pp. 441–442.

17. For example, Eisenhower recounts that in the 1954 Congressional campaign, Senator Paul Douglas, one of the intellectual forces behind the Social Security Act, "seemed to be prepared to run on the administration's record; he claimed to have supported me on foreign policy, the Bricker Amendment, housing, social security, and health. He charged his Republican opponent, Joseph Meek, with wanting to scuttle everything I proposed. . . . I told him [Meek] I would not back him until he announced he would support my program. . . . I could see no sense in working for office seekers who were ready to object to every proposal I made." *Mandate for Change*, p. 433.

18. This contention is made most convincingly by Andrew Shonfield, *Modern Capitalism* (London: Oxford University Press, 1965).

19. This estimate is given by Daniel Bell, "The Revolution of Rising Expectations," *Fortune* (April 1975), 99. A fine overview of these programs has been provided by Gilbert Steiner, *The State of Welfare* (Washington, D.C.: Brookings, 1971).

20. An excellent overview of the relationship is presented by Edward Greenberg, *Serving the Few: Corporate Capitalism and the Bias of Government Policy.*

21. Recently, the Defense Department decided to celebrate the bicentennial by attempting to increase the profitability of these contracts in a program appropriately entitled "Profits '76." Senator Proxmire has called "Profits '76" the "capstone in a series of handouts to the military industrial complex and one of the biggest rip-offs the taxpayer has ever suffered." Quoted in the *New York Times* (May 23, 1976).

22. For a case study of the pressures to retain the "regulation" of the CAB see the *Wall Street Journal* (June 4, 1976).

23. The classic statement of this position in regional economic theory is by François Perroux. See his "Note sur la Notion de Pôle de Croissance," in Jean Boudeville, ed., *Espace et les Pôles de Croissance* (Paris, 1968). An excellent recent discussion is provided by Nicholas Lang, "An Approach to the Political Analysis of Regional Economic Policy," *Planning Comment* (October 1975). Billie Reid Gile has described the consequences for one peripheral area, Southwestern Indiana:

> The major truth revealed by this study of the twenty years from 1950–1970 is that there are few ways for the majority of the population in the counties to earn a comfortable living, even

fewer avenues by which to increase their earnings to a higher level, and almost nothing for the yearly graduating classes entering the employment field.

"An Inquiry into the Economic Conditions and History of Ten Southwestern Counties of Indiana 1950–1970" (M.A. Thesis, University of Oklahoma, 1975), p. 22.

24. "The Welfare State: The Costs of American Self-Sufficiency," in Richard Rose ed., *Lessons from America: An Exploration* (London: Macmillan, 1974), p. 259.

25. All the above statistics plus the data for the tables is taken from Alfred Skolnik and Sophie Dales, "Social Welfare Expenditures, Fiscal Year 1974," *Social Security Bulletin,* 38, 1 (January 1975). It might be noted that the introduction of "revenue sharing" has had the effect of slightly underestimating the federal role.

26. A helpful description is offered by Robert J. Myers, *Social Security* (Bryn Mawr, Pa: McCahan Foundation, 1975), pp. 21–177.

27. The material presented in this paragraph is drawn from Joint Economic Committee *Studies in Public Welfare Paper,* No. 20 *Handbook of Public Income Transfer Programs: 1975* (Washington, D.C.: U.S. Government Printing Office, 1974).

28. Ibid.

29. These data are reported by Gayle Thompson, "Blacks and Social Security Benefits: Trends, 1960–63," *Social Security Bulletin,* 38, 4 (April 1975), 30–40.

30. See the discussion in Michael Barth et al., *Toward an Effective Income Support System* (Madison: University of Wisconsin Press, 1974). The quotation is from p. 168.

31. Myers, *Social Security,* p. 417.

32. Data from "Welfare Reform and Its Financing" (Committee for Economic Development: July 1976), p. 9.

33. Barth et al., *Toward an Effective Income Support System,* p. 22. See also Gilbert Steiner, *The State of Welfare* (Washington, D.C.: Brookings, 1971), chs. 4–5.

34. This change in emphasis was recommended in the fall 1973 report of the Housing Task Force which discovered that the main reason people live in shoddy housing is that they have insufficient incomes.

35. Myers, *Social Security,* p. 413.

36. Nevertheless, Richard P. Nathan has argued that the dramatic growth of the food stamp program is the single most important welfare change in America since the passage of the Social Security Act of 1935, providing more aid to the working poor, for example, than President Nixon's abortive Family Assistance Plan, *The Wall Street Journal* (April 24,

1974). Unfortunately, despite the obvious limitations of the program, Nathan may well be correct in his assessment.

37. This is the appropriate phrase of David Stockman, *The Public Interest* (Spring 1975), 3–30.

38. Data taken from Walter Kolodrubetz, "Employee-Benefit Plans, 1973," *Social Security Bulletin*, 38, 5 (May 1975), 22–29.

39. The provisions of the bill, including the alternative vesting standards, are detailed in the *New York Times* (August 1, 21, 1974).

40. The *New York Times* (August 23, 1974).

41. "Health Insurance and the Unemployed." Background Information Prepared by the Staff of the Committee on Finance, U.S. Senate (March 7, 1975), p. 26.

42. Kolodrubetz, "Employee-Benefit Plans," p. 27.

43. Cf. Alvin Rosenfeld, "Sick and Out of Work," *The New Republic* (May 24, 1975), 7–9.

44. "Health Insurance and the Unemployed," p. 31.

45. Table taken from data presented by Nancy Worthington, "National Health Expenditures, 1929–74," *Social Security Bulletin*, 38, 2 (February 1975), 16.

46. For a useful compendium see the Hearings before the Subcommittee of Health and the Environment of the Committee on Interstate and Foreign Commerce (House of Representatives), "National Health Insurance: Major Proposals," Serial 94–60: December 8–10, 1975.

47. Sylvia Law, *Blue Cross: What Went Wrong?* (New Haven, Conn.: Yale University Press, 1974) discusses the process in great detail. The quotation is from p. 2.

48. Eliot Freidson for one argues cogently that "by their very nature, professions in general and medicine in particular cannot live up to their professed ideals as long as they possess thoroughgoing autonomy. . . ." *Professional Dominance* (New York: Atherton, 1970), p. 234. In any event, it is becoming evident that they cannot live up to them at a monetary cost most people can afford.

49. Witte, *The Development of the Social Security Act*, pp. 78–79.

50. Reports of the study appear periodically in the *Social Security Bulletin*. We have also consulted with relevant members of the Office of Research and Statistics. Where noted, the data are taken from the unpublished marginals of the 1969 Microfilm Tables. The table is adapted from Sally Sherman, "Assets on the Threshold of Retirement," *Social Security Bulletin* 36, 8 (August 1973), 11.

51. Variable 169. N-2971.

52. Variables 145–149.

53. Variable 153.

54. Variable 117. In Question 27B "help from relatives" was to be

checked by the interviewer only if the answer was given spontaneously as a source of support.

55. Richard P. Nathan elaborates on this point in "Food Stamps and Welfare Reform" (a paper prepared for delivery at a conference held by the Food and Nutrition Service, U.S. Department of Agriculture, Fredericksburg, Virginia, February 1975). The history and provisions of Nixon's Family Assistance Plan are set forth well by Vincent and Vee Burke, *Nixon's Good Deed* (New York: Columbia University Press, 1974).

56. Nathan, "Food Stamps and Welfare Reform," p. 7.

57. U.S. Supreme Court, *Goldberg* vs. *Kelley,* 1970 397 US 254.

58. "Reform Follows Reality: The Growth of Welfare," *The Public Interest* (Winter 1974), 48.

59. As Anne Angus relates, "to back up all these weapons [untrained caseworkers, Work Incentive Programs, the "New Federalism"] against liberal welfare, the audit measures instituted by the federal government through the state welfare offices really frighten the professionals. Crudely, the state tells the county to cut its welfare numbers, or else, and if it doesn't then the auditors descend to find ineligibles at all costs. There is no real appeal from these audits." "The Gains and Losses of Poverty Programme," *New Society* (April 3, 1975), 15.

60. Even among those just about to receive social security retirement benefits, 84% of the Retirement History Study sample did not know what the amount was expected to be.

61. Barth et al., *Toward An Effective Income Support System,* p. 24.

62. *Economic Report of the President, Annual Report of the Council of Economic Advisors* (Washington, D.C.: U.S. Government Printing Office, 1974), p. 168.

63. Barth et al., *Toward An Effective Income Support System,* pp. 165–166.

64. *Economic Report of the President, Annual Report of the Council of Economic Advisors* (Washington, D.C.: U.S. Government Printing Office, 1975), p. 119.

65. For the propriety of stressing inequality rather than income deficiency as the criterion for poverty, see the powerful argument of S. M. Miller and Pamela Roby, *The Future of Inequality* (New York: Basic Books, 1970).

66. Figures from a useful review by Arthur Okun, "Equal Rights but Unequal Incomes," *The New York Times Magazine* (July 4, 1976), 104.

Chapter 8

1. Christopher Green, *Negative Taxes and the Poverty Problem* (Washington, D.C.: Brookings, 1966), p. 61.

2.   This account is based on John Inglehart, "Welfare Report/HEW Wants Welfare Programs Replaced by Negative Income Tax," *National Journal Reports*, 6, 42 (October 19, 1974), 1559–1566. Inglehart appears to have had access to the internal HEW documents ("black books") describing ISP.

3.   Ibid.

4.   S. M. Miller and Pamela Roby, *The Future of Inequality* (New York: Basic Books, 1970), pp. 128–129.

5.   Robert Levine, *The Poor Ye Need Not Have With You* (Cambridge, Mass.: M.I.T. Press, 1970) p. 220, sees a continuing role for community action, though he eschews the "systematic agitation model." Peter Marris and Martin Rein, *Dilemmas of Social Reform* (Chicago: Aldine, 1973) argue persuasively that a satisfactory redistribution of resources toward the poor will include the redistribution of power as well as of income.

6.   U.S. Congress, Joint Economic Committee, *Studies in Public Welfare*, Papers 1–20 (Washington, D.C., 1972–1974).

7.   Michael Barth, George Carcagno, and John Palmer, *Toward an Effective Income Support System* (Madison, Wis.: Institute for Research on Poverty, 1974).

8.   Ibid., pp. 39–40.

9.   Ibid., p. 42.

10.   Ibid.

11.   Ibid.

12.   One answer to the question, "Do the poor want to work," is an emphatic yes—just what one might expect in a society saturated with the work ethic. See Ibid, ch. 3, and Leonard Goodwin, *Do the Poor Want to Work?* (Washington, D.C.: Brookings, 1972). In a private letter Barrington Moore, Jr., has pointed out to us, however, that the inability to hold down a job may be socially created. Both of these things may well be true. One may want to work, but lack the skills and disciplines necessary to retain employment. Furthermore, both of the types mentioned by Goodwin and Moore are undoubtedly represented among the unemployed, but we know of no data which establish the proportions.

13.   Richard Titmuss, *Commitment to Welfare* (London: Allen & Unwin, 1968), p. 164. Cf. Jan Nasenius and Kristin Ritter, *Delad Välfärd* (Stockholm: Scandinavian University Books, 1974), p. 2.

14.   *Towards Equality* (Stockholm: Prisma, 1970).

15.   Gunnar Adler-Karlsson, *Reclaiming the Canadian Economy* (Toronto: House of Anansi Press, 1970), p. 1. Originally published under the title *Functional Socialism*.

16.   The notion that the public longs for a gradual dismantling of American social welfare institutions is suitably deflated by John Kenneth Galbraith, "The Conservative Majority Fallacy," *New York* (December 22, 1975), pp. 53–57.

17. An argument as to how this ironic situation evolved is provided by James Q. Wilson, "The Riddle of the Middle Class," *Public Interest,* 39 (Spring 1975) 125–129.

18. Harold L. Wilensky, *The Welfare State and Equality* (Berkeley: University of California Press, 1975), p. 37.

19. Barrington Moore, *Political Power and Social Theory* (Cambridge, Mass.: Harvard University Press, 1958), p. 7. It goes without saying that our fundamental objective in this volume is to present the social welfare state model as persuasively as we can to various strategic groups in the American population.

20. Arthur Okun, *Equality and Efficiency: The Big Trade-off* (Washington, D.C.: Brookings, 1975), p. 2.

21. Ibid., p. 97. The diminished work effort of secondary earners can have beneficial effects, allowing teen-agers to complete their education or mothers to spend more time with their families.

22. Ibid., p. 98.

23. This is, of course, the thesis of Friedrich Hayek, *The Road to Serfdom* (Chicago: University of Chicago Press, 1944).

24. "The two dozen largest, federally funded income support programs are under the jurisdiction of eleven federal agencies, as well as ten House and nine Senate committees; moreover, these programs usually involve innumerable state and local administrative authorites." Arnold Heidenheimer, Hugh Heclo, and Carolyn Adams, *Comparative Public Policy* (New York: St. Martin's), p. 260.

25. The Swedish Social Democrats, by contrast, exercised power for over forty years in a centralized parliamentary system and with the aid of a comprehensive union movement.

INDEX

DATE DUE